The Texts of 'Othello' and Shakespearian Revision

By the same author:

The Stability of Shakespeare's Text
Shakespeare: Seven Tragedies – The Dramatist's
    Manipulation of Response
Shakespeare's Impact on his Contemporaries
Shakespeare: The 'Lost Years'
John Weever, A Biography of a Literary Associate
    of Shakespeare and Jonson
Myriad-Minded Shakespeare: Essays, Chiefly on
    the Tragedies and Problem Comedies

Edited by Ernst Honigmann:

King John (the Arden Shakespeare)
Richard III (the New Penguin Shakespeare)
Twelfth Night (the Macmillan Shakespeare)
Milton's Sonnets
Paradise Lost, book 10 (with C.A. Patrides)
Shakespeare and his Contemporaries: Essays in Comparison
Playhouse Wills 1558–1642 (with Susan Brock)
Othello (the Arden Shakespeare: 1996)

Introduced by Ernst Honigmann:

British Academy Shakespeare Lectures 1980–89

The Texts of 'Othello' and Shakespearian Revision

E.A.J. Honigmann

ROUTLEDGE

London and New York

First published 1996
by Routledge
11 New Fetter Lane, London EC4P 4EE

Simultaneously published in the USA and Canada
by Routledge
29 West 35th Street, New York, NY 10001

Routledge is an International Thomson company

© 1996 E.A.J. Honigmann

Typeset in Baskerville by Datix International Limited, Bungay, Suffolk

Printed and bound in Great Britain by TJ Press (Padstow) Ltd,
Padstow, Cornwall

British Library Cataloguing in Publication Data
A catalogue record for this book is available from the British Library

Library of Congress Cataloguing in Publication Data
A catalogue record for this book has been requested

ISBN 0-415-09271-X

For
Harold Jenkins

Contents

List of illustrations

All illustrations are reproduced by courtesy of the British Library, as follows: Quarto, C34 k33; Folio, G 11631; Ralph Crane, Lansdowne MS. 690.

Foreword

Since the publication of *The Stability of Shakespeare's Text* (1965), which followed his Arden edition of *King John* (1954), Ernst Honigmann has been recognised as among the most innovative, acute and learned of Shakespearian textual scholars. As a preliminary to editing *Othello* – once more for the Arden Shakespeare – he has reviewed, with characteristic sharpness and openness of mind, the problems posed by the early editions of one of the most notoriously problematic of Shakespeare's texts.

The present study, in which he argues persuasively and in detail for a new understanding of the nature and interrelation of the first quarto of 1622 and the text printed in the 1623 First Folio, is, however, much more than an important monograph on a single play. In the course of his examination of the early editions of *Othello*, Honigmann scrutinises and reassesses many current textual orthodoxies and assumptions and significantly extends discussion of the role of the scribe Ralph Crane in preparing printer's copy for the First Folio. As he points out, his book is in part a detective story. It is also a reassertion of faith in the ability of analytic bibliography to improve knowledge of early seventeenth-century play texts – Shakespeare's and those of his contemporaries – in a manner which has pervasive implications for editors.

Himself an energetic proponent of the 'instability' of Shakespeare's texts, Honigmann now reminds us of the need for patience and an open mind in face of too great an eagerness to mount a root and branch attack on the New Bibliography and all its works. For *Othello*, he argues, revision may not, after all, provide the best explanation of the many textual variations between quarto and folio, nor need a single edited text which makes controlled eclectic use of both be a chimera.

This book will be indispensable to all serious students of *Othello*, but it also has important implications for editors of other plays from the First Folio, not least for its scrupulous attention to the minutiae of editing, such as elision, versification and punctuation – matters too often deemed beneath the conscious notice of editors and readers. Detailed analysis of many well-known passages in *Othello* affords strong grounds for editorial introduction of unfamiliar punctuation and verse-lining. Once more we have reason for gratitude to Ernst Honigmann for helping us to see more clearly what patient textual analysis can teach us and for indicating the wider significance of a particular textual puzzle.

Richard Proudfoot
King's College London

Preface

This book is intended as a companion volume to my edition of *Othello* (1996) in the third series of the Arden Shakespeare (Arden 3). The edition succeeds those of H.C. Hart (Arden 1, 1903) and of M.R. Ridley (Arden 2, 1958), but is in every way independent of its predecessors, particularly in its editorial thinking and in the text that resulted. I began work on the edition in 1982 and signed the contract for *The Texts of 'Othello'* on 19 May 1992. The ten-year gap does not, however, signify that *Texts* was an afterthought: much of the writing of *Texts* preceded 1992, and, except for the later insertion of cross-references, this volume was completed first, a year ahead of the edition. Indeed, although the two books were written simultaneously, I could not make a start on the edition until I knew what were to be the conclusions of *Texts*: from the reader's point of view they may be seen as companion volumes but from the author's they constitute a single project.

Inevitably the two volumes sometimes cover the same ground. I have tried to reduce repetition to the minimum, especially in the edition, which frequently cross-refers to the fuller discussion in *Texts*, to save space. Nevertheless, for the benefit of readers who do not have access to this companion volume, Appendix 2 in the edition summarises the principal conclusions of *Texts* and indicates their editorial consequences.

Chapter 3 of *Texts* was originally composed as a lecture for the fortieth anniversary of the Shakespeare Institute, Stratford-upon-Avon (in 1991: I was a Fellow of the Institute from 1951 to 1954). I am grateful to the Institute's Director, Stanley Wells, for the invitation to lecture, and for other kindnesses.

Jane Armstrong, of Routledge, politely expressed delight when I offered to send her an old-style manuscript of *Texts*, not the customary neat typescript of these degenerate days. I fear that her delight may have been short-lived, but perhaps it will console her to reflect that she now has first-hand experience of foul papers, authorial second thoughts, underpunctuation, overwriting, misreading, eye-skip, etc., and is therefore ideally qualified to be the publisher of this book. Her colleague, Penny Wheeler, was also resilient, efficient and amazingly courteous in trying circumstances: they both deserve the gold medal of the Bibliographical Society. I am equally grateful to my vigilant copy editor, Judith Ravenscroft.

For permission to print published and unpublished extracts from manuscripts in their collections, I have to thank the Bodleian Library, the British Library, Cambridge University Library and Trinity College, Cambridge, the Public Record Office, and, in the USA, the Folger and Huntington libraries. For permission to cite the Through Line Numbering of the *Norton Facsimile* of Shakespeare's First Folio I thank W.W. Norton & Company of New York. For all the essential 'reader services' that one now takes for granted it is a pleasure to thank colleagues in Newcastle University Library (the Robinson Library).

In the years since 1982 many friends and colleagues have helped me, in various ways. I must mention in particular Peter Beal, the late Fredson Bowers, Susan Brock, T.W. Craik, R.A. Foakes, and the late Charlton Hinman. Trevor Howard-Hill lent me his microfilm and photostat copies of the works of Ralph Crane, and gave me the benefit of his unique knowledge of Crane's scribal habits. Richard Proudfoot, the General Editor initially responsible for Arden 3 *Othello*, accepted that a separate volume on *The Texts of 'Othello'* would be needed, and (with a sinking heart?) that the General Editor would have to read it. I am deeply indebted to him for his advice and support, and also for writing the Foreword. Harold Jenkins read this book in its early stages, gently corrected its blunders and taught me much, in conversation and in his own books. My wife, Elsie, double-checked the 'swibs' and other statistics (which is not to say that they are always correct: sometimes we both found it difficult to confirm our own figures), and assured me that I was probably right even when we both knew that I was wrong. For these and other reasons I dedicate the less hard-hitting of the two companion volumes to her memory.

July, 1995

Abbreviations

The following abbreviations have been used for periodicals, the publications of learned societies, works of reference, libraries, etc. If a book was published or co-published in London, no place of publication is indicated.

AEB	*Analytical and Enumerative Bibliography*
The Library	*The Library: Transactions of the Bibliographical Society*
MP	*Modern Philology*
MSR	Malone Society Reprints
NYRB	*New York Review of Books*
OED	*The Oxford English Dictionary*, ed. James A.H. Murray *et al.* (13 vols, 1933)
PMLA	*Publications of the Modern Language Association of America*
PQ	*Philological Quarterly*
PRO	Public Record Office
RES	*Review of English Studies*
SB	*Studies in Bibliography: Papers of the Bibliographical Society of the University of Virginia*
SQ	*Shakespeare Quarterly*
SS	*Shakespeare Survey*
STC	*A Short-Title Catalogue of Books Printed in England, Scotland & Ireland and of English Books Printed Abroad 1475–1640*, 2nd edn, ed. W.A. Jackson, F.S. Ferguson, Katharine F. Pantzer (3 vols, 1976, etc.)
TLS	*Times Literary Supplement*
YES	*Yearbook of English Studies*

Editions of Shakespeare are cited by short title as follows:

Arden 1 refers to *Othello* in the first Arden Shakespeare, ed. H.C. Hart (1903); Arden 2, to the play in the second Arden Shakespeare, ed. M.R. Ridley (1958); Arden 3, to the play in the third Arden Shakespeare, ed. E.A.J. Honigmann (1996).

Cambridge 1
   The Works of William Shakespeare, ed. W.G. Clark, J. Glover, W.A. Wright (9 vols, 1863–6); rev. Wright (1891–3).

Cambridge 2
  Othello, ed. J. Dover Wilson and Alice Walker (1957: 'The New Shakespeare').
Cambridge 3
  Othello, ed. Norman Sanders (1984: 'The New Cambridge Shakespeare').

Line references to Shakespeare's other works are usually to *The Riverside Shakespeare*, ed. G. Blakemore Evans *et al.* (Boston, 1974). TLN (Through Line Numbers) are taken from the Norton Facsimile of the First Folio of Shakespeare (New York, 1968) by courtesy of W.W. Norton & Co. The titles of Shakespeare's works are abbreviated as in Arden 3, as follows:

AC	*Antony and Cleopatra*
AW	*All's Well That Ends Well*
AYL	*As You Like It*
CE	*The Comedy of Errors*
Cor	*Coriolanus*
Cym	*Cymbeline*
Ham	*Hamlet*
1H4	*King Henry IV Part 1*
2H4	*King Henry IV Part 2*
H5	*King Henry V*
1H6	*King Henry VI Part 1*
2H6	*King Henry VI Part 2*
3H6	*King Henry VI Part 3*
H8	*King Henry VIII*
JC	*Julius Caesar*
KJ	*King John*
KL	*King Lear*
LLL	*Love's Labour's Lost*
Luc	*The Rape of Lucrece*
MA	*Much Ado About Nothing*
Mac	*Macbeth*
MM	*Measure for Measure*
MND	*A Midsummer Night's Dream*
MV	*The Merchant of Venice*
MW	*The Merry Wives of Windsor*
Oth	*Othello*
Per	*Pericles*
PP	*The Passionate Pilgrim*
R2	*King Richard II*
R3	*King Richard III*
RJ	*Romeo and Juliet*
Son	*Sonnets*

STM	*Sir Thomas More*
TC	*Troilus and Cressida*
Tem	*The Tempest*
TGV	*The Two Gentlemen of Verona*
Tim	*Timon of Athens*
Tit	*Titus Andronicus*
TN	*Twelfth Night*
TNK	*The Two Noble Kinsmen*
TS	*The Taming of the Shrew*
VA	*Venus and Adonis*
WT	*The Winter's Tale*

Books and articles frequently referred to are cited by author and short title or by author and date or, in some cases, simply by author, as indicated below.

Abbott
A Shakespearian Grammar, by E.A. Abbott (1869: I have used the edition of 1884).

Arber, *Transcript*
Transcript of the Registers of the Company of Stationers, 1554–1640, ed. Edward Arber (5 vols, 1875–94).

Bowers, 1964
Bibliography and Textual Criticism, by Fredson Bowers (Oxford, 1964) (ch. 6: 'The Copy for the Folio *Othello*').

Bowers, 'Authority, Copy'
'Authority, Copy, and Transmission in Shakespeare's Texts', by Fredson Bowers, in *Shakespeare Study Today*, ed. Georgianna Ziegler, (New York, 1986, AMS Studies in the Renaissance, no. 13).

Chambers, *Elizabethan Stage*
The Elizabethan Stage, by E.K. Chambers (Oxford, 4 vols, 1923).

Chambers, *William Shakespeare*
William Shakespeare: A Study of Facts and Problems, by E.K. Chambers (Oxford, 2 vols, 1930).

Crane, Ralph
see Fletcher, Massinger, Middleton.

Fletcher, *Demetrius*
Demetrius and Enanthe, by John Fletcher (Malone Society Reprints, 1951: a 'Crane' transcript).

Fletcher
see also Massinger.

Greg, *Bibliography*
Bibliography of the English Printed Drama to the Restoration, by W.W. Greg (4 vols, 1940–59).

Greg, *Editorial Problem*
>*The Editorial Problem in Shakespeare: A Survey of the Foundations of the Text*, by W.W. Greg (Oxford, 1942).

Greg, *First Folio*
>*The Shakespeare First Folio, Its Bibliographical and Textual History*, by W.W. Greg (Oxford, 1955).

Hinman, *Facsimile*
>*The Norton Facsimile, The First Folio of Shakespeare*, prepared by Charlton Hinman (New York, 1968).

Hinman, *Othello 1622*
>*Othello 1622* (Shakespeare Quarto Facsimiles, no. 16). Introduction by Charlton Hinman (Oxford, 1975).

Hinman, *Printing and Proof-Reading*
>*The Printing and Proof-Reading of the First Folio of Shakespeare* (Oxford, 2 vols, 1963).

Honigmann, 'Indifferent Variants'
>'On the Indifferent and One-Way Variants in Shakespeare', by E.A.J. Honigmann, *The Library*, 5th Series (1967), XXII, pp. 189–204.

Honigmann, 'Re-Enter the Stage Direction'
>'Re-Enter the Stage Direction: Shakespeare and Some Contemporaries', by E.A.J. Honigmann, *SS* (1976), 29, pp. 117–25; revised in *Myriad-Minded Shakespeare* (1989), as 'On Not Trusting Shakespeare's Stage-Directions', pp. 169–87.

Honigmann, *Stability*
>*The Stability of Shakespeare's Text*, by E.A.J. Honigmann (1965).

Howard-Hill, *Ralph Crane*
>*Ralph Crane and Some Shakespeare First Folio Comedies*, by T.H. Howard-Hill (Charlottesville, 1972).

Howard-Hill, 'Shakespeare's Earliest Editor'
>'Shakespeare's Earliest Editor, Ralph Crane', by T.H. Howard-Hill, *SS* (1992), 44, 113–29.

Massinger, *Barnavelt*
>*Sir John Van Olden Barnavelt*, by John Fletcher and Philip Massinger (Malone Society Reprints, 1980: a 'Crane' transcript).

Middleton, *Game*
>*A Game at Chess*, by Thomas Middleton. The following manuscripts are cited: (1) T (Trinity College, Cambridge, MS. 0.2.66: in Middleton's hand); (2) H (Huntington Library, California, MS. EL 34.B.17: partly in Middleton's hand); (3) L (British Library, MS. Lansdowne 690: a 'Crane' transcript); (4) M (Bodleian Library, MS. Malone 25: a 'Crane' transcript); (5) F (Folger Shakespeare Library, Washington DC, MS. V.a.231: a 'Crane' transcript). Several of these manuscripts have now been edited for the Malone Society: T in 1990; H (Middleton's transcription) also in 1990; M in 1993 (Malone Society Reprints, *Collections*, vol. XV).

Middleton, *Witch*
>   *The Witch*, by Thomas Middleton (Malone Society Reprints, 1950: a 'Crane' transcript).

Revels
>   The Revels Plays (Manchester 1958–   ); The Revels Plays Companion Library (Manchester, 1984–   ).

Sir Thomas More
>   *The Book of Sir Thomas More*, by Anthony Munday *et al.* (Malone Society Reprints, 1911).

Spevack, *Concordance*
>   *The Harvard Concordance to Shakespeare*, by Marvin Spevack (Cambridge, Mass., 1973).

Taylor, 1983
>   'The Folio Copy for *Hamlet, King Lear*, and *Othello*', by Gary Taylor, *SQ* (1983), 34, pp. 44–61.

Taylor and Jowett, *Shakespeare Reshaped*
>   *Shakespeare Reshaped 1606–1623*, by Gary Taylor and John Jowett (Oxford Shakespeare Studies, 1993).

Walker, 1952
>   'The 1622 Quarto and the First Folio Texts of *Othello*', by Alice Walker, *SS* (1952), 5, pp. 16–24.

Walker, *Textual Problems*
>   *Textual Problems of the First Folio 'Richard III', 'King Lear', 'Troilus and Cressida', '2 Henry IV', 'Hamlet', 'Othello'*, by Alice Walker (Cambridge, 1953).

Walton, *Quarto Copy*
>   *The Quarto Copy for the First Folio of Shakespeare*, by J.K. Walton (Dublin, 1971).

Wells and Taylor, *Textual Companion*
>   *William Shakespeare: A Textual Companion*, by Stanley Wells and Gary Taylor with John Jowett and William Montgomery (Oxford, 1987).

Wilson, *The Manuscript of 'Hamlet'*
>   *The Manuscript of Shakespeare's 'Hamlet' and the Problems of its Transmission: An Essay in Critical Bibliography*, by J. Dover Wilson (Cambridge, 2 vols, 1934).

In extracts from early books and manuscripts, long 's' is printed as 's'; in passages where variant readings are italicised, names (often printed in italics in early books) are sometimes changed to roman.

Chapter 1

Introduction

The two earliest printed versions of *Othello*, the Quarto of 1622 (Q) and the Folio of 1623 (F), were not the very first texts of the play, for a manuscript in Shakespeare's hand must have preceded them. In this study of 'the texts of *Othello*' I suggest that Shakespeare (like other dramatists of the period) wrote a first draft or 'foul papers'[1] and also a fair copy, and that these two authorial versions were both copied by professional scribes, the scribal transcripts serving as printer's copy for Q and F. So the 'texts' of my title refer not to two but, in the first instance, to six versions of the play, which it will be convenient to designate A (foul papers) and Aa (scribal copy taken from the foul papers), B (authorial fair copy) and Bb (scribal copy), and Q and F. The six texts might then be arranged in a family tree, growing from left to right:

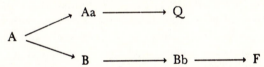

Unfortunately textual relationships can turn out to be almost as complicated as human relationships. As will appear, Q and F are not entirely independent strains, since F shows signs of 'contamination' directly from Q, a cross-fertilisation as unwelcome (from the editor's point of view) as are other kinds of incest.

The six early texts are the most important ones, but they are not the end of the story. I shall have to keep an eye on the Second Quarto (Q2, 1630) and later printed editions – especially Arden 3, the third version of the play to be published in The Arden Shakespeare. Arden 3 follows Arden 1 (edited by H.C. Hart in 1903) and Arden 2 (edited by M.R. Ridley in 1958), and is the 'only begetter' of *The Texts of 'Othello'*: that is, the two studies of *Othello* were planned as companion volumes, each self-sufficient and yet each lacking much detailed information found only in the other.

To return to the six early texts: four of the six have perished and cannot be inspected, so it may seem that I propose to build on insecure foundations. To some extent this is true, though not more true than in the case of any other editor of *Othello*. Every editor has to explain the provenance and transmission of his text or texts, whatever the number of lost intermediate versions. I have a significant advantage over previous editors of the play if, as I would like to think, I have identified the scribe of Bb, a man with quite distinctive scribal habits that can be checked in surviving manuscripts: this identification, if correct, solves dozens of textual problems in *Othello* and brings not only Bb but also B into sharper focus, which, in turn, throws new light on A and Aa. Four of the six texts may have disappeared, but the editor's task is far from a hopeless one. On the contrary, what with the new information that follows about the publisher of Q (chapter 3), the scribe of Bb (chapter 6), and about Shakespeare's often illegible writing (chapter 8), we are in a good position to rub away the film of old theories and to see the textual problems of *Othello* more clearly. As might be expected, some of these problems are not peculiar to *Othello*: the argument has to be tested against other Shakespearian texts, and opens up larger issues. In the first place this is a study of the texts of one play, but at the same time the reader should be prepared to reconsider some of the basic assumptions of our textual criticism of Shakespeare.

This, then, is a book that has much in common with J. Dover Wilson's *The Manuscript of Shakespeare's 'Hamlet' and the Problems of its Transmission* (Cambridge, 2 vols, 1934), being similarly concerned to track down scribes, compositors, the sources of error, etc., even though in some ways more wide-ranging – for instance, in its archival dimension, and in the use made of the 'Pavier quartos' and the Crane manuscripts. Like Dover Wilson's book, it has a 'detective' interest as the evidence accumulates and is gradually fitted together. I can only hope that, though not endowed with Dover Wilson's skills, I communicate the excitement of such work, and that readers will understand the need to master so much textual detail. The words, after all, are the words of Shakespeare, even if the hands are the hands of Aa or Bb, or of compositors B and E. If it turns out (among other things) that some of Shakespeare's most sublime poetry has been mislined and consequently misread for centuries (chapter 10), for that reason alone the effort should be worthwhile.

Having introduced my aims and hinted at some conclusions, I have two other introductory duties. First, to describe Q and F, and to outline some of the extraordinary differences of the two texts; and, second, to provide a preliminary survey of recent editorial thinking about these two texts.

The Quarto was entered in the Stationers' Register on 6 October 1621. 'Thomas Walkley Entred for his copie vnder the hands of Sir George Buck, and Master Swinhowe warden, *The Tragedie of Othello, the moore of Venice . . . vjd*'.[2] Q printed the same title, and added 'As it hath beene diuerse times acted at the Globe, and at the Black-Friers, by his Maiesties Seruants. Written by William Shakespeare. [Ornament] London, Printed by N.O. for Thomas Walkley, and are to be sold at his shop, at the Eagle and Child, in Brittans Bursse. 1622'. Q collates A², B–M⁴, N², and consists of forty-eight leaves; after an epistle, 'The Stationer to the Reader' signed 'Thomas Walkley', the text follows on pages numbered 1 to 99.

The other early text of *Othello* was published in the Folio collection of 1623; placed third from the end, it precedes *Antony and Cleopatra* and *Cymbeline*. Like Q it has the title *The Tragedie of Othello, the Moore of Venice*. It occupies thirty pages, printed in double columns; on the last page, after 'FINIS', it gives a list of 'The Names of the Actors' (Fig. 4).

According to Charlton Hinman's Through Line Numbering,[3] F – one of Shakespeare's longest texts – contains 3,685 lines, about 160 lines more than Q. F's 160 additional lines include more than thirty passages of 1 to 22 lines; amongst F's most interesting additions we may note Roderigo's account of Desdemona's elopement (1.1.119–35), Desdemona's Willow Song (4.3.29–52, 54–6, 59–62) and Emilia's speech on marital fidelity (4.3.85–102).

'Apart from passages in which the texts are divergent', said W.W. Greg,[4] 'Q has only some five half-lines that are not in F.' A slight understatement, but it remains true, I think, that 'the F omissions are trifling and doubtless due to error'.[5] In addition, it has been estimated, Q and F diverge in about a thousand readings (hence the need for a more systematic scrutiny of 'the texts of *Othello*' than has appeared to date). The figure depends on how we define divergence; if differences of punctuation are included the figure would be much higher. Whatever their precise number, the many variants of the play pose editorial problems of exceptional complexity, equalled (in the Shakespeare canon) only by *Hamlet* and *King Lear*.

Both Q and F were press-corrected, which added yet more variants.[6] The press corrections may but need not restore manuscript readings, since proof-readers sometimes examined the first 'pulls' or rough proofs without checking the printer's copy, i.e. sometimes corrected without authority.

More than fifty oaths, printed by Q, were deleted in F or replaced by less offensive words. Editors used to assume that F was purged because of the Act of Abuses, 1606, which prohibited profanity and swearing, but we now know that some scribes omitted profanity for purely 'literary' reasons and that not only prompt-books but even private transcripts were purged. On the assumption that the profanity stems from Shakespeare, modern editors revert to Q's readings. If more QF variants could be shown to point back to a single cause, as with F's purgation of profanity, the editor's task would be easier: as will appear, the identification of the scribe of Bb helps us to make some progress.

Both Q and F divide the play into acts and scenes. Q numbers only Acts 2, 4 and 5, and one scene (2.1); F numbers the acts and scenes as in modern editions, except that F's 2.2 combines two scenes (2.2 and 2.3 in Arden 3). Nevertheless, scene divisions are marked in Q with the usual *Exeunt*, and in effect Q initiated the divisions adopted by all subsequent texts. Q, however, was the first of Shakespeare's 'good quartos' to be divided into acts, and its act divisions (like F's) may have no authority.

The stage directions in Q and F 'have a common basis' (Greg[7]). Q's are more complete, and, said Greg, 'might all have been written by the author'; some give essential information that could not have been inferred from the dialogue. I list some of Q's more revealing stage directions, adding F's (if any) in square brackets.[8] 1.1.80 'Brabantio at a window' ['Bra.Aboue', speech prefix]; 157 'Enter Barbantio in his night gowne, ...' ['Enter Brabantio, ...']; 1.3.0 'Enter Duke and Senators, set at a Table with lights and Attend-ants' ['Enter Duke, Senators, and Officers']; 124 'Exit two or three'; 170 'Enter Desdemona, Iago, and the rest' ['... Iago, Attendants']; 2.1.0 'Enter Montanio, Gouernor of Cypres, ...' ['Enter Montano, ...']; 55 'A shot'; 177 'Trumpets within'; 196 'they kisse'; 2.3.140 'Enter Cassio, driuing in Roderigo' ['... pursuing Rodorigo']; 152 'they fight'; 153 'A bell rung'; 3.3.454 'he kneeles'; 465 'Iago kneeles'; 4.1.43 'He fals downe' ['Falls in a Traunce']; 210 'A Trumpet'; 5.1.45 'Enter Iago with a light' ['Enter Iago']; 5.2.0 'Enter Othello with a light' ['Enter Othello, and Desdemona in her bed']; 17 'He kisses her'; 82 'he stifles her. / Emillia calls within' ['Smothers her./Æmilia at the doore']; 123 'she dies'; 195 'Oth. fals on the bed'; 232 'The Moore runnes at Iago. Iago kils his wife'; 249 'she dies'; 279 '... Cassio in a Chaire' ['Cassio']; 354 'He stabs himselfe'; 357 'He dies'['Dyes'].

As this selection shows, Q supplies more detail than F, and F lacks many directions that one would expect from a prompt-book: sound effects, stage movement and lighting are all neglected. On the other hand, Q is sometimes vague ('two or three', 'and the rest') and omits some essential equipment (Desdemona's bed) – quite like other Shakespearian texts that supposedly derive from foul papers. Some of Q's unusual phrasing can be matched in the stage directions in other plays (cf. p. 161).

Next, a quick survey of editorial thinking about the provenance and trans-mission of Q and F. Opinions have differed, and my summary is meant to highlight the differences, without pretending that this is a survey of all the possibilities.

(1) E.K. Chambers, 1930. 'Q and F are both good and fairly well-printed texts; and they clearly rest substantially upon the same original'. F was 'printed from the original and Q from a not very faithful transcript, without a few passages cut in representation. It must have been an early transcript, in view of the profanities. Whether it was made for stage purposes or for a private collector one can hardly say. . . . The Q stage directions may well be the author's, but the transcriber might have added some marginal notes for action, not in F.'

(2) Alice Walker, 1952, 1953. Q 'was a memorially contaminated text, printed from a manuscript for which a book-keeper was possibly responsible and based on the play as acted'; F 'was printed from a copy of the quarto which had been corrected by collation with a more authoritative manuscript.'

(3) W.W. Greg, 1955. 'Q appears to have been printed from a transcript, perhaps of the foul papers . . . The date of the transcript is unlikely to have been earlier than 1620'. Greg agreed, following Miss Walker, that F was

printed from a copy of Q collated with a manuscript. The manuscript, he thought, was probably the prompt-book, prepared by a scribe. Hence 'we get a picture of two different scribes struggling with, and at times variously interpreting, much and carelessly altered foul papers – perhaps even of alterations made by the author or with his authority after his draft had been officially copied'.

(4) Fredson Bowers, 1964. 'Dr. Walker's case (though correct) is not nearly so copious or rigorous in its evidence as to make for an acceptable demonstration'. Concluded that 'once the necessary compositor studies have been made, the rigorous application of this evidence ... may hopefully lead to a final determination of disputed printed versus manuscript copy in the Folio'.

(5) J.K. Walton, 1971. Argued that F *Othello* was not printed from corrected Q (as Miss Walker had claimed), but from a manuscript.

(6) Stanley Wells, 1987.[9] 'Q represents a scribal copy of foul papers. F represents a scribal copy of Shakespeare's own revised manuscript of the play'. 'There must have existed a transcript by Shakespeare himself.'

Here we may pause to pick out some of the more interesting differences. Chambers, Greg, etc., consider Q a good text; Miss Walker thinks it contains 'a solid core of variant readings only explicable as memorial perversions.' Chambers dates the Q transcript 'early' (i.e. before 1606), and Greg 'late', not earlier than 1620. Chambers, Walker and Greg assume that there was only one authorial text, Wells that there were two. The F manuscript puzzles some of the commentators, including Greg who confesses that he has 'slipped into thinking of the manuscript that lies at the back of F as the prompt-book', but notes some evidence to the contrary. Wells observes that F's stage directions 'are not strongly theatrical . . . . Particularly striking is the total absence from F of music cues'; unusual spelling and punctuation suggest that 'another hand intervened' between Shakespeare's transcript and F's printed version.

One other difference deserves immediate attention. J.K. Walton's *The Quarto Copy for the First Folio of Shakespeare* (1971) received mostly neutral or unfavourable reviews,[10] yet his rebuttal of Miss Walker's theory gradually won support.

(7) Richard Proudfoot, 1972.[11] Agreed that Miss Walker's 'clinching argument' for F's being printed from corrected Q, an argument based on preterite endings (-t, -d, etc.) that was accepted by Greg as conclusive, had been shown to be less than conclusive by Walton, who 'may well be right'.

(8) Gary Taylor, 1983. Agreed with Walton against Miss Walker. When compositor E set up Folio texts from printed Quarto texts, he followed Q punctuation closely; in F *Othello* compositor E's punctuation, and especially his brackets, differ sharply from Q *Othello*, therefore F was printed from a manuscript, not from corrected Q.[12]

My drastic summaries may suggest, unfairly, that the textual experts resemble those readers of the *Boston Evening Transcript* who 'sway in the wind like a field of ripe corn'. Not so: the experts assessed the evidence available to them, with great care. As more evidence emerged the picture changed. I believe that it is about to change again, as a result of the collective effort of many individuals, whose abandoned theories and disagreements have not been in vain.

The most divisive issue of all, though not one that has featured prominently in my preliminary survey, revolves round F's additional passages, and raises the question of authorial revision. If Shakespeare added more than a hundred lines at several points in the play, he himself might be responsible for some of the perhaps one thousand other variants. F's additional passages lead straight on to a major parting of the ways for editors. I turn to these passages in the next chapter, and warn in advance that I have modified my previous position (see pp. 9–10).

Chapter 2

Revision?

Many textual specialists and recent editors of *Othello* have taken it for granted that the play shows signs of authorial revision. About the extent of this revision they have been less unanimous, some arguing for two authorial versions, the later one (F) involving 'a strategy of revision', whilst others hold that Shakespeare only wrote one complete version but improved some words or short passages, with the result that Q and F now and then print 'first and second thoughts'. In this chapter I turn first to the 'strategy of revision', and begin with an important paper by Nevill Coghill, its leading spokesman.

Coghill's argument centred on the longer passages omitted by Q and first printed by F. Editors had previously assumed that these passages were deliberate or accidental omissions from Q; Coghill contended that they were later additions, from Shakespeare's own pen. 'The immediate occasion that prompted Shakespeare to revise the play was perhaps the Act of that year [1606] against profanity and swearing in stage-plays, but the real motive can, I think, be shown to have been Shakespeare's dissatisfaction with certain features in the play as it was first written.'[1]

Before we examine Coghill's 'strategy' it will be useful to list some of the longer passages first printed by F, upon which he based his claims. They are the following (some start or end in mid-line: they can be identified more exactly from Arden 3): 1.1.119–35, 1.2.72–7; 1.3.25–31; 2.3.275–7; 3.3.386–93; 3.3.456–63; 4.1.38–43; 4.1.172–4; 4.2.74–7; 4.2.153–66; 4.3.29–52; 4.3.54–6; 4.3.59–62; 4.3.85–102; 5.2.147–50; 5.2.181–90; 5.2.244–6. Not all the 'longer passages' are long. I shall deal with shorter passages later; here, merely for convenience, I define passages of two or more lines as 'longer'. Coghill, it should be added, did not consider all the 'longer passages', nor was it necessary that he should; he dealt with most of F's significant additions, and the case for a 'strategy of revision' can be stated, initially, from his selected passages.

Coghill, an experienced director, argued from the point of view of the theatre, showing that passages first printed in F aim at theatrical effects that greatly strengthen the play. The traditional view that these lines were cut in Q, rather than added by Shakespeare after he had completed the play, makes little sense, according to Coghill, for only a fool would have cut such passages:

without them the play loses some of its most magical moments. 'Nothing
entitles us to assume stupid cutting, still less destructive cutting, except a blind
reliance on the supposed axiom that Shakespeare never revised his work'.[2] For
example, why does F add the 'Pontic sea' speech in 3.3?

> *Oth.*   O blood, Iago, blood.
> *Iag.*   Patience I say, your mind perhaps may change.
> *Oth.*   Neuer:
> In the due reuerence of a sacred vow,
> I here ingage my words.
> > *Iag.*   Doe not rise yet:
> > > (3.3.454 ff., Q)

F expands Othello's speech:

> *Oth.*   Neuer, Iago. Like to the Ponticke Sea,
> Whose Icie Current, and compulsiue course,
> Neu'r keepes retyring ebbe, but keepes due on
> To the Proponticke, and the Hellespont:
> Euen so my bloody thoughts, with violent pace
> Shall neu'r looke backe, neu'r ebbe to humble Loue,
> Till that a capeable, and wide Reuenge
> Swallow them vp. Now by yond Marble Heauen,
> In the due reuerence of a Sacred vow,
> I heere engage my words.
> > (F)

These magnificent lines not only build up the scene's climax more effectively,
said Coghill, 'they are also there to herald, by the importance given to
Othello's kneel, a still more important kneel that is to come in the next act,
and appears in Folio, but not in Quarto'.[3]

> > Heere I kneele:
> If ere my will did trespasse 'gainst his Loue, . . .
> > (4.2.153–66, F)

Desdemona and Othello are both brought to their knees before their trusted
tormentor, said Coghill, and this 'is a stroke of stage-craft of great visual force
and point, a double demonstration of Iago's triumph'.

Again, F expands one of Roderigo's speeches by seventeen lines, adding:

> If't be your pleasure, and most wise consent,
> (As partly I find it is) that your faire Daughter,
> At this odde Euen and dull watch o'th' night
> Transported with no worse nor better guard,
> But with a knaue of common hire, a Gundelier,
> To the grosse claspes of a Lasciuious Moore: . . .
> > (1.1.119–35, F)

The function of these lines, said Coghill, 'could hardly be clearer: it is to state exactly what is happening between some Moor and Brabantio's daughter . . . . It is the purest, most lucid piece of exposition in the scene', needed because 'nobody knew the story of *Othello*'.[4]

Some of F's added passages, Coghill went on, are 'serially connected', thus revealing Shakespeare's 'strategy of revision'. The two kneels are one example; in Acts 4 and 5 Emilia is the common factor in four additions.

> It is the character of Emilia that receives the fullest benefit, though others profit as well. It is as if Shakespeare had set himself methodically to strengthen her part at the four key-points we have considered; his purpose seems to have been to *endear* it to the audience: it is as if he had sensed that Emilia's guilt in the matter of the handkerchief had been insufficiently wiped out in the eyes of her critics.[5]

Years later I drew attention to another group of 'serially connected' differences between Q and F, where F is more 'sexually specific', adding 'images or turns of phrase that throw new light on sexual behaviour or fantasy, notably reinforcing the play's central concern with normal and abnormal sexuality'.[6] Emilia's diatribe against selfish husbands is a good example:

> But I do thinke it is their Husbands faults
> If Wiues do fall: (Say, that they slacke their duties, . . .)
> $\qquad$ (4.3.85–102, F)

I wanted to show that the 'strategies of revision' discovered in *King Lear* by Michael Warren, Gary Taylor and others[7] were very similar to Coghill's thinking about *Othello*: in both plays various 'revised' passages were said to be 'serially connected', and towards the end of each play a secondary character, Edgar and Emilia, seems to be strengthened in the revised text. These similarities appeared to support the revision theory, indicating that *King Lear* was not a 'one off' instance of revision but, on the contrary, characteristic of its author. At the same time I issued a warning.

> Yet Coghill's assumption, that all the 'F only' passages discussed by him can be detached from the hypothetical original version, still needs to be proved. It is important to remember this, since F restores much (chiefly words, phrases or single lines rather than longer passages) that undoubtedly formed part of the original text.
>
> How carefully did Coghill check that the 'F only' passages discussed by him are not necessary to Q's continuity? This is not clear, but I believe that closer scrutiny will show that the Q text hangs together without Coghill's 'F only' passages.[8]

Yes, Q 'hangs together', though not quite as securely as F. A closer study of F's 'longer passages' has made me think again about this crucial point and consequently about the revision of *Othello*. Whether or not this affects the case for the revision of *King Lear* I leave to others to determine.

In 1982 I was aware that some of the arguments for the revision of *Othello* could be reversed. For example, it was not impossible that the 'sexually specific' passages in *Othello* were there from the start, and were altered or deleted in Q by a bowdlerising editor. I thought this unlikely, for the Folio *adds* sexually specific passages yet *loses* much of the play's profanity (which survives in Q). Are we to assume that F and Q were both bowdlerised, in quite different ways? That would be most unusual – different forms of censorship in two different substantive texts of the same play – therefore the revision theory seemed to be on the right track.

More damagingly, Coghill's argument can be reversed as well. He contended that if *Othello* was shortened, if Q was a shortened version rather than the original version, the person responsible was guilty of 'stupid cutting' and 'destructive cutting'. True: yet we still have to ask whether stupid and destructive cutting should be ruled out as inconceivable in the Elizabethan theatre. After all, the most extraordinary things happen to Shakespeare's text even in our enlightened modern theatres, even in the holy of holies: I dare not say that some productions by the Royal Shakespeare Company have been guilty of stupid and destructive cutting, yet no one would deny that producers have sometimes cut the plays in strangely 'creative' ways. And – this is the awkward point – it could also happen in Shakespeare's own day, in his own company. Whoever shortened the only text we have of *Macbeth*, this person left textual tangles and stupidly introduced 'the other three Witches'.[9] At least one early production of *Henry V* omitted Chorus, arguably the second most important part in the play. And if *King Lear* was revised, some of the most powerful episodes were removed in the Folio, the 'revised' version – for instance, the mock-trial in 3.6, where Lear, Edgar and the Fool vie with each other in madness. 'The omission of the mad trial is, without question, the Folio's most surprising cut', said Gary Taylor, explaining that it was cut because it failed: 'uncertainty of focus is apparent in the scene's detail as well as its structure'.[10] Others have also tried to justify this 'cut' – without, however, grappling with a related question. Isn't this episode indispensable, as the geometric centre of the whole play? And if it can succeed in the modern theatre, why should it have failed at the Globe? Is there any evidence that it failed?

In other words, stupid and destructive cutting did occur in the 'Elizabethan' theatre, as indeed in our own, and this weakens Coghill's argument. It is another weakness that most of the instances of Shakespeare's professional skill outlined by Coghill – lucid exposition, the kneel that 'is a stroke of stage-craft of great visual force', and so on – remain Shakespeare's, whether we think of them as part of the play's original composition or as revision. To take the alternative view to Coghill's is not to deny Shakespeare's professional skill but only to claim that what Coghill saw as brilliant afterthoughts were equally brilliant strokes of stagecraft when the play was first written.

Furthermore, we have to concede that one 'added passage' in F is likely to be a Q 'cut' rather than a later addition, namely the Willow Song (4.3.29–52). Q prints the preceding lines, which explain and lead into the song:

> *Des.*   My mother had a maid cald *Barbary*,
> She was in loue, and he she lou'd, prou'd mad,
> And did forsake her, she has a song of willow,
> An old thing 'twas, but it exprest her fortune,
> And she died singing it, that Song to night,
> Will not goe from my minde -- harke, who's that knocks?
>
> (4.3.24 ff., Q)

The absence from Q of the song, and of two shorter passages that almost immediately follow in F (4.3.54–6, 59–62), makes Desdemona's 'Wouldst thou doe such a deed, for all the world' (l. 63, Q) strangely abrupt; in effect, Desdemona's 'lead in' lines and her 'lead out' line ('Wouldst thou doe such a deed . . . ') appear to presuppose the passages missing from Q. A popular explanation is that a boy actor cast as Desdemona after the first production was unable to sing, and so the song and three[11] connected passages had to be dropped. Other play-texts seem to have dropped songs for the same reason;[12] these other texts, however, are thought to be late and 'theatrical' in origin. If the *Othello* Q is based on an early text, perhaps a transcript of the foul papers, a different explanation would have to be found for the song's omission from Q.[13]

We must now ask whether Q's omission of the song, and of the shorter passages that follow, should be treated as a special case (because a boy actor could not sing), or whether any other passages found only in F look like Q 'cuts' rather than F 'additions'. The continuity of both Q and F makes sense, either with or without these passages – hence our difficulty. Yet although the person who changed one of the texts took some care, other omissions from Q introduce awkwardnesses or worse, and this convinces me that in these instances at least Q was cut.

(1) Seventeen lines disappear from Roderigo's account of Desdemona's flight (1.1.119–35, F), an amputation so clinically clean that we are not immediately aware of problems.

> *Bra.*   This thou shalt answer, I know thee *Roderigo*.
> *Rod.*   Sir, I will answer any thing: But I beseech you, [118, F]
> If she be in her chamber, or your house, [136, F]
> Let loose on me the Iustice of the state . . .
>
> (Q)

A patient, however, may suffer from post-operative developments, and even a text can suffer in this way. After an interval Brabantio refers back to the cut passage.

Where didst thou see her; O vnhappy girle,
With the Moore saist thou? who would be a father?
How didst thou know twas she? O *thou deceiuest me* [F: *she deceiues me*]
Past thought: what said she to you? get more tapers,
Raise all my kindred, are they married thinke you?

(1.1.161–5, Q)

Leaving aside the seventeen lines not found in Q, to what does Brabantio allude? In the preceding dialogue Iago, not Roderigo, had been the principal speaker, and there was no suggestion that Roderigo had been an eye-witness. Yet Brabantio now assumes that Roderigo had been close to events, and implies that Roderigo, not Iago, had described them ('With the Moore *saist thou?*') The natural explanation of Brabantio's 'lead out' lines is that he refers back to Roderigo's account of Desdemona's elopement, the seventeen lines cut by Q.

(2) So, too, another long cut (4.3.85–102) is followed by a 'lead out' couplet that appears to presuppose the cut lines.

Then let them vse vs well: else let them know,
The illes we do, their illes instruct vs so.
   Des.   Good night, good night:
Heauen me such vses send,
Not to picke bad, from bad; but by bad, mend.

(4.3.101–4, F)

Curiously, Desdemona's final couplet makes sense in Q, despite the absence of eighteen lines.

   Em.   Why, the wrong is but a wrong i'the world; and hauing the
world for your labour, tis a wrong in your owne world, and you might
quickly make it right.
   Des.   I doe not thinke there is any such woman.
   Em.   Yes, a dozen, and as many to the vantage, as would store the
world they played for.
   Des.   Good night, good night: God me such vsage send,
Not to picke bad from bad, but by bad mend.

(Q)[14]

The 'bad' of the closing line points back to 'ills' in F and to 'wrong' in Q, and we would accept either text if the other one did not exist. Yet F's last *two* lines latch on to the previous *two*, for 'vses' (or 'vsage') refers back to 'Then let them *vse* vs well' (line 102), and to the whole of Emilia's 'cut' speech, which deals with the ways husbands and wives use (or treat) each other. F's final couplet, being more precisely related to the immediate context, suggests that F's version here preceded Q's. One would not expect a reviser to knit in new material and make a better, more complex 'join' than already existed.

One question touched on by Coghill rather than fully explained concerns the very small saving of time if Q represents a cut text - just 8 minutes out of a total of 2¾ hours. Why reduce so long a play by a mere 8 minutes?[15] If Q was cut, however, it does not follow that the Q text was ever performed. Here is an alternative hypothesis: the manuscript behind Q was 'marked up' to indicate possible cuts by someone asked to shorten the play. We know from plays of the period that cuts could be marked up in various ways; we know from Shakespearian texts apparently printed from foul papers, or from manuscripts not far removed from foul papers, that passages marked as cancelled were sometimes misunderstood and printed, in the upshot giving us two versions of the same passage.[16] I deduce that such marks in Shakespeare's texts could be light and confusing; in the case of the *Othello* Q, either the printer omitted only some of the passages marked as cancelled, or, more probably, the person marking the cuts made a start, saw that he was damaging the play and gave up in disgust.

Some of Q's omissions may well have been accidental, resulting from eye-skip. This is likely when the same words are repeated – for example, 1.3.195, where 'with all my heart' repeats from l. 194, or 4.2.74–7, where 'What committed' comes at the end of l. 73 and l. 77. I am not proposing that all the passages missing from Q were marked for omission. The 'lead in' and 'lead out' lines give some support to this hypothesis in the instances discussed above; here, though, and in most of the other instances the 'cuts', if cuts they are, were made so cleverly that the result looks very like seamless stitching. The same would be true if Q's 'cuts' were actually later additions to the text: the person responsible took care in inserting or removing these passages. We should note, however, that whereas the flow of thought is sufficiently smooth in Q to persuade some experts that the Q version came first, the metrical flow is sometimes impaired when F's 'additions' are removed.

(A) (1)   Let's to the Sea-side (hoa)
            As well to see the Vessell that's come in,
            As to throw-out our eyes for braue Othello,
            [Euen till we make the Maine, and th'Eriall blew,
            An indistinct regard].
               Gent.   Come, let's do so.
                                            (2.1.36 ff., F)

I have added square brackets to indicate lines missing from Q. The metrical 'join' is correct in F, not in Q – and, significantly, other F 'additions' are also metrically more acceptable than the Q text at the same point.

   (2)   *Iago.*   I should be wise; for Honestie's a Foole,
         And looses that it workes for.
            [*Oth.*   By the World,
         I thinke my Wife be honest, and thinke she is not: . . .

Ile not indure it. Would I were satisfied.
   Iago.] I see you are eaten vp with Passion:
                  (3.3.385 ff., F)

(3)   *Oth*.   Neuer [Iago. Like to the Ponticke Sea,
Whose Icie Current, and compulsiue course, . . .
Euen so my bloody thoughts, with violent pace
Shall neu'r looke backe, neu'r ebbe to humble Loue,
Till that a capeable, and wide Reuenge
Swallow them vp. Now by yond Marble Heauen,]
In the due reuerence of a Sacred vow,
I heere engage my words.
   Iago. Do not rise yet:
                  (3.3.456 ff., F)

(4) Good Friend, go to him: for by this light of Heauen,
I know not how I lost him. [Heere I kneele: . . .
Not the worlds Masse of vanitie could make me.]
                  (4.2.152 ff., F)

(5) But why should Honor out-liue Honesty?
Let it go all. ·
   Æmil. [What did thy Song boad Lady?
Hearke, canst thou heare me? I will play the Swan,
And dye in Musicke: Willough, Willough, Willough.]
Moore, she was chaste: She lou'd thee, cruell Moore,
                  (5.2.243 ff., F)

Metrical considerations, of course, must not be allowed to weigh too heavily in *Othello*, a play that contains many irregular lines. All the same, is it more likely that in disputed passages, which can be seen as either cuts or additions, the person responsible for the 'additions' straightened out irregular metre – or that the person responsible for the 'cuts' introduced metrical irregularities? And, let us remember, one of the passages in question (5) reverts to the Willow Song, which is widely thought to be a 'cut'. Furthermore, while the flow of thought seems more or less undislocated in both Q and F, other small telltale signs strengthen the view that Q is a 'cut' text. In (3) Othello's vow is surprisingly abrupt and Iago's supporting vow too emphatic in comparison: F's version, with a vow and an echo-speech of roughly the same length, picking up similar images (yond Marble Heauen – Elements, that clip vs round about; my bloody thoughts – What bloody businesse euer), seems much more natural.

Pursuing the 'mark up' hypothesis, it follows that the Willow Song passages are not a special case, in so far as other 'long passages' are more likely to have been cuts than later additions. Why, though, should Shakespeare write a song

I craue fit difpofition for my wife,
Due reuerence of place and exhibition,
Which fuch accomodation ? and befort
As leuels with her breeding.
    Du. If you pleafe, bee't at her fathers.
    Bra. Ile not haue it fo.
    Oth. Nor I.
    Defd. Nor I, I would not there refide,
To put my father in impatient thoughts,
By being in his eye: moft gracious Duke,
To my vnfolding lend a gracious eare,
And let me finde a charter in your voyce,
And if my fimpleneffe. - - - -
    Du. What would you - - - - fpeake.
    Def. That I did loue the Moore, to liue with him,
My downe right violence, and fcorne of Fortunes,

Figure 1a Quarto version of *Othello* 1.3.237 ff.

I craue fit difpofition for my Wife,
Due reference of Place, and Exhibition,
With fuch Accomodation and befort
As leuels with her breeding.
    Duke. Why at her Fathers?
    Bra. I will not haue it fo.
    Othe. Nor I.
    Def. Nor would I there recide,
To put my Father in impatient thoughts
By being in his eye. Moft Greaious Duke,
To my vnfolding, lend your profperous eare,
And let me finde a Charter in your voice
T'affift my fimpleneffe.
    Duke. What would you *Defdemona?*
    Def. That I loue the Moore, to liue with him,
My downe-right violence, and ftorme of Fortunes,

Figure 1b Folio version of *Othello* 1.3.237 ff.

for a boy actor who could not sing? Two reasons suggest themselves: (1) it is never possible to predict accurately when a boy's voice will break: the first Desdemona actor may have had to be replaced sooner than expected;[17] (2) although one thinks of the first production as the obvious time for the 'marking up' exercise, plays were lengthened and shortened for later revivals, and this could have been the fate of *Othello*. Nevertheless, as already stated, we must not assume that the shorter (i.e. Q) version of *Othello* was ever performed.

The combined evidence of 'lead in' and 'lead out' lines and of metrical irregularity favours the view that at least some of the disputed longer passages were cut, rather than added. And, we must ask, if at least some – why not the others as well? Is it not unlikely that some were omitted by Q (as I have tried to show) and that others were authorial afterthoughts, first printed in F (as Coghill suggested)? We are moving away from Coghill's theory; this does not mean that Shakespeare did not revise the play, only that one kind of evidence – the longer passages – must now be discounted.

What other evidence remains? We may divide it into three categories. (i) Shorter passages that differ in Q and F (some being very similar in length to F's shortest 'longer passages'); (ii) what I call 'high-quality' single word variants, where both Q and F transmit excellent readings that could well be authorial, rather than unauthorised substitutions by a scribe or compositor; (iii) F's inferior variants, graphically related to Q's, which suggest that the F scribe was trying to decipher a second manuscript written in the same hand as the Q manuscript. Two other kinds of variant should be mentioned in passing, even though they may not seem to give much help in the debate about authorial revision. (iv) Indifferent variants, where it is difficult or impossible to choose between Q and F because grammar, metre and the author's characteristic style lead us to conclude that both are acceptable (e.g. singular–plural variants, these – those, the – that, I am – am I, and similar trifling alternatives); and (v) editorial variants, such as the elimination of profanity or of old-fashioned words or phrases. As will be seen, (iv) and (v) are not an entirely separate issue; in the first instance, however, we must concentrate on (i) to (iii) to resolve the all-important question for an editor of *Othello* – did Shakespeare himself revise or at any rate retouch the play?

I begin with (i), shorter passages that differ in Q and F. Here the play's metre is again significant, though now (cf. p. 13) we shall consider passages where Q is regular and F irregular. I have inserted a solidus (/) in (1) and (3) to indicate Q's 'correct' line-endings.

(B) (1)   As leuels with her breeding.
   Du. If you please, / bee't at her fathers.
   Bra. Ile not haue it so. /
   Oth. Nor I.
   Desd. Nor I, I would not there reside, /
  To put my father in impatient thoughts, /
         (1.3.240 ff., Q)

As leuels with her breeding.
 Duke. Why at her Fathers?
 Bra. I will not haue it so.
 Othe. Nor I.
 Des. Nor would I there recide,
To put my Father in impatient thoughts
(F)

(2) *Oth.* Your voyces Lords: beseech you let her will,
Haue a free way, I therefore beg it not
To please the pallat of my appetite.
(1.3.261 ff., Q)

 Othe. Let her haue your voice.
Vouch with me Heauen, I therefore beg it not
To please the pallate of my Appetite:
(F)

(3) Either for stay or going, the affaires cry hast, /
And speede must answer, you must hence to night, /
 Desd. To night my Lord?
 Du. This night.
 Oth. With all my heart. /
(1.3.277 ff., Q)

Either for her stay, or going: th'Affaire cries hast:
And speed must answer it.
 Sen. You must away to night.
 Othe. With all my heart.
(F)

(4) Cry out, sweete creature, and then kisse me hard,
As if he pluckt vp kisses by the rootes,
That grew vpon my lips, then layed his leg
Ouer my thigh, and sigh'd, and kissed, and then
Cried, cursed fate, that gaue thee to the Moore.
(3.3.424 ff., Q)

Cry, oh sweete Creature: then kisse me hard,
As if he pluckt vp kisses by the rootes,
That grew vpon my lippes, laid his Leg ore my Thigh,
And sigh, and kisse, and then cry cursed Fate,
That gaue thee to the Moore.
(F)

(5) *Em.* 'Twill out, 'twill: I hold my peace sir, no,
I'le be in speaking, liberall as the ayre,
(5.2.217 ff., Q)

>   *Emil.*   'Twill out, 'twill out. I peace?
>   No, I will speake as liberall as the North;
>
>   (F)

Greg, who discussed three of these five passages, said of (5) that

> what strikes one most is the Shakespearian quality of both versions, and it
> is by no means easy to decide which is preferable . . . . With regard to the
> second line in F it might be objected that the wind does not in fact speak. Q
> might therefore be preferred . . . . [But] the reading 'North' itself may seem
> a rather violent ellipsis unless prepared for by the 'ayre' of Q. Everything
> therefore points to F's version having been reached by way of Q's, rather
> than Q's being a corruption of F's.[18]

In Shakespeare's mind the wind *could* speak (*Troilus* 1.3.253: 'speak frankly as
the wind'), and this 'image' supports F, whilst 'liberal as the air' or free as air
(*OED*, liberal, 3) also sounds right. If we agree with Greg that Q's first line
should be emended as in Q2 ('Twill out, 'twill [out]), authorial revision best
accounts for the two versions. In that case revision sharpened the sense and
left a short line.

So with (3). This is not simply an instance of omission, as the lines preceding
the 'omission' are changed as well. And a reason for F's change is not hard to
find: Desdemona's 'To night my Lord?' might be thought immodest, making
her reluctant to give up her wedding night. As in an earlier line, 'my hearts
subdued, / [E]uen to the *vtmost pleasure* of my Lord' (1.3.251–2, Q; *very quality*,
F), the possibility that Desdemona has sexual pleasure in mind is eliminated
in F. In (2) F again rescues Desdemona from a possible unkind reflection –
that she has behaved wilfully – and in (1) F softens Desdemona, making her
refusal to live at her father's house less emphatic. Four times in less than thirty
lines F retouches Q to protect Desdemona, and three of the four involve more
than simple verbal substitution, that is, depart from the normal course of
corruption in Q: authorial revision is therefore the more likely explanation.
(See also p. 35: the suggestion that Shakespeare intended to delete one of two
alternative passages, 4.3.63–6, again to protect Desdemona.) If so, it is significant that the F versions of (1)–(3) and (5) condense, leaving irregular lines,
and that F scans irregularly in (4) as well, which may have a bearing on
other lines where F omits or changes words, producing irregular metre but
acceptable continuity.[19]

Greg said of (3) that 'the impression is of deliberate revision in F rather
than of corruption in Q',[20] a remark that applies equally to the other passages.
And it must be stressed that in these instances Q, a text not noticeably
sensitive to the play's metre, transmits metrically correct lines, even though
(1) and (3) are not laid out on the page as metrical lines, whereas F prints
long and short lines.

Let us now compare the five passages headed (B)(1)–(5) and the five other passages cited earlier as (A)(1)–(5). In passages (A)(1)–(5) I was struck by the common factor that the Q versions contain long and/or short lines, whereas F scans regularly; in passages (B)(1)–(5) by the common factor that Q scans regularly and F contains long and/or short lines. I suggested that, in passages (A)(1)–(5), Q's metrical irregularities indicate that the F text was cut to produce Q, and that, in passages (B)(1)–(5), F's metrical irregularities indicate that the F text followed Q. Is this a self-cancelling argument by a damnable both-sides rogue? It appears to suggest that Q's metrical irregularity identifies F as the later text, and that F's metrical irregularity also identifies F as the later text: heads I win, tails you lose. We must remember, however, that the (A) and (B) passages differ textually in one important respect. The (A) passages all involve a clean cut (if the F version preceded Q) or a 'clean' addition (if Q preceded F), that is, without other rewriting; in the (B) passages some rewriting has undoubtedly taken place (and in three instances for a discernible reason, to 'protect' Desdemona (p. 35)). This difference, and the fact that Q so often mislines its verse even when it unknowingly preserves the verse pattern, persuades me that (A)(1)–(5) should be interpreted as Q cuts, and (B)(1)–(5) as F revisions.

Returning now to (ii) (p. 16), the 'high-quality' variants, I once wrote that in transcribing or revising his own play Shakespeare might well 'substitute literally related words. Some of these "related" variants in *Othello* are out of the way and would not spring to the mind of every copyist or compositor: *provulgate–promulgate* (1.2.21), *enscerped–ensteep'd* (2.1.70).'[21] Other poets and dramatists not infrequently substitute literally related variants in their holograph fair copies: I urged that Shakespeare might do the same. A more comprehensive study of misreading in *Othello* (chapter 8) now persuades me that, while it remains true that Shakespeare might do the same, it would be risky to argue for authorial revision on the evidence of such variants. Misreading is so pervasive in both Q and F that it can never be ruled out as a possible begetter of literally related variants.

As for (iii), F's inferior variants that point to a second authorial manuscript, this is a more complicated question, one that cannot be discussed in all its ramifications until we have identified the scribe of the F manuscript (chapter 6) and the misreading in both Q and F (chapter 8). The reader will have to take it on trust that (iii) gives strong support to (i), unless he or she wishes to turn immediately to pages 99ff., before I have laid out the evidence that leads to this conclusion.

Let us pause, then, and take stock. We have eliminated F's longer 'additions' and high-quality variants as evidence for revision, and are left with (i) and (iii). Greg, who came down on the side of revision in (i), nevertheless thought that both versions of *Othello* derive from the same authorial manuscript. The question whether Q and F originated in one authorial manuscript or in two is quite crucial for the editor and, as I have promised, will be examined later: here I want to prepare the ground for it by asking two related questions.

(1) Why did Greg disbelieve, in general, in two authorial manuscripts of Shakespeare's plays? (2) How have later textual critics reacted to Greg's position?

(1) Since I reviewed Greg's reasons for disbelief elsewhere[22] we can save space by summarising the principal ones, together with some replies. (a) Greg accepted as fairly close to the truth the claim of Heminges and Condell that 'we have scarce received from him [Shakespeare] a blot in his papers'. Answering Fredson Bowers, who disagreed with him, Greg said 'unless Professor Bowers can point to earlier examples of the like claim, what business has he to assert that in making it Heminges and Condell were merely following a fashion, rather than setting one that Moseley followed a quarter of a century later?'[23] Earlier examples were not hard to find; it was shown 'that the First Folio circle had heard of the wonders of free composition just before the Folio preliminaries were drafted'[24]: that is, what Heminges and Condell said about unblotted papers, a fairly standard compliment, need not be taken too literally. (b) Because he believed that 'Shakespeare doubtless composed fluently and seldom went back over what he had written', Greg thought that Shakespeare's foul papers would need little tidying, and therefore that Shakespeare could leave it to others to prepare his fair copies. Reaching this view, Greg disregarded his own account of some of Shakespeare's foul papers (e.g. those of *Othello*, 'a rather heavily corrected manuscript') and his own scattered conclusions about individual plays, quite a few of which he described as printed from Shakespeare's fair copies.[25] In addition (c) Greg ignored the evidence of surviving dramatic manuscripts: on his own showing, probably five out of fifteen extant prompt-books are in the author's hand, and other authorial fair copies apart from prompt-books have also come down to us.

(2) In 1955, when Greg published his definitive statement, *The Shakespeare First Folio*, Fredson Bowers brought out *On Editing Shakespeare and the Elizabethan Dramatists*. Here Bowers emphasised that 'there is no evidence whatever . . . in Henslowe that an author ever submitted for payment anything but a fair copy', and noted some of the inconsistencies in Greg's opposition to Shakespearian fair copies (hence the irritation in Greg's review of *On Editing*, quoted in the previous paragraph). But was Shakespeare just 'an author', any author? Bowers later qualified his generalisation:

> It may seem probable, however, in my opinion, that a commissioned playwright like Shakespeare, a shareholder in the company, need not have been bound by the conventions applied to outsiders. Instead, I suggest, Shakespeare ordinarily submitted his working papers, and that the company thereupon had these transcribed.[26]

This may be right, for 'ordinarily' allows for exceptions, and Shakespeare's exceptions are likely to have been the plays that engaged him most deeply (including *Othello* and *King Lear*). But it should be noted that the reasons for thinking that Shakespeare need not have submitted fair copies are really quite flimsy. True, few of his plays have reached us in what might be thought to be two authorial versions (such as the Q and F versions of *Othello* and *King Lear*) – yet how many plays by other dramatists have survived in two authorial versions? If it was a convention that contemporary dramatists had to hand in a fair copy of every play, there is no evidence that Shakespeare was exempted, and we have some evidence to the contrary, insofar as Greg himself held that a number of Shakespeare's plays were printed from authorial fair copies. Moreover, if Shakespeare's writing had deteriorated by c. 1600, as I try to demonstrate (chapter 8), he would have had an added motive for wanting to give his colleagues legible copy, especially of his more important plays. So, taking 'ordinarily . . .' as a let-out clause, and refusing to attach too much significance to the absence of fair copies of some of Shakespeare's plays – an absence that seems natural enough, when one thinks about it, after four hundred years, and not unlike the fate of play-texts written by other dramatists – it would not be unreasonable to assume that sometimes, if not always, Shakespeare took the trouble to prepare a fair copy, and that the F texts of *Othello* and *King Lear* could be instances. For my present purposes that suffices, for no one is going to say that Shakespeare never wrote out a fair copy, or that there is positive evidence that he refused to submit fair copies of *Othello* and *King Lear*.

I have arrived at a position very like that of thirty years ago, when I argued that Shakespeare sometimes wrote out two copies of a play, both of which he regarded as 'finished', though not therefore beyond the reach of afterthoughts; that is, I believe that Q and F *Othello* are examples of textual instability, not of large-scale revision. Before we return to this issue, in chapter 9, we shall have to look much more closely at the textual detail of Q and F, which in turn necessitates an examination of the professional practices of the texts' printers and publishers, and scribes and compositors. I begin with new archive material concerning a fascinating rogue, Thomas Walkley, the publisher of Q *Othello*.

Chapter 3

The Quarto publisher and printer

Thomas Walkley, bookseller and publisher, took up his freedom on 19 January 1618 and remained an active stationer until 1658. In his first few years in business he entangled himself in serious financial difficulties, which led to law suits with another stationer and with one of his authors, and to his imprisonment. Indirectly, these difficulties have a bearing on his publications at this time, including several Beaumont and Fletcher plays and the first Quarto of *Othello*.

Walkley's law suits involved many individuals; the one that will chiefly interest students of *Othello* survives in unpublished records that are badly mutilated, therefore often illegible and confusing. To help readers I shall summarise the evidence, in so far as this is possible, relegating the details to Appendix B, where they can be checked.

Percy Simpson long ago drew attention to what may have been Walkley's first brush with the law.[1] 'A collection of Wither's Poems was fraudulently issued by the stationer Thomas Walkley in 1620', namely *The Workes of Master George Wither*, printed by John Beale for Thomas Walkley. The co-publisher of Wither's later *Faire-Virtue* (1622) denounced the earlier *Workes* as 'an imperfect and erronious Copie . . . which the Stationer hath . . . falsely affirmed to bee Corrected and Augmented for his owne Aduantage', without the author's knowledge. The stationer, Walkley, fell out with John Beale, his printer, and this is how we come to know of events that might have been better left concealed. Beale had sued Walkley for not paying his bills and, said Percy Simpson, 'Walkley, completely helpless, asks for the case to be heard in the Court of Requests'.

Although it was later objected that Simpson exaggerated Walkley's wickedness,[2] there can be little doubt that, in Simpson's phrase, Walkley was Beale's 'brother-rogue' in 1620. For our present purposes all that matters is that, whatever Walkley's precise degree of guilt, his case against Beale so strangely resembles his later account of his troubles with Dr John Everard. The two law suits were more or less contemporary, and both began with a bill of complaint brought by Walkley. *Walkley* v. *Everard* was heard in the Court of Chancery, and fortunately the defendant's answer also survives. I have the impression that Walkley, who once again presented himself as the injured party, was at least partly the victim of his own incompetence, and the same may be true of his dealings with Beale.

Walkley v. *Everard*, hitherto unknown, concerned a treatise, *Bellona's Embrion*, written by Sir Michael Everard, who died in 1621 or 1622. Sir Michael's widow, Lady Margaret Everard, asked her husband's cousin, Dr John Everard, to see to the publication of the treatise and he, said Walkley, 'did come and fly unto your orator [i.e. Walkley, addressing the court], as he had done many times before'. In fact Walkley had published two works by John Everard, in 1618 and 1622 (*STC* 10598, 10599), and it may be that Everard had also 'flown' unto him on other occasions, as authors are inclined to do when they think they know a friendly publisher. At any rate, Everard persuaded Walkley to publish *Bellona's Embrion*, 'undertook to make it fit for the press' and (Everard himself claimed) paid 20 shillings for the licensing of the book. Seven hundred and fifty copies were to be printed. Walkley's bill and Everard's answer explained their financial arrangements in some detail: it seems that Lady Margaret paid various sums to Dr Everard, who in turn paid Walkley who was supposed to buy paper and pay the printer. But Walkley, already heavily in debt, did not pay the printer – as he had failed to pay the printer of Wither's *Workes* in 1620 – using the money instead to settle with other creditors. In the upshot the printer, Bernard Alsop, apparently refused to continue after perfecting thirty-eight sheets, and Walkley prevailed upon a second printer, Thomas Snodham, to go on with the book. But, said Everard, Walkley was preoccupied with another book, 'which he called his *Nero*', and 'neglected to set *Bellona's Embrion* to the press'.

These events partly overlapped with the printing of Q *Othello* (late 1621 and / or early 1622), and dragged on thereafter. Walkley's financial difficulties, it transpires, had already begun by 1621, and Everard's account of them suggests that the publisher of Q *Othello* had to resort to desperate measures to extricate himself: 'by prayers and tears' Walkley entreated Everard to help him, and 'protested with horrible oaths that he had paid all arrears', yet 'meant nothing but fraud and deceit'[3] – not, one hopes, the normal behaviour of a reputable London publisher. While Everard may have exaggerated a little, as authors tend to do when speaking about their publishers, his account of Walkley's difficulties is confirmed by what we know of the printing of Walkley's books. Alsop printed two books for him in 1622 (Chapman's *Pro Vere* and Juan de Luna's *The pursuit of the historie of Lazarillo de Tormes*: *STC* 4988, 16927); the only book that may have been published by Walkley in 1623 was Edmund Bolton's *Nero Caesar* (folio, T.S. for T. Walkley, 1624). The revised *Short-Title Catalogue* notes that the engraved title-page is dated 1623 and that 'Alsop printed B–M; Snodham the rest'. This is the book referred to by Everard, who complained that Walkley concentrated on the printing of a work 'which he called his *Nero*', neglecting *Bellona's Embrion*. Alsop, it seems, refused to go on with two of Walkley's books, and Snodham twice picked up the pieces, completing *Nero Caesar* and continuing – but not completing – *Bellona's Embrion*.

Here a brief digression is in order. Charlton Hinman noted in 1975 that there seems 'to have been a major break in the printing of [Quarto] *Othello* just after the composition of the second forme for sheet G was completed'.[4] We know that Walkley's difficulties had begun by 1620, when he and John Beale fell foul of each other. The fact that the printing of *Othello* was interrupted in late 1621 or early 1622, anticipating as it does the fate of *Nero Caesar* and *Bellona's Embrion*, again confirms that Walkley was already in serious trouble and was trying to survive by juggling with his commitments. He borrowed £100 from one George Humble;[5] also, having managed somehow to obtain a manuscript of *Othello* – the first Shakespeare text to 'escape' the King's Men since 1609 – he no doubt hoped that this popular play would bring him a much-needed profit and would reduce his debts.

Back to *Walkley* v. *Everard*. The printer Thomas Snodham set up other books for Walkley in 1624 (N. Flamel, *Exposition: STC* 11027) and in 1625 (*A King and No King*, second edition; J. Gee, *Steps of ascension unto God: STC* 1671, 11706.4). It is unlikely that he stepped in because he needed the cash (squeezing cash out of Walkley was clearly not easy) – for in his will, dated 16 October 1625, he was able to leave each of his three children £250, substantial sums at this time. He was a wealthy and well-connected stationer: his wife was the daughter of Cuthbert Burby, and both he and his wife named two important stationers, Edmund Weaver and William Stansby, as overseers of their wills.[6]

Two other printers who worked for Walkley, Nicholas Okes and John Beale, enjoyed a different reputation. Sir John Lambe wrote of the latter:

> Master John Beale succeeded his partner Master William Hall about 15 yeares since [i.e. in 1620], never admitted (of great estate but a very contentious person), he tooke 50 li to furnish ye pore with bread and doth not do it. He bought Hall [out] and took Thomas Brudenell to be his partner for £140, which Brudenell had much a doe to recover.[7]

Okes, the printer of Q *Othello*, is a central actor in our story, and I return to him later. Let us note immediately, though, that Okes and Beale both got into trouble for printing pirated texts around 1620, and that both men printed play-texts that were later replaced by better versions, a strange sequence of events probably not unrelated to Walkley's financial difficulties. Six Beaumont and Fletcher plays were published from 1619 to 1625 in nine editions, five of the nine for Walkley. These five plays need to be considered as a group, as K.W. Cameron observed in 1932, adding that 'the crux of the matter is the young bookseller, Thomas Walkley'.[8]

1619 *Cupid's revenge* (2nd edition) [A. Mathewes] for T. Jones. Assigned 15 April 1619.

A King and No King [J. Beale] for T. Walkley [Entered to E. Blount, 7 August 1618].

The maides tragedy [N. Okes] for F. Constable [SR 28 April].

1620 Phylaster [N. Okes] for T. Walkley [SR 10 January].

1621 Thierry and Theodoret [N. Okes] for T. Walkley.

1622 The maides tragedy ['second impression']. Newly perused, augmented, and enlarged. [G. Purslowe] for F. Constable.

Phylaster ['second impression'], corrected and amended. [N. Okes] for T. Walkley.

1625 A King and No King [The second time printed] [T. Snodham] for T. Walkley [a revised edition, with additions].

The scornful ladie (another ed.) [A. Mathewes] for M.P[artrich?] sold by T. Jones. Assigned by Partrich to T. Jones 8 May 1617.

Two points must be noted at once. In 1622, the year in which 'augmented' and 'corrected' versions of two plays appeared, Walkley also published the first quarto of Othello, printed by N. Okes; and Othello, a third play belonging to the King's Men, again survives in two versions. Secondly, also in 1622, Bernard Alsop printed for Walkley The pursuit of the historie of Lazarillo de Tormes with a dedication signed T.W. which refers to the book as 'this strangely recouered Continuation' – meaning, it seems, this strangely acquired manuscript.[9] One wonders therefore how Walkley acquired his play-texts: 'strangely', perhaps?

It is not impossible that the King's Men released three play-texts for publication in 1622. Greg thought that Q Othello, registered on 6 October 1621 and issued in the year before the Folio, 'is unlikely to have been published without the sanction of the King's company',[10] a view now difficult to sustain, because of Hinman's revised chronology of the printing of the Folio (see p. 30). I think 'the sanction of the King's Company' more probable in the case of the two Beaumont and Fletcher plays, both of which replaced inferior quartos, than of Q Othello, where the same motive could not apply. Why should the King's Men allow the Othello quarto when they had opposed all quarto publications of Shakespeare for many years, ever since 1609?

Seeking an answer to this question we must not overlook a lost letter sent by the Lord Chamberlain to the Stationers. Greg explained it as follows: 'On 3 May 1619 the Court of the Stationers' Company had before it for consideration a letter from the Lord Chamberlain, whereupon it was ordered that in future no plays belonging to the King's men should be printed without their consent. There can be no reasonable doubt that the players were behind it'.[11] The letter itself has disappeared, but 'it seems to be recapitulated in a subsequent letter of like tenor addressed to the Company on 10 June 1637 by Philip, Earl of Pembroke and Montgomery, who had succeeded his brother in his title and office in 1630'.[12]

Wheras complaint was heertofore presented to my Deare brother &

predecessor by his Maiestes servantes the Players, that some of the Company of Printers & Stationers had procured, published & printed diuerse of their bookes of Comædyes, Tragedyes, Cronicle Historyes, and the like, which they had (for the speciall service of his Maiestye & for their owne vse) bought and provided at very Deare & high rates, By meanes wherof not onely they themselues had much preiudice, but the bookes much corruption to the iniury and disgrace of the Authors; And therupon the Masters & Wardens of the company of printers & stationers were advised by my Brother to take notice therof & to take Order for the stay of any further Impression of any of the Playes or Interludes of his Maiestes servantes without their consentes.

The letter of 1619, we have been told,[13] was triggered off by the so-called Pavier quartos of 1619, the first abortive attempt to bring out Shakespeare's plays as a collection. Yet the statement that 'stationers had procured, published & printed diverse of their books' suggests that these books were now published for the first time, unlike the Pavier quartos, which were all reprints. At a later point in the 1637 letter the Lord Chamberlain complains that the first warning had not been heeded, and now he writes even more explicitly:

Notwithstanding which I am informed that some Coppyes of Playes belonging to the King & Queenes servantes the Players, & purchased by them at Deare rates, haueing beene lately stollen or gotten from them by indirect meanes, are now attempted to bee printed.

As the players were more likely to object to the first printing of a play than to its being reprinted, and as the Lord Chamberlain's letter appears to refer to the procuring (i.e. stealing) of play-texts from the players, we must ask whether the Lord Chamberlain's letter of 1619 pointed to the Pavier quartos or, in the first instance, to the Beaumont and Fletcher plays published in 1619 and thereafter. At any rate, it is a curious coincidence that the Lord Chamberlain's letter was considered by the Stationers on 3 May 1619, that *The Maid's Tragedy* was registered on 28 April – and that this same play was reissued in 1622 in an augmented, improved text.[14]

I want to propose another possible explanation of the letter of 1619, aided by the knowledge that Walkley and his associates resorted to piracy and other dubious practices on a greater scale than Greg could have suspected. In 1618–19 a number of manuscripts belonging to the King's Men went missing. Edward Blount registered *A King and No King* on 7 August 1618, without publishing the play: this looks like a 'blocking entry' to prevent piracy, like Blount's entry of *Antony and Cleopatra* and *Pericles* in 1608, the former not published till 1623, the latter followed by a bad quarto in 1609. So far as we know, Walkley published *A King and No King* in 1619 without Blount's authority. As soon as the players heard that *The Maid's Tragedy* had been entered in the Stationers' Register (28 April) they felt that they had to act, as decisively as they could, and they asked the Lord Chamberlain to intervene. He wrote at once to the Stationers. The man or men who held the other missing manuscripts therefore had to proceed with caution, and issued them one by one, in the hope that the Lord Chamberlain's letter would be forgotten. We should keep in mind that 'blocking entries', if intended to prevent unauthorised publication (as is generally but not universally assumed[15]), were sometimes followed a year or so later by a text, often a suspicious text; that is, unauthorised publishers saw that there were advantages in biding their time.

We should also notice that, contrary to custom, four plays – *A King and No King, The Maid's Tragedy, Philaster, Othello* – were entered in the Stationers' Register without any hint of their author(s) or of the companies that had performed them. When the author was famous and the play had been a success in the theatre, more often than not one or both facts would be recorded in the Register entry – whereas this group of plays, once one recognises it as a group, seems to have been sneaked into the Register as quietly as possible.

Four Beaumont and Fletcher plays and perhaps *Othello* could have gone 'missing' in 1618–19, I suggest, three or four of these five plays being later replaced by improved texts[16] – which would seem to indicate that the players had not sanctioned the first printing of at least three, and, it may be, of all five. Yet, looking at the situation from the point of view of the King's Men, we have only identified the tip of an iceberg. We know from Sir Henry Herbert's office-book that the allowed text of *The Winter's Tale* was 'missing' in 1623; other First Folio plays were also unavailable for a while (for example, *Troilus and Cressida*) or had to be printed from imperfect texts (*Timon of Athens*). Further, since two manuscripts existed for some plays, who knows how many more 'second texts' may have been found to be missing at this time? And at this very time, in April 1619, John Witter started legal proceedings against Heminges and Condell concerning the ownership of the Globe theatre. Witter, an unsavoury opportunist, had married the widow of one of their colleagues, later deserting her; after her death he claimed to have rights in the Globe, which Heminges and Condell disputed, with good reason. It would not be out of character if Witter had something to do with the missing play-texts. Be that as it may, the King's Men were sorely afflicted: missing manuscripts, the Okes–Walkley quartos, the Pavier quartos, the Witter law-suit and, last but not least, the unexpected death[17] of their leading actor, Richard Burbage, in March 1619. The company must have seemed particularly vulnerable in these months: no wonder that unscrupulous stationers thought that now was the time to pounce.

Who were these stationers, and how were they connected? Evidently Pavier and Jaggard acted together. Jaggard had previously issued the unauthorised *Passionate Pilgrim* in 1599, had reissued it with additions in 1612, both times as 'By W. Shakespeare', and was later deeply involved in the First Folio: a committed printer of Shakespeare, if not an entirely honest one. While we do not know much about the relationship of Jaggard and Pavier, in his will (23

March 1623)[18] Jaggard called Thomas Pavier, stationer, and Thomas Evans, grocer, 'my very good friends', asking them to act as his overseers. The plays issued by Jaggard and Pavier in 1619 are known as 'the Pavier quartos', perhaps because Pavier owned the copy for five of the ten plays, yet it may well be that Jaggard rather than Pavier was the instigator, and a new study of Pavier's career confirms me in this belief.[19]

How closely the other stationers acted together can only be surmised. The printers, again, may have had as great a say in their private arrangements as the publishers, for the printers were established men and the publishers mere novices in comparison: the printers Okes and Beale became freemen in 1603 and 1608, and the publishers, Constable and Walkley, in 1614 and 1618. Percy Simpson described Walkley as Beale's 'victim' in the piracy of Wither's *Workes* (1620) and, be it noted, Beale also printed *A King and No King* for Walkley in 1619. Okes printed *The Maid's Tragedy* (1619, for Constable), and *Philaster* (1620), *Thierry* (1621) and *Othello* (1622) for Walkley. Like Beale, Okes got into trouble for piratical texts of Wither, in 1619 and 1621,[20] and on other occasions for other reasons. Peter Blayney has published a fairly comprehensive account of Okes and his professional activities – as it happens, not including the play-texts of 1619–25, yet surveying Okes's early and later work and outlining his many brushes with authority.

> One of the notable features of Okes's record is how much he managed to get away with, and for how long. At least once he was warned that if he printed another unlicensed book his presses would be dismantled . . . .
>
> [Okes] was seldom found in open defiance of the regulations [of the Stationers]: he merely broke them . . . whenever he thought he could remain undiscovered. The known actions against him probably reveal only a fraction of his illicit activity. He seems to have had few compunctions about printing other men's copyrights; was quite prepared to make a little extra money by working on books known to be unlicensed.[21]

Okes's record reflects on Walkley, who chose Okes as his printer for so many play-texts that came into being in – shall we say? – unusual circumstances.

The printers and publishers who issued several Beaumont and Fletcher plays and Q *Othello* appear to have been not entirely blameless in their professional dealings. Nevertheless, a wicked stationer may 'procure' a good text: should they have handled stolen goods, as we may suspect, their texts are not necessarily bad. And if the manuscripts were stolen directly from the King's Men we have cause to be grateful to Walkley and his associates for texts, good or bad, that might otherwise have disappeared. So we need to know whether these texts, four of which were replaced by augmented and/or corrected versions, can be classified as good or bad. The careful analysis of the Beaumont and Fletcher texts by Fredson Bowers and his experienced editors does not help, however, except for one point that must interest editors of *Othello*: some of the Beaumont and Fletcher texts, like the *Othello* Quarto, could be either 'good' or 'bad'. Robert K. Turner concluded in 1966 – note the date – that 'the middle part of *Philaster* Q1 may be like *Othello* Q1, corrupt but essentially authoritative, or it may be like *Richard III* Q1 or *Lear* Q1, an unusually faithful report. I am inclined, but with some reservations, to think it a bad text'.[22] Editing *The Maid's Tragedy* Turner was also pulled in two directions, and came down on the other side: Q1 was printed from 'an essentially authoritative manuscript . . . sometimes hard to read . . . sometimes heavily worked over. . . . These are the characteristics of rough foul papers'.[23] He warned, however, that 'it is possible that Walkley garnered five scribal copies which may have differed considerably in physical state but have come into being under the same or similar circumstances'.[24] Having suggested, very tentatively, that the printer or printers rather than the publisher may have done the 'garnering', I have to add that the one other Shakespeare text printed by Okes – namely, *King Lear* Q1 – resembles *Othello* Q1 and some of the Beaumont and Fletcher texts in its textual characteristics, making it either a good 'bad quarto' or a badly printed 'good quarto', according to taste. Taste has changed since 1966, but the possibility that some of the Walkley texts and the *King Lear* quarto came into existence in 'similar circumstances' could have far-reaching consequences.

In this chapter I have tried to show that Walkley and Okes arouse misgivings as to their professional dealings at the very time when they produced the Quarto version of *Othello*.[25] Editors of plays printed or published by one or both must fear the worst. I suggest in the next chapter that the Quarto suffers from many faults – misreading, deliberate omissions due to inaccurate 'casting off', perhaps even additions for the same reason – but, as will emerge later, the Folio also printed a deeply flawed text, in many respects a text inferior to the Quarto's. Whilst it will be as well to fear the worst, we shall find that Walkley's Quarto also helps us to correct the Folio in many scores of readings.

Chapter 4

The Quarto text

Thomas Walkley entered *Othello* in the Stationers' Register on 6 October 1621 (see p. 2). It was a perfectly normal entry. Greg thought that the date makes it unlikely that Q was 'published without the sanction of the King's company, and they doubtless reserved the right of reprinting, since the Folio was already in hand'.[1] Charlton Hinman later expressed a different view, based on his more detailed study of the printing of the Folio.

> Precisely when and with whom Walkley agreed that *Othello* might be included in the Folio is of course not very important. Agreement there must have been at *some* time, in any event . . . . But it can no longer be argued that the players gave Walkley permission to publish when work on the collection was already going forward. The quarto, indeed, may well have been on sale to the public for some little time before a single Folio forme had been set into type.[2]

'Much if not all of [Q *Othello*] probably went through the press in late 1621'.[3] In other words, Walkley did not have to ask the King's Men or Folio publishers for permission to print: he was first in the field and so they would have to ask him, even if he had acquired and printed his text against the wishes of 'the grand possessors'. This may explain how Walkley acquired the corrected text of *Philaster*, which he published in the same year as Q *Othello*: the King's Men were allowed to issue F *Othello*, a play in which Walkley had established his 'copy-right', and in exchange Walkley was given a better text of *Philaster*. One of Greg's brilliant papers proved long ago that 'copy-right' quarrels between stationers could be resolved by just such a compromise.[4]

The epistle printed in the second issue of the first quarto of *Troilus and Cressida* (1609) coined the phrase 'the grand possessors', referring to the King's Men and their reluctance to publish their best plays. After 1609 no other Shakespearian text repeated 'the scape it [*Troilus*] hath made' until Q *Othello* some twelve years later, a remarkable contrast with the years before 1609, when so many quartos were published. The tone of the *Troilus* epistle, the total cessation of new quartos for twelve years and, most explicitly, the Lord Chamberlain's letters to the Stationers' Company (see p. 25), concur in suggesting that the King's Men resisted the publication of their Shakespeare plays, and that Walkley acted on his own when he issued Q *Othello*, without wasting time on the usual courtesies.

He might nevertheless have acquired a 'good' text, rather than one 'maimed, and deformed by the frauds and stealthes of iniurious impostors' (the words of Heminges and Condell in the Folio, referring to earlier 'bad' quartos). A rogue may sell blameless goods – therefore we must examine Q *Othello* carefully, taking Walkley's professional career into account. Was Q printed from an authorial manuscript or from copy at one remove from the author, or was it printed from seriously flawed copy? Editors have backed these very different explanations; Walkley's career, as I have outlined it, is bound to check optimism, but should not be allowed to decide the issue.

We must make our decision from the 'internal evidence' of the Q text itself, comparing it with other good and bad Shakespearian texts and, if necessary, with other contemporary play-texts. Comparing it with other Shakespearian good quartos one is immediately struck by several differences. Unlike the quartos published before 1623, Q *Othello* is divided into acts – incompletely, but the intention remains visible in the opening lines of each act.

(1)   Enter *Iago* and *Roderigo*.
                            Roderigo.
        TVsh, neuer tell me, I take it much vnkindly

(2)   *Actus* 2.
                            Scoena I.
            Enter Montanio, *Gouernor of* Cypres, *with*
                        two other Gentlemen.
                            Montanio.
        WHat from the Cape can you discerne at Sea?

(3)   *Enter* Cassio, *with Musitians and the Clowne*.
        Cas.   MAsters, play here, I will content your paines,

(4)   *Actus*. 4.
                    Enter Iago *and* Othello.
        Iag.   Will you thinke so?

(5)   *Actus*. 5.
                    Enter Iago *and* Roderigo,
            Iag.   Here stand behind this Bulke, straite will he come,

No scene division was marked, apart from '*Actus* 2. | *Scoena* I', but the use of large or dropped capitals (found nowhere else in the play-text) confirms that (3) was meant to begin Act 3, and therefore that act division of some sort was marked in the Q manuscript. This could have been done by Walkley or Okes in 1621, though one might have expected more consistency if act division was inserted to 'dress up' the text for publication.

Its heavier punctuation, especially its colons and dashes, also distinguishes Q *Othello* from most of the earlier good quartos; the quartos naturally differ from one another as well, being the work of many printers.[5] By contrast Shakespeare's Hand D in *Sir Thomas More* used no colons or dashes, omitted many necessary question marks and other stops, and failed to punctuate the end of all but two of its four dozen speeches. The dashes in Q *Othello* usually consist of two, three or four hyphens and presumably came from the Q manuscript. If we decide that this manuscript had more in common with good than with bad quartos, we shall have to keep in mind the possibility that it was a scribal copy, not Shakespeare's own papers.[6]

Before we attempt a more refined solution we must try to weigh the 'good' against the 'bad' textual characteristics of Q *Othello*. I take the bad first, and begin with examples of mishearing.

(1)   Or put vpon you what restraint, and greeuance,
        That law with all his might to inforce it on,
        Weele giue him cable.
                                            (1.2.15–17; *Will* F)

(2)   *Ia.*   Hee's married,
          Cas.   To who?
          Ia.   Marry to. – Come Captaine, will you goe?
          Oth.   *Ha, with who?*
                                            (1.2.52 ff.; *Haue with you* F)

(3)   But with a little art, vpon the blood,
        Burne like the *mindes* of sulphure . . .
                                    (3.3.331–2; *Mines* F)

In these striking examples Q must be corrupt, and others are not hard to find.[7] At one time such mishearing would have counted as damning evidence – a reporter would have been blamed for it – but we now accept that even in the best of texts some mishearing may occur, since a tired compositor can 'mishear' what he has just read. Thus two recent editors of *Hamlet* seem to have thought that the compositor of the 'good' quarto (Q2) 'misheard' will–we'll, as in (1) above:[8]

                her father and my selfe,
        Wee'le so bestow our selues, that seeing vnseene,
                                    (3.1.31–2, Q2; *Will* F)

The variants due to mishearing do not prove that Q *Othello* is a reported text, though there are more than one normally looks for in a 'good' text.[9] They need to be considered together with another group of variants that may be due to 'hearing'. Stabbed by Iago, Roderigo cried 'O dambd *Iago*, O inhumaine dog, – –o, o, o' (5.1.62, Q). F omits 'o, o, o', which is sometimes described as an 'actor's vulgarisation'. Othello sees himself as 'A fixed figure, for the time of scorne, / To point his slow vnmouing fingers at -- oh, oh' (4.2.56, Q); again, F omits 'oh, oh'. Instead of 'O *Desdemona, Desdemoua* [*sic*], dead, O, o, o' (5.2.279, Q), F prints 'Oh *Desdemon*! dead *Desdemon*: dead. Oh, oh!' If actors were responsible, how did their 'O, o, o', etc., intrude into the manuscript? Could Q, after all, be a reported text? The same question arises in other plays – 'The rest is silence. O, o, o, o. *Dyes*.' (*Hamlet*, 5.2.358, F: Q2 omits 'O . . . o'); 'pray you vndo this button, thanke you sir, O, o, o, o' (*King Lear* 5.3.310, Q; F omits 'O . . . o'). Are we to suppose that the quartos of *Othello* and *King Lear* and the Folio of *Hamlet* are all reported texts? Some years ago I analysed a number of 'O, o, o' readings in Shakespeare and other Elizabethan dramatists[10] and concluded that they were crypto-directions, signals to the actor to make whatever noise was appropriate – a sigh in *Macbeth* ('all the perfumes of Arabia will not sweeten this little hand. Oh, oh, oh. *Doct*[or] What a sigh is there?' (5.1.50–3, F)), or a roar in *Othello* ('*Oth*. Oh, oh, oh. / *Em*[*ilia*]. Nay, lay thee downe, and rore' (5.2.195–6, Q; so F)). As these and other examples demonstrate, the author must sometimes be responsible for 'O, o, o', so we are not bound to conclude that Q *Othello* was a reported text.

Another kind of variant in Q *Othello* resembles 'O, o, o', namely 'actors' connectives', words or phrases that are said to be interpolated or substituted at the beginning of a speech, presumably to ease the transition from one thing to another. Thus:

(1)   *Rod.*   I will incontinently drowne my selfe.
        Iago.   *If* thou do'st, I shall neuer loue thee after.
                                (1.3.306–7, F; *Well, if* Q)

(2)   *Rod.*   O Villaine that I am.
        Oth.   *It is* euen so.
                (5.1.29, F; *Harke tis* Q)

If there are any 'actors' connectives' in Q they may include some profanity, when this is either replaced by other words in F or simply omitted. When F fails to provide a counterpart to Q's profanity this might mean that an actor has added a 'connective'.

(3)   *Ia.*   *But* you'l not heare me. If euer I did dream
        Of such a matter, abhorre me.
              Rodo.   Thou told'st me,
                                (1.1.4, F; *S'blood, but* Q)

(4)   And makes me poore indeed.
        Oth.   *Ile* know thy Thoughts.
              (3.3.164, F; *By heauen I'le* Q)

On the other hand, F also adds words that look like 'connectives': is it sensible then to argue that both texts had non-authorial words inserted by actors?

(5)   As doth import you.
      Othe.   *So please* your Grace, my Ancient,
                     (1.3.284, F; *Please* Q)

(6)   *Iago.*   She's the worse for all this.
      Othe.   *Oh, a* thousand, a thousand times:
                    (4.1.188–9, F; *A* Q)

The alternative is to explain all such differences – mishearing, so-called actors' vulgarisation and connectives – as part of the overall variation of Q and F, attributable to authorial second thoughts or scribal changes or 'normal' textual corruption and not to special factors such as Q's being a reported text. Although Q's stage directions make it look more like a 'performance' text than F's (see p. 4), it would be premature to assume that a layer of Q errors originated in performance. On the other hand, the evidence suggesting a reported text cannot be dismissed as negligible.

Textual dislocation, where a speech or line fails to follow on smoothly from its predecessor, may also arouse misgivings in Q *Othello*. Some of it can be explained as resulting from Q omissions, so the 'rough' state of the text here and there need not mean that it was an unauthorised publication. Again, Q includes perhaps more than its fair share of misprints, if a 'good' text, and of odd spellings that look like misprints: it turns out, though, that a large number of these spellings, odd as they may appear to modern readers, are actually 'Shakespearian' – that is, they occur elsewhere in the canon. Some were rare spellings, others were accepted alternative spellings: while the spelling preferences of Nicholas Okes's printing house may account for some, so many are also found in Shakespearian texts issued by other printers that their presence in Q *Othello* compels us to consider the alternatives to a 'bad' text provenance, namely foul papers or a scribal copy of foul papers. I refer to spellings such as battell, coffe, deuide, ecchoes, ghesse, Lethergie, musique, Physition, Qu. (= cue), syen (= scion) (for a longer list see Appendix C).

What more can be said in favour of Q's foul-paper provenance? 'In general, and *a priori*, we should expect an author's foul papers to show quite a lot of deletion, alteration, interlining, false starts, and the like', W.W. Greg explained.[11] 'Quite a lot' in a manuscript, and inevitably less in a printed text, where the printer will have spotted some of the superseded material and omitted it. Are there any signs of such material in Q? Editors, I believe, have been so preoccupied with the possibility of revision coming *between* Q and F that they have failed to pay attention to the signs of authorial alterations *within* Q.

(1) (i)   *Des.*   Wouldst thou doe such a deed, for all the world?
      Em.   Why would not you.
      Des.   No, by this heauenly light.
      Em.   Nor I neither, by this heauenly light,
I might doe it as well in the darke.

(ii)   *Des.*   Would thou doe such a *thing* for all the world?
       Em.   The world is a huge thing, it is a great price,
    For a small vice.
       Des.   Good troth I thinke thou wouldst not.

(4.3.63–9, Q; deed F)

F prints more or less the same passage, the most significant difference being *deed* for *thing*, and this 'independent' support may have thrown editors off the scent: nevertheless, as we shall see (p. 94), F sometimes copies Q and should not always count as an 'independent' authority. The virtual repetition in Q of 'Wouldst thou doe such a deed, for all the world?' alerts us to the possible survival of a false start, and may give us a glimpse of Shakespeare in the act of composition. He saw the opportunity for a joke – doing the 'deed' not by this heavenly light but in the dark – no sooner thought than written. Then he realised that Emilia could not possibly say 'Why, would not you?', since she overheard Desdemona's horrified reaction on being charged with just such a deed (4.2.72 ff.), and knows how it devastated her – 'my lord hath so bewhored her / Thrown such despite and heavy terms upon her / That true hearts cannot bear it' (4.2.117–19). After what has happened not even someone as slow-witted as Emilia could make a joke of Desdemona's marital fidelity – so out goes the joke, to be replaced by an alternative version, one that bypasses Desdemona's own sexual behaviour. Shakespeare, I think, saw the problem at once, and failed to delete the first version clearly, as in other texts where false starts were printed by accident. Had he inserted the second version in the margin, at a later date, it would have been more obvious that the two passages were alternatives. If this explanation is correct it leads to the depressing conclusion that the Q scribe or compositor probably made at least three mistakes: he or they misunderstood a cancellation, misprinted 'Wouldst' as 'Would', and substituted 'thing' (from the next line) for 'deed'. It should be noted that in cancelling (i) and replacing it with (ii) Shakespeare 'protected' Desdemona, as he had done several times in 1.3 (see p. 18).

    Assuming that F *Othello* followed Q in reprinting a false start, one naturally asks whether other traces of false starts survive. Greg suggested two.[12]

(2)   The *Anthropophagie*, and men whose heads
    Doe grow beneath their shoulders: this to heare,
    Would *Desdemona* seriously incline;

(1.3.145 ff., Q)

F printed the second line as 'Grew beneath their shoulders. These things to heare'. 'This is, as it stands, impossible', said Greg, 'and editors have perforce followed Q. But as a reference to the narrative that precedes, F's "These things" is preferable to Q's "This". It looks as though Shakespeare wrote the overweighted line "Do grow beneath their shoulders. These things to hear" and that Q and F each sought to lighten it in a different fashion.'

(3)   My seruices which I haue done the Seigniorie,
        Shall out tongue his complaints, tis yet to know,
        [Which when I know,] That boasting is an honour,
        I shall provulgate, I fetch my life and being,
                        (1.2.18 ff, Q; [*Which . . . know*] from F)

'Neither version will do', said Greg. 'It would appear that the "tis yet to know" was a false start immediately replaced by "Which when I know", but inadequately deleted. Hence the appearance of both phrases in F, while Q left out the wrong one.'

I feel less strongly than Greg about what will or will not do. For (2) I am content to follow Q; for (3) I accept F (Greg's omission of 'tis yet to know' produces a short line). These cannot count as certain false starts. What, though, of lines that no one has explained satisfactorily, and that could be deleted without loss?

(4)   Forsooth, a great Arithmetition,
        One *Michael Cassio*, a Florentine,
        A fellow almost dambd in a faire wife,
        That neuer set a squadron in the field,
                        (1.1.18 ff., Q; so F)

Not only does line 20 fail to make sense, it appears to point forward to a married Cassio. I suspect that, as soon as he had written the line, Shakespeare realised that a bachelor would suit the plot better, and marked it for deletion. As no emendation has won more than very limited agreement, the simplest solution is to postulate another false start.

Loose half-lines that are not strictly necessary and are just as easy to remove could have been marked for omission as well.

(5)   And spoke such scuruy, and prouoking tearmes
        [Against your Houor,] that with the little godlinesse I haue,
        I did full hard forbeare him: but I pray sir,
                        (1.2.7 ff., Q)

(6)   Still questioned me the story of my life,
        From yeare to yeare, the battailes, seiges, fortunes
        That I haue past:
        I ran it through, euen from my boyish dayes,
                        (1.3.130 ff., Q)

(7)   My wife must moue for *Cassio* to her mistris,
        I'le set her on.
        My selfe a while, to draw the Moore apart,
                        (2.3.378 ff., Q)

(8)   That he you hurt is of great fame in *Cypres*,
       And great affinity, and that in wholesome wisedome,
       He might not but refuse you: but he protests he loues you,

                                        (3.1.46 ff., Q)

F repeats the half-lines that hang loose metrically – Q's 'Against your
Houor'(5), 'I'le set her on' (7), 'And great affinity' (8) – half-lines without
which the sense is perfectly clear. In (6) F repeats Q's 'From yeare to yeare'
and 'That I haue past': this passage differs from (5), (7) and (8) in so far as
one of the two half-lines in (6) probably replaced the other. This is pure
speculation, but I think legitimate speculation when one considers (a) that
many Shakespearian texts, not just the Folio, print words and lines that were
meant to be deleted, (b) that so many lines and half-lines in *Othello* seem to fall
into this category. But of course Shakespeare left other metrically unattached
half-lines in the play which are needed to finish sentences: metrical irregularity
must not be taken too seriously, even when the removal of a loose half-line
yields a clean cut.

   Imperfectly cancelled first thoughts give some support to the theory that Q
derives from foul papers, without being decisive. The stage directions in Q are
more helpful.

   The Q directions might all have been written by the author. At I.iii.171
   'and the rest' can only be his; the erroneous inclusion of Desdemona at l.47
   has many parallels; at II.i.1 the 'Gouernor of Cypres' is quite in Shakespeare's manner, and so are the 'two or three' at I.iii.120. On the other
   hand, several directions peculiar to Q have a literary flavour, and some
   definitely point to a transcriber.

Thus Greg, who believed that Q's 'frequent spellings "'em" and "ha" (for
"haue", in place of the earlier "a")' point to a late Jacobean original [i.e.
transcript]'.[13]

   Some stage directions deserve special attention. (1) '*Enter* Montanio, *Gouernor of* Cypres' (2.1.0). Shakespeare seems to have intended Montano to be the
governor of Cyprus replaced by Othello, though this is never made quite
explicit. Hence the message sent back to Venice:

   Seignior *Montano*,
   Your trusty and most valiant seruitor,
   With his free duty recommends you thus,
   And prayes you to beleeue him.

                                        (1.3.40 ff., Q)

– where the feeble 'beleeue' is probably a misprint for 'releeue' (appropriate,
since Cyprus expects an attack). Hence, too, Montano's remarks on hearing
that Othello 'is in full Commission here for Cypres': 'I am glad on't, tis a
worthy Gouernour' and 'I haue seru'd him, and the man commands / Like a

full Soldier' (2.1.29–36, Q). Unlike Iago, who resents being passed over for promotion, Montano cheerfully accepts the governor sent to replace him, a Shakespearian touch. The fact that Othello replaces the governor *in situ* is one that we are not allowed to forget ('we haue there a substitute of most allowed sufficiency', says the Duke at 1.3.224–5, Q).

(2) '*Enter* Cassio, *driuing in* Roderigo' (2.3.140, Q). This unusual stage direction should be compared with '*Enter Ariell, driuing in Caliban*' (*Tempest* 5.1.256). *Othello* pre-dates *The Tempest*, and Q *Othello* was printed before *The Tempest*: 'driving in' must be Shakespeare's own phrasing, so Q *Othello* is unlikely to be a reported text.[14]

(3) The author's stage directions may at times have been indistinguishable from the dialogue, causing some confusion.

(i)   *Oth,*   What is the matter here?
         Mon.   Zouns, I bleed still, I am hurt, to the death:
         Oth.   Hold, for your liues

                                    (2.3.160–1, Q)

For the second line F reads 'I bleed still, I am hurt to th' death. He dies.' Q may have omitted 'He dies' because it looked like a stage direction and Montano goes on speaking (i.e. doesn't die), yet the words make good sense (meaning 'I'll kill him') and improve the scansion: 'Zouns, I bleed still, I'm hurt to th' death. He dies.'

(ii)   I'le make thee an example.
         Desd.   What is the matter?
         Oth.   All's well now sweeting:
       Come away to bed: sir, for your hurts,
       My selfe will be your surgeon; leade him off;
       Iago, looke with care about the Towne,

                                    (2.3.247 ff., Q)

This divides into perfectly regular verse lines, leaving out 'leade him off':

       I'll make thee an example.
         Desd.   What's the matter?
         Oth.   All's well now, sweeting, come away to bed.
       Sir, for your hurts, myself will be your surgeon [*lead him off*]
       Iago, look with care about the town,

Compare *A Midsummer Night's Dream*: '*The Lion roares, Thisby runs off* (TLN 2065, F), where *off* is used similarly (= off stage). If we follow F, as I do in Arden 3 with some reluctance, we have to print two short lines in a total of four lines. This is because F adds the word *Deere* – 'What is the matter (Deere?)' – and, like Q, incorporates *lead him off* in the dialogue ('My selfe will be your Surgeon. Lead him off:'). As we have seen (p. 16), what looks like F revision sometimes does introduce metrical irregularity. In the present instance I feel that Q may well print Shakespeare's correct words, but dividing the lines incorrectly, as often elsewhere, and misunderstanding *leade him off* as part of Othello's speech.

Having stated the case for Q's foul-papers origin, I have to acknowledge a difficulty. The Willow Song seems to have been removed from the Q text – carefully removed from 4.3.29–52, 54–6, 59–62, and from 5.2.244–6 – why would anyone want to remove a song from the foul papers? It is sometimes assumed that the song was not cut from the Q text at the same time as Q's other omitted passages. So Greg – 'A cut text more usually goes back to prompt-copy, but the cuts (except the Willow Song) may have been marked in the foul papers.'[15] The Willow Song, it was thought, had to be removed at a later date, when the boy actor of Desdemona lost his voice. The fate of the Willow Song should be connected, I believe, with that of a song in *Twelfth Night*.

> It is almost certain from the insistence on Viola's musical accomplishments at I.ii.57–58 that she was meant to be a singer, and from the awkward opening of II.iv that the song 'Come away, come away death' has been transferred from her to Feste. We must therefore suppose that when the play was originally produced the company had a singing boy who was no longer available on the occasion of some revival.[16]

Here Greg expressed a widely shared view. If, however, *Othello* has been post-dated and really dates from late 1601 or 1602, as, following Alfred Hart, I have recently argued,[17] the tragedy could have been an almost exact contemporary of Shakespeare's final romantic comedy, and the Willow Song and 'Come away' might have been composed for the same boy, the original actor of Viola and Desdemona.

Hart observed long ago that the bad quarto of *Hamlet* (1603) echoes *Othello*, as well as many other plays. *Hamlet* was entered in the Stationers' Register on 26 July 1602, so *Othello* needs to be dated earlier. John Manningham saw *Twelfth Night* at the Middle Temple on 2 February 1602:

> At our feast we had a play called 'Twelue Night, or What you Will', much like *The Comedy of Errors*, or *Menaechmi* in Plautus, but most like and near to that in Italian called *Inganni*. A good practice in it to make the Steward believe his lady widow was in love with him . . .[18]

Had *Twelfth Night* been anything other than a fairly recent play an enthusiast like Manningham would surely have known it. The entry in his diary shows that it was new to him, and therefore the most likely date for the play's *première* is 6 January 1602,[19] while Shakespeare was hard at work finishing *Othello*. Dating the two plays close together, which others have failed to do because they accepted the traditional dating of *Othello* (1603 or 1604), we see that the reallocation of Viola's song to Feste and the dropping of the Willow Song are best explained by a new hypothesis. Instead of postulating revivals of the two plays, at a time when the boy actors of Viola and Desdemona were unable to sing, I suggest that the original boy actor's voice broke earlier than expected, and that adjustments were hurriedly made in both plays at much the same time. This is a preferable solution, for three reasons. (1) The leading boy actor's loss of voice did not normally lead to such drastic measures; (2) there are now good reasons for dating the two plays close together and for thinking that the same boy was involved; (3) a change introduced in a late revival would not normally be marked in the foul papers.

Othello, the later of the two plays, was either just completed or nearing completion when the Willow Song was removed. It would be not unreasonable to think that the other Q cuts (see p. 11) were made at the same time, probably by someone other than Shakespeare, but this need not follow. Some Q 'cuts' look like accidental omissions, others might have been lightly or wrongly marked, or omitted to save time (see p. 13) Be that as it may, the removal of the Willow Song from Q is not incompatible with the theory that Q derives, perhaps by way of a scribal copy, from the author's foul papers.

*   *   *

A word about the intermediate scribal copy (Aa). As I have mentioned (above, p. 37), Greg thought that Q's frequent spellings *em* and *ha* reveal the 'late Jacobean' date of Aa. He added a footnote that may confuse inattentive readers.

> Fredson Bowers queries (privately) whether these forms may not be compositorial and points out that in *Westward Ho* (1607) the spelling changes from ''em' to ''hem' when a fresh compositor takes over. But the forms ''em' and 'ha' are certainly not characteristic of any of the habitual Folio compositors.[20]

Here Greg wrote 'Folio' instead of 'Quarto' (it is Q that frequently prints *em* and *ha*), but I believe that his 'late Jacobean' scribal copy was on the right scent. Consider, first, a passage quoted on p. 32, where Q's 'Ha, with who?' corresponds to F's 'Haue with you.' The Q manuscript (Aa) must have read 'Ha with you' and, I suspect, this became 'Ha, with who?' under the influence of 'To who?', printed just above; that is, *Ha* must have stood in Q's copy (Aa) before it could be misunderstood and turned into an exclamation by the Q compositor. (Shakespeare, of course, might have written *ha* himself.)

Another Q spelling that belongs with *em* and *ha* is *tho*, Q's preferred spelling (*tho* occurs 18 times, *though* 4 times). Q's preference for *tho* is significant, because neither Shakespeare's good quartos nor the first published versions of *Venus and Adonis*, *Lucrece* and the *Sonnets* contain a single *tho* − yet *tho* was misread as *the* in Q *Othello* (2.1.241: I quote and discuss the passage on p. 43).

The misreading can only mean that *tho* was the spelling of an intermediate text, one that came between Shakespeare's holograph (since *tho* was not his spelling) and Q. I believe that the profusion of dashes in Q, and the large or dropped capital M at the start of Act 3, are other hangovers from an intermediate text (see p. 46).

Neither *ha* nor *em* can be classified as exclusively 'late Jacobean', for both forms occur in Shakespeare's texts before 1600. They become more common in the Jacobean period, and I feel that Greg's date, 'late Jacobean', is probably correct, yet this is only a matter of feeling. The *the–tho* error in Q, together with the other points mentioned above, supports the hypothesis of a scribal copy (Aa); I would not, however, rule out the possibility that Q could have been printed directly from the foul papers. If there was a scribal copy, as I think, Thomas Walkley could have commissioned it in 1621, for the use of the Q printer.

*   *   *

The misreading in Q, already touched upon, must now be considered in more detail. I begin with some typical examples.

(1) Of thirtie Saile: and now they do *re-stem*
     Their backward course
                    (1.3.38, F; *resterine* Q)

(2) If after euery Tempest, come such *Calmes*
                    (2.1.183, F; *calmenesse* Q)

(3)   Or for I am declin'd
     Into the *vale* of yeares (yet that's not much)
                    (3.3.270, F; *valt* Q)

(4) Whil'st you were heere, *o're-whelmed* with your griefe
                    (4.1.77, F; *ere while, mad* Q)

(5) Lay not your blame on me: if you haue *lost* him,
     I haue *lost* him too
                    (4.2.47–8, F; *left . . . left* Q)

(6) I haue rub'd this yong *Quat* almost to the sense
                    (5.1.11, F; *gnat* Q)

(7)   Now, whether he kill *Cassio*,
     Or *Cassio* him, or each do kill the other,
     Euery way makes my *gaine*
                    (5.1.14, F: *game* Q)

(8) I know not where is that *Promethœan* heate
     That can thy Light *re-Lume*
                    (5.2.13, F; *returne* Q)

These and many similar variants are graphically related. Most, if not all, must have resulted from misreading: Q fails to make sense, or prints an improbable variant, and we are entitled to assume that usually the Q scribe copied or the compositor set up the words that he thought he saw in his manuscript. (A few single-letter variants, such as *vale–valt*, could be due to foul case but, as will be seen from further examples, graphically related variants frequently involve more than one letter.) The Q scribe or compositor, I take it, misread (1) *resteme* or *resteme̅*; (2) *calmes*; (3) *vale*; (4) *orewhelmed*; (5) *lost . . . lost*; (6) *quat*; (7) *gaine*; (8) *relume*. In accordance with its usual practice, F switched several times to emphasis capitals (*Calmes, Quat, re-Lume*) which we may discount (they throw no light on Q's closeness to copy, my present concern). It transpires that minim confusion led to several of Q's errors, namely (1), (2), (6)–(8). In (2) and (8) *m* may have been written hurriedly, with more than three minim strokes (in Hand D of *Sir Thomas More*, usually identified as Shakespeare's, there are too few or too many minim strokes in *Linco, dung, sounde* [ll. 27, 134, 240]). Thus (2) *calmes* could have looked like *calmnes*: as elsewhere in the same scene, Q opted for *-(e)nesse* rather than *-nes*, on the assumption that it was dealing with the suffix *-ness*,[21] corrupting *calmes* to *calmenesse*.

Taken together, Q's misreadings show that someone found it difficult at times to decipher even the most familiar words. (I shall refer to the corrupter as one person, the Q scribe, though it is not impossible that the Q compositor was responsible or that scribe and compositor both multiplied misreading errors.) He did not hesitate to copy nonsense, if that was what the manuscript seemed to require – the easy way out, when the alternative was to pause and inspect the manuscript carefully. While the scribe cannot be said to inspire confidence, Q's graphical closeness to copy, and very willingness to transcribe nonsense, deserves the modern editor's gratitude. Whenever Q prints multiple variants, including some that make no sense, we may guess that the scribe had to wrestle with an illegible passage and hurriedly did his best – not a very good best, yet still a botch that is useful, from our point of view, in so far as it gives us an opportunity to reconstruct the manuscript reading and to assess his general reliability.

The scribe's hit-and-miss procedure can be illustrated from a large number of QF variants which are graphically similar yet less close than those listed above. It seems that he was able to read – or misread – some letters and had to guess the rest, not always sensibly.

(9)   I fetch my life and being,
    From Men of Royall *Seige*
        (1.2.22, F; *height* Q)

(10)   Rude am I, in my speech,
    And little bless'd with the *soft* phrase of Peace
                (1.3.83, F; *set* Q)

(11) To *vouch* this, is no proofe
          (1.3.107, F; *youth* Q)

(12)   *A Noble* ship of Venice,
       Hath seene a greeuous wracke and sufferance
                    (2.1.22, F; *Another* Q)

(13)   And your name is great
       In *mouthes* of wisest Censure.
              (2.3.188–9, F; *men* Q)

(14)   *Oth.*   This Fortification (Gentlemen) shall we see't?
        Gent.   *Well* waite vpon your Lordship.
                    (3.2.6, F: *We* Q)

(15)   No sure, I cannot thinke it
       That he would *steale* away so guilty-like
                 (3.3.39, F; *sneake* Q)

(16) Why *do you speake so faintly?*
       (3.3.286, F; *is your speech so faint?* Q)

Using dots to indicate letters illegible in the manuscript, we may reconstruct what the scribe thought he saw. (9) .eig.; (10) se.t; (11) .ou.h; (12) Ano. .e.; (13) men. . . .; (14) We. . ; (15) s.ea.e; (16) . .you. spee. . so faint. . − and these few examples already reveal a habit that we shall find to be characteristic. If he could not think of a word composed of the correct number of letters, the scribe treated extra letters as if they did not exist: the *f* in (10), *-thes* in (13), *-ll* in (14) (I assume that Shakespeare wrote *We'll*), *-ly* in (16). This is not as reprehensible as we may initially think for, as will emerge (p. 86), there could have been genuine doubt whether or not a letter was intended.

   We can observe the same man solving his problems in the same way in longer passages, where the simple expedient of omission sometimes has unfortunate consequences (see Figure 2).

(17) (i) a knaue very voluble, no farder conscionable, then in putting on the meere forme of ciuill and hand-seeming, for the better compassing of his salt and hidden ∧ affections: ∧ A subtle slippery knaue, a finder out of occasions; that has an eye, can stampe and counterfeit ∧ the true aduantages neuer present themselues. ∧ Besides, the knaue is handsome . . .

                                             (2.1.235 ff., Q)

   (ii) a knaue very voluble: no further conscionable, then in putting on the meere forme of Ciuill, and Humaine seeming, for the better compasse of his salt, and most hidden loose Affection? Why none, why none: A slipper, and subtle knaue, a finder of occasion: that he's an eye can stampe, and counterfeit Aduantages, though true

Aduantage neuer present it selfe. A diuelish knaue: besides, the
knaue is handsome . . .

(F)

I have inserted carets to indicate missing words in the Q text: some could have
been added to the F text by a 'reviser', but at least one Q line ('counterfeit the
true aduantages') makes no sense without F's addition, and I suspect that all
are Q omissions. It is reassuring, however, that although Q appears to omit
and transpose, it again shows signs of trying to decipher copy. *Humaine* and
hand are not graphically far apart if the first was written *hūane* or *humane*: final
-d and *e* were often confused, so the Q scribe could have thought that the word
was h..and. Equally, *e* and *o* were easily confused, *though* could be spelt *tho* (see
p. 40: this was actually Q's preferred spelling), and *tho* could be misread as *the*.
In short, the Q scribe solved his problems by writing two words (*hand*, *the*)
which he thought he saw in his manuscript, two words that cannot be right,
and otherwise he simply omitted words or letters (and perhaps transposed
words) – exactly the procedure that we have already identified.

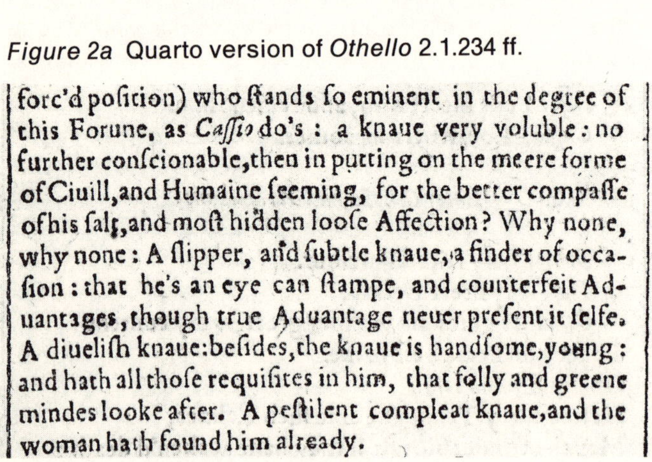

*   *   *

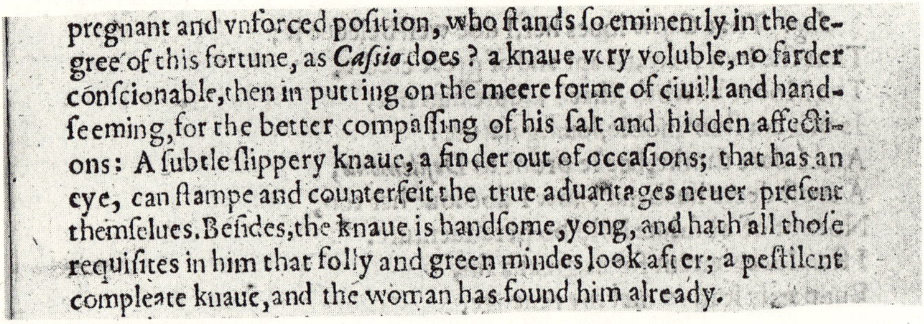

Figure 2a Quarto version of *Othello* 2.1.234 ff.

Figure 2b Folio version of *Othello* 2.1.234 ff.

The scribe's treatment of prose and verse is equally revealing. Because we can compare his text with F we can say categorically that often – far too often – Q mislines its verse; F's verse lineation is much more confidence-inspiring, except when F divides single verse lines into two, having miscalculated its casting off. The Q scribe, it seems, had no ear for verse, and even relined unmistakable prose as verse.

> *Rod.* Euery day, thou dofftst me, with some deuise *Iago*;
> And rather, as it seemes to me, thou keepest from me,
> All conueniency, then suppliest me, with the least
> Aduantage of hope: I will indeed no longer indure it,
> Nor am I yet perswaded to put vp in peace, what already
> I haue foolishly sufferd . . .
>
> *Iag.* Sir, there is especiall command come from *Venice*,
> To depute *Cassio* in *Othello's* place.
> *Rod.* Is that true? why then *Othello* and *Desdemona*
> Returne againe to *Venice*.
> *Iag.* O no, he goes into *Mauritania*, and takes away with him
> The faire *Desdemona*, vnlesse his abode be [l]inger'd
> Here by some accident, wherein none can be so
> determinate, as the remouing of *Cassio*.
>
> (4.2.177 ff., 222 ff., Q)

Here Q's 'verse' line endings probably indicate the length of each line of prose in the scribe's copy (Shakespeare's foul papers, manuscript A, as I have suggested). Remembering that Shakespeare did not begin verse lines with capital letters in *Sir Thomas More* – a not unusual procedure at this time – we can see that a scribe with no ear for verse might the more easily confuse prose and verse, though not many others would have erred as idiotically as the Q scribe. Again we find that this scribe has reproduced copy in his own peculiar way, transmitting the 'true' text in see-through disguise. This should encourage us to take a special interest in Q's manifest corruptions, which may still help us to reconstruct 'true' readings.

* * *

Next, what do we know about the writer of the Q manuscript (Aa), and about Q's compositor or compositors? Many years ago I suggested that two or possibly three compositors set Q from a manuscript prepared by two scribes. Charlton Hinman, more experienced in such matters, later declared that bibliographical evidence

> makes it quite certain that most of the Okes quarto of *Othello* was set by formes; and spelling peculiarities make it reasonably sure that the whole book was set by the same compositor. The evidence from types that shows

setting by formes is especially clear in the first half of the book – in sheets B through G. . . . Recurrences of this kind show that the setting was at least for the most part by formes throughout.[22]

Hinman was partly indebted to a University of Kansas doctoral dissertation which I have not seen.[23] I accept that my argument of thirty years ago is flawed,[24] but find the alternative puzzling. Why set Q by formes if only one compositor was involved? The chief benefit of casting off would be that two compositors could work simultaneously and speed up the printing. Other Okes quartos are thought to have been set by two compositors at this time (e.g. *Thierry and Theodoret*, 1621; *The Duchess of Malfi*, 1623[25]). And why are there no dashes on p. 18 and eight on p. 19, commencing in mid-scene? This ocular proof, together with other spelling and typographical peculiarities, persuades me that at least two men collaborated, either as compositors or as scribes. (For the sake of brevity I refer henceforth to one compositor and a single scribe, leaving open the possibility of more than one of each.) One day others may untangle this mystery; for the present I pick up the point that is not in dispute, that Q was set by formes.

As is well known, setting by formes could lead to trouble, especially if the text mingled prose and verse, thus complicating the counting of lines. Miscalculations in casting off could be fudged by printing prose as verse, or verse as prose, or by the simple expedient of omission. Now Q sometimes omits short passages as the compositor approaches the bottom of a page: taken together with the evidence for setting by formes, which explains why they were necessary, these omissions confirm the view (see p. 47) that Q cuts corners and sometimes doctors the text.

(1)   *Cas.*   I will rather sue to be despis'd, then to deceiue so good a
         Commander, with so slight, so drunken, and so indiscreet an Officer.
         Drunke? And speake Parrat? And squabble? Swagger? Sweare? And
         discourse Fustian with ones owne shadow? Oh thou invisible spirit of
         Wine, if thou hast no name to be knowne // by, let vs call thee
         Diuell.

                                                              (2.3.273–9)

(2)   *Iago.*   And did you see the Handkerchiefe?
         Oth.   Was that mine? //
         Iago.   Yours by this hand: and to see how he prizes the foolish woman
         your wife: she gaue it him, and he hath giu'n it his whore.
         Oth.   I would haue him nine yeeres a killing:

                                                              (4.1.170 ff.)

(3)   *Gra.*   I am sorry to finde you thus;
         I haue beene to seeke you.
             Iago.   Lend me a Garter. So: – Oh for a Chaire
         To beare him easily hence.

> *Bian.*   Alas he faints. Oh Cassio, Cassio, Cassio.
> *Iago.*   Gentlemen all, I do suspect this Trash //
> (5.1.80 ff.)

These extracts are from F, with Q omissions in italics and a double solidus indicating where Q pages end. Q gives itself away in (2) by printing the wrong catchword and by repeating the speech prefix *Oth.* (unnecessary, since Othello continues speaking on the next page if Iago's speech is dropped). There are several other omissions near the bottom of a page, and II^a repeats the last line of $H4^b$, another probable consequence of imperfect casting off. At the end of sheet M ($M4^b$) Q omits seven lines; the transition is abrupt, and again casting off could be responsible (a seven-line miscalculation, however, would be unusual).

More disturbing, from an editor's point of view, is the possibility that the Q compositor may have interpolated lines of his own invention, when he reached the end of a page and had run out of text.

(1)   *Oth.*   Fetch me that handkercher, my mind misgiues.
　　　Des.   Come, come, you'll neuer meete a more sufficient man.
　　　Oth.   The handkercher.
　　　Des.   *I pray talke me of Cassio.*
　　　Oth.   *The handkercher.* //
　　　Des.   A man that all his time, . . .
　　　Oth.   The handkercher
(3.4.91 ff., Q)

(2)   *Iag.*   Go to, farewell: – doe you heare Roderigo?
　　　Rod.   *what say you?*
　　　Iag.   *No more of drowning, doe you heare?*
　　　Rod.   *I am chang'd.*　　　　　　　*Exit Roderigo.*
　　　Iag.   *Goe to, farewell, put money enough in your purse:*
(1.3.377 ff., Q)

In these extracts from Q, F omissions are italicised. I am uneasy about the passages omitted by F, for several reasons: (i) they come at or near the bottom of the Q page, where incorrect casting off might leave the compositor with insufficient material; (ii) in both cases repeated phrases are repeated yet again; (iii) 'talke me of Cassio' does not sound right ('talk me' is not found elsewhere in Shakespeare). In (2) the four lines omitted by F are there replaced by '*Rod.* Ile sell all my Land.', and authorial revision might account for the changes, or even poor casting off in F (where the passage falls four lines from the bottom of the page). Yet if (1) looks like a compositor's patchwork, as I think, either the Q or F compositor, or both, may be responsible for the differences in (2).

Casting-off problems also shed light on Q's frequent mislineation.

> *Des.* It is my wretched fortune.
> *Iag.* Beshrew him for it; how comes this tricke vpon him? //
> *Des.* Nay, heauen doth know.

(4.2.130–1, Q)

> *Des.* It is my wretched Fortune.
> *Iago.* Beshrew him for't:
> How comes this Tricke vpon him?
> *Des.* Nay, Heauen doth know.

(F)

Two iambic pentameters, preceded and followed by regular verse lines: F divides correctly, whereas Q, having run out of space at the end of the page, makes one line of 130b ('Beshrew . . .') and 131a ('How comes . . .'). Better so, we may say, than to lose a half-line, the obvious alternative: yet the compositor's attitude to lineation should be remembered whenever F or later editors arrange verse lines more attractively than Q.

The compositor seems to have tampered with the text in many ways, omitting lines for which casting off had left insufficient space, perhaps adding lines of his own devising, re-lining the verse and, unless someone else is to blame, misreading many words. Was the scribe equally unreliable? If, following Greg, we describe his transcript as 'late Jacobean', it would have been intended either as a private transcript of an unpublished play or as printer's copy for Q. In other words, it was not prepared for use in the theatre, where omitted passages and verbal substitutions would have been spotted by the actors, but rather for a purchaser or printer who had no means of assessing its accuracy. Since we know that a conscientious scribe like Ralph Crane was quite capable of omitting lines and longer passages, partly from carelessness and partly to speed up a tedious task,[26] the scribe of Q *Othello* may also have chosen to save himself work by skipping longer passages, such as 1.1.119–35, which cannot be regarded as accidental omissions. These Q omissions have been explained by others as 'cuts for performance' or as Folio 'additions', two theories open to serious objections (see p. 13). If we look for an explanation not in the Q text's 'theatrical' career but in its transmission by an unscrupulous scribe and compositor, probably working for Thomas Walkley, we bypass these objections. It would be neater, of course, to assign the cutting of the Willow Song and omission of other Q passages to a single cause. Remembering, though, that Q seems to have been preceded by two manuscripts (A → Aa → Q), and that at least three individuals could have introduced confusion and error, we have to admit that it is one thing to identify corruption and quite another to identify its cause. Omissions, in particular, can be plausibly explained in a variety of ways.

The Quarto text emerges at the end of this chapter with a blackened character. Partly illegible foul papers were copied by one or more scribes who misread Shakespeare's hand repeatedly, and who perhaps saved themselves time and trouble by omitting bits of text; then one or more compositors manhandled the text in other ways. Has the chapter been unduly influenced by the new information about Thomas Walkley? I hope not: but if it has, the next two chapters will compensate by being equally pessimistic about the Folio text.

Chapter 5

The printer of the Folio text

The printing house of William Jaggard, responsible for the Folio text of *Othello*, has received much more attention than the publisher of the Quarto. Charlton Hinman's *The Printing and Proof-Reading of the First Folio of Shakespeare* deserves pride of place in any account of Jaggard and his professional activities: I begin, however, with an important biography of Jaggard by E.E. Willoughby, and with Willoughby's summary of Jaggard's feud with one of his authors, Ralph Brooke. Neither Willoughby nor later textual specialists unravelled all the implications of this feud for editors of Shakespeare.

Brooke published in 1619 a revision of Thomas Milles's *Catalogue of Honor* (1610), entitled *A Catalogue and Succession of Kings, Princes, Dukes . . . to the present yeare, 1619*, printed and published by Jaggard. After Jaggard had printed the text, Brooke demanded that a long list of 'Faultes escaped in Printing' be inserted, although only a minority of the 'faults', according to Willoughby, 'could by any stretch of the imagination be attributed to the printer'. Unfortunately Brooke's *Catalogue* contained many more errors: in 1621 he persuaded William Stansby to issue a 'corrected' edition, one that blamed all the errors on Jaggard.

Brooke, the York Herald, had previously engaged in bitter quarrels with other heralds, notably with William Camden, the Clarenceux King of Arms. A young protégé of Camden called Augustine Vincent offered Jaggard a further list of errors in Brooke's *Catalogue* of 1619, and Jaggard entered this in the Stationers' Register on 29 October 1621, calling it *A Discoverie of Errours*. It was 'an exact reprint of [Brooke's] 1619 edition with a caustic commentary by Vincent'.[1] Stansby now 'worked night and day . . . to forestall the publication of Vincent's *Discoverie*', and Jaggard stopped other work to speed up Vincent's book. Stansby won the race, but Vincent 'was able to convict the York Herald of gross carelessness in many places. . . . In short, he pulverized Brooke's pretensions.'

The story is of particular interest to students of Shakespeare's text because Jaggard inserted a defence of his workmen in Vincent's *Discoverie* shortly before his men were engaged on the First Folio. In an epistle headed simply 'The Printer' he ridiculed Brooke's claim that ordinary misprints and lost syllables necessitated a new edition of Brooke's *Catalogue*: 'there was no feare that the meanest Reader were like to stumble at such strawes, nor the most captious Aduersarie would go a hawking after syllables'. He went on:

> Master *Yorke* [i.e. Brooke] must giue me leaue, to acquaint him with the *Worke-mens* answer, who will at no hand yeelde themselues to bee fathers of those syllabicall faults, whereof (they say) if his owne blindenesse were not the mother, yet at least it was the Midwife, to helpe them into the world.

The workmen alleged that Brooke's handwritten errors were 'yet extant in his Copie':

> which if the Worke-men had bene so madly disposed to tye themselues too, and haue giuen him leaue to print his owne English (which they now repent they did not) hee would (they say) haue made his Reader, as good sport in his Catalogue, as euer *Tarleton* did his Audience, in a Clownes part.[2]

So Jaggard said quite explicitly that his workmen corrected Brooke's English. Brooke was known to be arrogant about his scholarship, and quarrelsome: one therefore wonders whether the same workmen also tampered with Shakespeare's English. If they dared to correct Brooke, a peppery herald, what might they not have done to correct − or corrupt − the texts of a dead dramatist? Some years earlier Thomas Heywood accused Jaggard and his men of negligence in 'mistaking of syllables, misplacing half-lines, coining of strange and never heard of words' (see p. 57). Consciously and unconsciously Jaggard's men changed the words in their 'Copie', as Jaggard conceded, and this has far-reaching implications for editors of Shakespeare.

We can check how Jaggard's men corrected their copy without much difficulty, by studying reprints produced by them. Being specially interested in their treatment of play-texts, let us look at their reprinted plays. The ten 'Pavier' quartos of 1619[3] select themselves as the obvious targets for attention: they were close to the Folio in time, and were probably set by some of the very compositors who worked on the Folio,[4] including compositor B, who was also responsible for about half of the text of F *Othello*.

D.F. McKenzie saw long ago that 'the patient analysis of reprints, where the compositor or compositors can be positively identified and the copy is not seriously disputed, offers the surest method of determining the nature of compositorial corruption'.[5] In a useful comparison of the 1619 ('Pavier') quarto of *The Merchant of Venice* (Q2) and the 1600 quarto (Q1), he assembled the evidence for various kinds of corruption in Q2.

> The total number of variants introduced into Q2 is something like 3,200. Whether all of these are in fact compositorial is not easy to determine. Some apparently new readings may derive from variant forms in the copy of Q1 used by B but no longer extant . . . . Similarly, it may even be that a

Q2 proof-reader introduced some variants and removed others, although there is no evidence of this. But we meet by far the greatest difficulty in deciding whether any of the new readings are the work of an independent reviser . . . . In fact, as we shall see, it is neither difficult nor unreasonable to attribute all the so-called revisions in the text itself to compositor B.

McKenzie analysed the changes in substantive readings in Q2 and also the changes in accidentals (spelling, punctuation, etc.). He found 'some 715 changes' in punctuation: 'the addition of 347 commas makes up by far the largest single group. By contrast, only 23 commas were deleted.'

A very large number of new Q2 readings can be safely attributed to the compositor, but what of the rest? Consider these lines (2.2.21 ff., Q1):

fiend say I you counsaile *well* . . . certainely the Iewe is the very deuill *incarnation* . . . I will runne fiend, my heeles are at your *commaundement* . . . O heauens, this is my true begotten Father . . . I will try *confusions* with him.

For the words that I have italicised, Q2 reads *ill, incarnall, command, conclusions*: *command* could have resulted from justification (McKenzie, p. 79); the other three variants look like conscious corrections. But whose corrections?

The issue cannot be decided by analysing just one of the Pavier quartos, since the corrections in these texts differ quite markedly. One, Q2 of *Sir John Oldcastle* (reprinted from Q1, 1600), 'revised' its text much more drastically than did Q2 of *The Merchant of Venice*, rewriting many speeches, censoring profanity and 'editing' in other ways. These changes in Q2 *Oldcastle* strangely resemble some of the variants in the F text of *Othello*, as compared with Q *Othello*, and deserve some attention.[6] (My line references are to the edition of *Oldcastle* by Peter Corbin and Douglas Sedge in *The Revels Plays Companion Library*, Manchester, 1991, where my collations can be checked.)

(a) Profanity is often censored (though not eliminated) in Q2: iii.5, 51; iv.62, 91, 180; xi.47, 53, 70, 136; xiii.44; xvi.13, 31–2; xviii.2. In these instances profanity either disappears or is replaced by other words. In addition, profanity is sometimes softened: *God haue mercy* becomes *Gramercy* (iii.158) or *God a mercy* (xi.108, xvii.19); *Gods* becomes *Cuds* (iv.148) or *Uds* (xvii.22, 25).

(b) Colloquial contractions are introduced: *I am > I'me; thou art > th'art; you are > y'are; you will > youle; they will > they'l* (iii.36, 75, 157; iv.104; vii.196; viii.14; x.66; xvi.28; xviii.1). Other contractions introduced in Q2 include *never > nere, over > o'er, into > to, in his > in's, escape > scape, open > ope*. In general, Q2 switches to the shorter form, but the reverse happens as well: *tis > it is* (x.51, xiv.37), *though > although* (xviii.12, 16). Q2 also switches some words in both directions (*you > ye* and *ye > you; is > 's* and *'s > is*). Justification must be responsible now and then; the later text nevertheless pulls more often than not towards the colloquial or shorter forms.

(c) As a result of (b), Q2 introduces metrically irregular lines.

(1)   Hold villaines hold, my Lords, what *do ye* meane,
                          (xi.121, Q1; *d'ye* Q2)

Sheer carelessness and insensitivity to metre are responsible for other metrical lapses.

(2)   Nay, pray *ye take it, trust me but* you shal,
                          (ii.61, Q1; *take it, trust me* Q2)

(3)   *None none* my Lord, but sir Iohn Old-castle.
                          (xii.46, Q1; *None* Q2)

Heywood and Brooke complained of Jaggard's men's 'mistaking of syllables', exactly what we find in (b) and (c).

When we turn to Pavier's *King Lear* (Q2, 1619) we find that some of the characteristic changes of Q2 *Oldcastle* are reversed. In *King Lear* colloquial contractions are expanded quite often, as follows (line references are to the Through Line Numbering of Q2 in Michael Warren's *The Complete King Lear 1608–1623* [1989]): *ith* > *in the* 607, 916, 1810; *at'h* > *of the* 1629, 2249; *'t* > *it* 538, 584, 719, 1005, 1018, 1112, 1113, etc.; *thar't* > *thou art* 497–8; *you'l* > *you will* 971; *You'r* > *You are* 3048; *tha're* > *they are* 2401; etc. Again these changes are not wholly consistent, but the general tendency of Q2 *King Lear* contradicts that of Q2 *Oldcastle*, and suggests that a single compositor (B) could not have set both texts.

Another feature of Q2 *King Lear* that has a bearing on the text of *Othello* is its treatment of final -*s*. In the following instances I cite Q1 first, adding an asterisk if Q1 is probably wrong (in which case the Q2 change will be deliberate; the other Q2 changes, I assume, are unconscious).

>   *stande – 763 stands; right – 842 rights; *Cõmand – 1195 Commands;
>   *life – 1364 life's; garments – 1806 garment; letters – 2242 letter; peeble
>   chaffes – 2302 peebles chafe; me thoughts – 2354 methought; *sonne in
>   lawes – 2447 sonnes in law; one – 2468 ones; bossome – 2806 blossomes;
>   thing – 2997 things; *honor – 3060 honors.

I may have missed one or two examples; it is immediately clear, however, that while Q2 adds or drops a final -*s* now and then, the problem is on an entirely different scale in *Othello* (see p. 85) and cannot be explained as merely due to the compositor's usual carelessness.

We shall return to the unauthorised alterations in the Pavier reprints, and to their significance for editors of First Folio texts. It may be helpful, though, to illustrate some of the editorial implications immediately: to do so I have selected, first, the use of the question mark in two Pavier reprints and in F *Othello*.

(A) (1)   *S.Iohn.*   How now my *Lord?* why stand you discontent?
                          (*Oldcastle*, 1619, B₃a [ii.136]; *lord*, 1600, B₃a)

(2)   *Har.*   Hast thou bene at the *Ale-house?* hast thou sought there?
(1619, C$_3$b [iv.97]; *Alehouse,* 1600, C$_3$b)

(3)   *Cam.*   Then perish may my *soule?* what thinke you so?
(1619, E$_2$b [vii.162]; *soule:* 1600, E$_2$b)

(B) (1)   O ho, are you there with me? No eyes in your head nor money in your purse? your eyes are in a heauy case . . .

(2)   Speake *Edmund,* where's the king, and wher's *Cordelia?*
Seest thou this obiect Kent?

(3)   To who my Lord? who hath the office?
(*King Lear,* 1619, I$_3$a, L$_3$a, L$_3$a)

The *Oldcastle* quotations (A) show how Jaggard's printing house multiplied question marks by sub-dividing questions. As for (B), every one of the question marks here was added in 1619: several dozen were added in *King Lear* alone. (Neither the Variorum *King Lear* (ed. H.H. Furness, 1880) nor the Revels *Oldcastle* gives a full collation of the punctuation of the 1619 quartos. The question marks added in 1619, in (A) and (B) above, are not collated in these editions). What, then, are we to make of the dozens of question marks in F *Othello,* produced in the same printing house?

(C) (1)   *Iago.*   How *now?* What do you heere alone?
(3.3.304, F; *now,* Q)

(2)   Are you a *Man?* Haue you a *Soule?* or Sense?
(3.3.377, F; *man,* . . . *soule* Q)

(3)   *Oth.*   *Would?* Nay, and I will.
(3.3.396, F; *Would,* Q)

(4)   *Æmil.*   Hath she forsooke so many Noble *Matches?*
Her *Father?* And her *Country?* And her *Friends?*
To be call'd Whore? Would it not make one weepe?
(4.2.127–9, F; *matches,* . . . *Father,* . . . *Countrey,* . . . *friends,* Q)

Although some question marks in F *Othello* were probably taken over from Q, F added many more, and they can make a difference to the way we read or speak the dialogue. F's new question marks suggest pauses, or a change of inflection – with what authority? It should be borne in mind (1) that Jaggard's men added question marks in the 1619 Pavier reprints; (2) that not a single question mark appears in the three Shakespearian pages of *Sir Thomas More,* whereas at least twelve are required. I deduce that many, if not most, of F's question marks have no authority, and that editors of Folio texts like *Othello* should feel free to disregard F's question marks unless the sense of the passage positively supports them. Needless to say it takes courage to let go of F's punctuation: some editors cling to it as if they have no other option, apparently unaware that they are merely clutching at the whims of unreliable compositors.

Editors, again, may simply perpetuate the whims or carelessness of Jaggard's compositors when they choose to follow F rather than Q *Othello* in variants involving verbal transposition.

(A) (1) We cannot *all be* Masters, nor all Masters
             (1.1.42, F; *be all* Q)

    (2) For such proceeding *I am* charg'd withall
             (1.3.94, F; *am I* Q)

    (3) Is of a constant, *louing, Noble* Nature
             (2.1.287, F; *noble, louing* Q)

Compare the 'Pavier' text of *Henry V* (Q3) and Q 1600:[7]

(B) (1) Or should or should not, stop *vs in* our clayme
             (1.2.8., Q; *in vs* Q3)

    (2) For in the booke of Numbers *is it* writ
             (1.2.64, Q; *it is* Q3)

See also 1.2.196, 3.6.96, 4.3.2, 4.8.77. Editors of *Othello* used to think F 'the better text', and adopted its readings when choosing between Q and F indifferent variants, including transpositions.[8] Such a policy assumes that the 'better text' will be more reliable no matter what kinds of variant are involved – an assumption that is entirely unwarranted. For, as the question marks and transpositions in the 'Pavier' quartos show, a printing house or compositor can introduce substantive and indifferent variants in any text, even in the 'better text'. The editor of a First Folio text needs to know more about (1) editorial policy for the Folio (this may change from play to play); (2) the policy or preference of Jaggard's printing house; (3) the preferences of individual compositors. Thanks to Alice Walker, Charlton Hinman and others, we know a little about some of the tendencies of Jaggard's compositors, but much more needs to be done before editors will be able to replace the 'better text' policy in dealing with indifferent variants. Among other things, they will have to look beyond individual texts at the general output of a printing house or a known compositor.

McKenzie wondered whether the changes in Q2 *Merchant of Venice* involved anyone apart from the compositor. He thought not, and it seems a reasonable verdict if we examine this text on its own. Once we look beyond this single text, at the 'Pavier' quartos collectively, the question becomes more problematic. Why would the compositor of Q2 *Oldcastle* change stage directions, as at xi.121? 'Here as they are ready to strike, enter Butler and drawes his weapon and steps betwixt them' (Q1); 'As they proffer, enter Butler, and drawes his sword to part them' (Q2). Both stage directions occupy two lines, and space-saving cannot have been the motive for the change. Why are names changed in stage directions and speech prefixes (Harry to Henry, Oldcastle to Cobham, Wrotham to Priest)? Above all, would a compositor have censored profanity in Q2?

It may be said that Q2 *Oldcastle* is a special case, and to some extent this is true. Consider, then, an unusual feature of this text, that it censors the harmless word *yea*, substituting another or simply omitting it: ii.138 (twice); iii.68, 75 (twice); vii.171; xxii.24 (twice). Long ago I observed that *yea* disappeared from the F texts of *1* and *2 Henry IV* and *Richard III* twenty-eight times, and surmised that 'the F editor felt uneasy about the word',[9] perhaps because of its being a common asseveration in the Bible, one that might just be construed as profanity. As it happens, F *2 Henry IV* also changed Harry to Henry now and then (1.1.109, 2.1.134; 4.5.119),[10] so this text has at least two unusual 'links' with *Oldcastle*; the Folio's *yea* changes, however, involved the work of several compositors (chiefly B, but also A and/or C: e.g., sigs g5b, r1b), and this suggests that a scribe or editor, not a compositor, was responsible – not only in *2 Henry IV* but also in Q2 *Oldcastle*. That being so, some of the less obvious changes introduced in other 'Pavier' quartos may after all point to interference from someone other than the compositor (e.g. *incarnall* and *conclusions* in *The Merchant of Venice*: see p. 52; the 1619 *Pericles* also seems to me to include corrections unlikely to have been made by a compositor).

The possibility that an editor may have interfered in the 'Pavier' quartos serves as a reminder that we still know very little about the procedures followed in Jaggard's printing house. It seems that the compositors dealt with textual 'accidentals', such as spelling and punctuation, as was normal. What guidance were they given, if any? How much discretion did they have when they thought that Ralph Brooke or William Shakespeare could not have meant what they read in their copy?

*   *   *

Editors of Shakespeare, whenever they have to choose between a quarto and folio text, as in the case of *Othello*, have traditionally given one of the two the status of a preferred or 'better' text (see p. 142). With the notable exception of M.R. Ridley, the editor of Arden 2, recent editors have preferred F *Othello* to Q, and my account of the professional careers of Jaggard, Walkley and Okes may seem to support the majority view. Jaggard, though criticised by Ralph Brooke, was the printer selected by Heminges and Condell, whereas no one knows how Walkley and Okes acquired their copy; Jaggard was trusted by the players, who had little cause to trust Walkley and Okes. By a curious coincidence the two printers, Okes and Jaggard, were compared by a contemporary for the quality of their work, and his verdict went the other way.

To my approued good Friend, Mr. *Nicholas Okes*. The infinite faults escaped
in my booke of *Britaines Troy*, by the negligence of the Printer [Jaggard], as
the misquotations, mistaking of sillables, misplacing halfe lines, coining of
strange and neuer heard of words. These being without number, when I
would haue taken a particular account of the *Errata*, the Printer answered
me, hee would not publish his owne disworkemanship, but rather let his
owne fault lye vpon the necke of the Author . . . finding you on the contrary,
so carefull, and industrious, so serious and laborious to doe the Author all
the rights of the presse, I could not choose but gratulate your honest
indeauours with this short remembrance.

The writer was Thomas Heywood, in an epistle appended to *An Apology for
Actors* (1612). Admittedly this was some time before Okes and Jaggard came
to print *Othello*, in two versions that differ in hundreds of readings: it serves as
a warning, though, that we must beware of simplifying the editorial situation
– as if Okes was always unreliable and Jaggard could do no wrong. Heywood
complained of Jaggard's 'misplacing of sillables', Brooke of Jaggard's 'syllabi-
call faults', and there are certainly syllabical differences between Q and F
Othello, some of which, as will emerge (p. 141), we may have to attribute to the
'disworkemanship' of Jaggard's compositors.

Four years before Heywood, Edward Topsell condemned Jaggard's workmanship more diplomatically for 'the manifolde escapes in the presse, which
turned and sometimes ouerturned the sence in many places, (especially in the
Latine:) which fault as it may in parte concerne me, so yet it toucheth another
more deeply'.[11] The unnamed other was Jaggard. He, 'wanting the true
knowledge of the Latine tongue', had printed Topsell's *Historie of Foure-Footed
Beastes* not at all to the author's satisfaction: Topsell expressed himself
diplomatically because he asked Jaggard to print their joint apology.

No less than three of Jaggard's authors were displeased with his workmanship, and said so publicly. Heywood, in his *Apology for Actors*, mentioned a
fourth, under whose name Jaggard had issued *The Passionate Pilgrim*: 'the
Author I know much offended with M. *Jaggard* that (altogether vnknowne to
him) presumed to make so bold with his name.'[12] This author was William
Shakespeare. Would he have been entirely happy with the workmanship of
Jaggard's most famous book, the First Folio? As we have seen, Jaggard's men
took many liberties with the texts they printed.

Editorial preference for F *Othello* as against Q has coexisted for some time
with a growing awareness that the Folio contains many different kinds of text,
transmitted by more and sometimes less conscientious compositors, not to
mention scribes. Compositor B, responsible for about half of F *Othello*, was
careless and also high-handed. An editor, said Alice Walker, 'needs always to
be on his guard against the readings of Compositor B', and the Folio as a
whole 'requires more drastic editorial treatment than has been customary'.[13]
As for Compositor E, his 'work generally is full of errors' according to Charlton

Hinman, and E was the apprentice responsible for the other half of F *Othello*. The gradual accumulation of more knowledge of the shortcomings of the Folio's compositors undermines the status of F *Othello* as 'the better text' – or, at any rate, obliges us to look more sympathetically at Q variants. This is a topic to which I shall return here and there, and especially in chapter 12.

Chapter 6

The Folio scribe and text

Was F *Othello* printed from a corrected copy of Q, as Alice Walker contended, or from a manuscript, as J.K. Walton suggested? Although Greg, Bowers and others accepted Miss Walker's arguments when she published them, a growing number of voices now agrees with Walton.[1] In this chapter I try to support the manuscript theory, and ask what we may deduce from F about the writer of the manuscript.

Can we identify him? The F text has many distinctive features, including unusual spellings, which point to one man. For example, it contains thirty-four single words enclosed in brackets: in the three plays that precede *Othello* in the Folio the figures are quite different: *Macbeth*, 3; *Hamlet*, 3; *King Lear*, 4. Now it is well known that Ralph Crane, who worked for the King's Men or for their dramatists before and after 1623, added many brackets to the texts he transcribed: less familiar is the fact that he had a partiality for placing single words in brackets, a less common phenomenon than the use of brackets in general. In the five plays included in the Folio that are widely thought to have been printed from Crane transcripts, the figures for single words in brackets are closer to those for *Othello*: *Tempest*, 14; *Two Gentlemen*, 33; *Merry Wives*, 66; *Measure for Measure*, 17; *Winter's Tale*, 76 – an average of 41.[2] We cannot compare these five texts with a 'good' Quarto, as the plays were first printed in the Folio (except for *Merry Wives*, for which we have a 'bad' quarto); we can, however, compare the Q and F texts of *Othello*, and here the figures for single words in brackets are Q: 0; F: 34.

Could it be that Shakespeare's own writing habits fluctuated so markedly? We can check in the Quartos (excluding the 'bad' Quartos), with the following results, in chronological order of publication, for single words in brackets: *Venus and Adonis*, 0; *Lucrece*, 1; *Titus*, 2; *Richard II*, 7; *Love's Labour's Lost*, 3; *1 Henry IV*, 2; *Romeo*, 2; *Dream*, 3; *Merchant of Venice*, 0; *2 Henry IV*, 3; *Ado*, 0; *Hamlet*, 0; *Lear*, 0; *Troilus*, 4; *Sonnets*, 3. Although these figures may have been influenced by printing-house preferences, they involve so many printers and are sufficiently alike to prompt two inferences: (1) Shakespeare himself was probably responsible for some single words in brackets; (2) he is unlikely to have departed as far from his norm as would be the case if he acted as scribe for the Folio text of *Othello*.

If not Shakespeare, could it have been the compositors who were responsible? Two compositors are thought to have set the type for F *Othello*: an apprentice, E (Act 1, to TLN 731), and compositor B (TLN 732 to the end). Charlton Hinman, who first identified E, assigned only the first six pages of F *Othello* to him; Trevor Howard-Hill, employing a greater variety of tests, later reassigned the stints of E and B as follows:[3] E set TLN 1–731, and also TLN 855–1494, 2388–3026, and B set the rest. That is, Howard-Hill assigned not 6 but 16 pages to E. Thus compositor E set nine single words in brackets in F *Othello*, and B twenty-five, according to Hinman's compositor analysis; according to Howard-Hill's, E set twenty in 16 pages, B set fourteen in 14 pages. Whichever compositor analysis we prefer, the unusual number of single words in brackets in F *Othello* cannot be attributed to one of the compositors; it looks as if both compositors followed their copy in adopting these brackets.

We know a little about B's faithfulness to copy because B set the type for some of the ten 'Pavier quartos' of 1619, all reprints.[4] How many 'swibs' (single words in brackets, a convenient abbreviation) were added in the Pavier quartos, compared with the texts used in 1619 as copy? The figures are: *The Whole Contention*, Parts 1 and 2, 0; *Pericles*, 0; *Yorkshire Tragedy*, 0; *Merchant of Venice*, 1; *Merry Wives*, 0; *King Lear*, 0; *Henry V*, 0; *Oldcastle*, 1; *Midsummer Night's Dream*, 0. Jaggard's compositors, it seems, did not have a habit of wantonly multiplying swibs; on the other hand, they usually reproduced swibs if they found them in their copy-text (there are seven in *Pericles*, 1619, all present already in Q1 of 1609; three in *Dream*, 1619, again all present in Q1 of 1600).

I suspect that a compositor setting from manuscript may have changed punctuation more freely than one setting from printed copy (in fact, the punctuation of the Pavier quartos was changed quite extensively: see p. 51). Nevertheless, the figures given in the previous paragraph confirm the impression that swibs in F *Othello* should not be attributed to the two compositors. By a process of elimination we return to Ralph Crane. Other men no doubt worked for the King's company as scribes, and at least one needs further attention (cf. p. 76); the only other scribe who did so and whose name we know, Edward Knight, did not share Crane's partiality for swibs. Crane, however, is believed to have transcribed five texts for the Shakespeare Folio, so Crane must be given serious consideration as the man responsible for the manuscript used by the Folio compositors of *Othello*, if indeed a manuscript was used.

Crane varied the frequency of swibs in his transcripts, as in the First Folio texts customarily assigned to him (below, p. 62). Howard-Hill, considering brackets generally and not swibs, thought that higher-frequency texts could be explained as Crane transcripts from Crane transcripts, because we know that in some cases he certainly added to the number of brackets in his copy.[5] I do not rule out this possibility; a swib count for three Crane transcripts issued in the Malone Society Reprints, however, suggests a simpler explanation. The figures are: *Demetrius and Enanthe*, more than 250 swibs; *Sir John van Olden Barnavelt*, 3; *The Witch*, 81.

The likeliest explanation of these figures is that, as in his use of 'massed entries', Crane had no fixed principles, varying his practice according to the time available and the purpose for which his transcript was commissioned. Massed entries are found in the Malone manuscript of *A Game at Chess* but not in some other Crane transcripts; they are also found in three of the five Crane texts in the First Folio. Rearranging the entries so as to 'mass' them at the beginning of every scene clearly took up time, and adding many unnecessary brackets would also be time-consuming: being proud of his workmanship, Crane liked to produce at his best when there was time, and added not only massed entries and swibs but also many twirls and flourishes and rules, apostrophes, hyphens and other proofs of his devotion to his mystery.

The swib test must be applied with caution: we need to know more about the swib habits of other authors, scribes and printing houses. Nevertheless, since it seems possible that Shakespeare's Q and F texts divide into two groups – one with a low or nil swib count, another with a much higher count – it will be useful to list the swibs in some of his other texts, and to consider what they reveal. I list the words in the order in which they appear, omitting the brackets.

1 *Othello* (F): *Iago*, Sir, Sir, hoa, vnbonneted, Friends, Generall, Iewell, Moore, hoa, Cassio, Madam, Friends, Hony, Masters, Sir, Michaell, Deere, Iago, Iago, Gentlemen, Sweet, Iago, doubtlesse, Sir, indeed, Iago, pish, Iago, man, Cassio, indeed, belike, Cassio.
2 *Lucrece*: alas.
3 *Titus Andronicus* (Q): sweete, vnaduizd.
4 *Richard II* (Q): God, vncle, coward, Aumerle, sweet, vilaine, King.
5 *Love's Labour's Lost* (Q): companie, Lordes, Lady.
6 *1 Henry IV* (Q): zoundes, Hall.
7 *Romeo and Juliet* (Q2): exquisit, what.
8 *Midsummer Night's Dream* (Q): perforce, forsooth, forsooth.
9 *2 Henry IV* (Q): happy, gentlemen, Harry.
10 *Troilus and Cressida* (Q): slanderer, Achilles, alas, Lord.
11 *Troilus and Cressida* (F): Traitor, indeed, Vlysses, me, forsooth, ful, Achilles, alas, Lord.
12 *Sonnets*: perhaps, loue, Doctor-like.
13 *Macbeth* (F): Sir, Beldams, alas.
14 *Hamlet* (F): Horatio, sometimes, perhaps.
15 *King Lear* (F): Sir, perchance, Friend, Sir.

The important point to notice is that the use of swibs seems to be quite unsystematic. The very same words occur in the same texts without brackets, in some cases many times (e.g. 'hoa' and 'indeed' in *Othello*, 'zounds' in *1 Henry IV*, 'Harry' in *2 Henry IV*). These words therefore have the same significance as Shakespeare's unusual spellings (scilens, a leven, etc.), which are found in *Sir Thomas More* and in the good Quartos as well as more usual spellings: they identify an individual by his occasional and usual habits. Except that, in printed texts, we have to consider more than one individual – namely author, scribes and compositors. So it is reassuring that some swibs appear in several printed texts (but see also p. 163), and that the very unusual swib (hoa), found twice in F *Othello*, occurs on two different pages, set by two different compositors – that is, must have been present as a swib in the manuscript copy. Both Hinman and Howard-Hill assign the first swib (hoa) to compositor E (TLN 199) and the second to B (TLN 792).

As will be obvious from the list for F *Othello*, a large proportion of swibs consists of vocatives. Crane's other texts are also crammed with swib vocatives: non-vocative swibs are therefore more idiosyncratic, and of more evidential value as the thumb-prints of an individual. All the non-vocative swibs in the First Folio are listed in Appendix D; since our immediate concern is Ralph Crane, here is a list of non-vocative swibs in the five Folio plays usually ascribed to Crane.

16 *The Tempest*: *inuisible* (stage direction).
17 *Two Gentlemen*: hap'ly, vnworthily, *senceles*, Spaniel-like.
18 *Merry Wives*: la, I'faith, indeed, be-like, forsooth, alas, forsooth, *Faire*, *Lapis*, singly.
19 *Measure for Measure*: Authority, soe, oh, be-like.
20 *The Winter's Tale*: indeed, good-deed, Priest-like, Counsaile, alas, missingly, frighted.

Again it is reassuring that (be-like) in *Merry Wives* (D6^b) and in *Measure for Measure* (G2^b) was set by different compositors (C and B), which confirms that this swib probably stood in the printer's copy.

Can we distinguish Shakespeare's swibs from Crane's? It seems reasonable to assume that swibs repeated in different quartos will be Shakespeare's (alas, sweet, forsooth, indeed), as the quartos contain so few swibs in the first place, and that Crane, already partial to swibs on his own account, kept most of Shakespeare's when he transcribed his plays, and added others. But it is not impossible that some swibs were bracketed more generally at this time, just as some unusual spellings caught on more generally; before we attribute swibs to Shakespeare we need more information about general usage. Crane's are more easily tracked down, because we have so many manuscripts in his hand. Thus out-of-the-way swibs found in a Crane manuscript and in the Shakespeare Folio may point back to Crane: (Spaniel-like) in *Two Gentlemen* (TLN 1636) and (Priest-like) in *Winter's Tale* (TLN 326) – such hyphened *-like* words occur as swibs in F Crane texts and in no other F texts, and may be compared with Crane's (Epicurean-like), (Capon-like) and (wynner-like) in

Game at Chess, Malone manuscript, lines 2217, 2299 and 2442. Middleton's holograph text of *Game* (T) omits the brackets in all three instances; Crane's (L) and (F) transcripts of *Game* have some, but not all three, of these *-like* words as swibs, for, as already stated, Crane was never entirely consistent in his peculiar scribal habits. Yet despite Crane's evident partiality for hyphened -like swibs, the presence of (Doctor-like) in the *Sonnets* must not be overlooked.

The thirty-four swibs in F *Othello* cannot be said to identify Crane as the scribe. But they encourage us to look for other clues, such as unusual and characteristic spellings, which may be as revealing as a man's handwriting. Such clues are not as plentiful as one might expect, given the fact that Crane's surviving manuscripts seem to be crammed with distinctive spellings, because the Folio compositors 'corrected' most of these spellings. In the five Folio comedies usually accepted as printed from Crane transcripts some of his most habitual spellings have just about disappeared – spellings such as answeare, beutie, confes, holly (= holy), inocent, litle, noyce, noe, saffe, soe, theis, wellcom, and many more. Hence Howard-Hill's conclusion that the

> textual characteristics adduced to show that Crane influenced the texts of the early comedies are mainly accidentals – marks of elision, parentheses, hyphens and the like – and matters of substance supply little evidence for identification of the texts for which he made transcripts.[6]

Where distinctive spellings are concerned, we have to reckon with other complicating factors, apart from the tendency of compositors to eliminate them. Some 'unusual' spellings, by modern standards, were less unusual in Crane's day: thus many 'Crane' spellings occur in F *Othello* and / or in the five Crane comedies, yet are also found in other Folio texts. I mean intrusive or misplaced apostrophes (e.g. do's, ha's, was't [= wast], y'are) and a host of other spellings that appear to link F *Othello* and Crane (al, a-part, Curtsie, 'Faith, falce, Great-ones, guift, happely, he'ld, hir, Leacherie, neu'r, Noble [almost invariably capitalised], obay, pratle, recide, shrew'd, sodaine, ther, etc.): without a comprehensive analysis of the spelling in Shakespeare's texts we cannot know whether such 'unusual' spellings support the hypothesis that Crane prepared the copy for F *Othello*, or, in other F texts, strengthen the possibility that Crane acted as supervisor for texts that he did not transcribe personally (see p. 73).

*   *   *

Crane characteristics and spellings. (Line references for Crane manuscripts are to the Malone Society Reprints of *Barnavelt*, *Demetrius* and *The Witch*; for Crane's transcripts of *A Game at Chess*, which are not yet available in printed editions,[7] the line numbering follows that of the MSR of Middleton's holograph version, edited by T. Howard-Hill [1990]. *Othello* is cited from the *Norton Facsimile* of the Folio, edited by Charlton Hinman [1968], with the Norton Through Line

Numbering [TLN]. Letters A, B, etc., after the TLN indicate the compositor who set the page, as in Howard-Hill's compositor analysis; if Hinman's differs from Howard-Hill's, Hinman's follows in pointed brackets. Marvin Spevack's *Concordance* is my authority when I say that a word occurs so many times in Shakespeare: by this I also mean that I have checked all the instances of the word cited in the *Concordance* in the specified text [Q and / or F], except for *Passionate Pilgrim, A Lover's Complaint* and *Two Noble Kinsmen.*)

(1) For-sooth ('For-sooth, a great Arithmatician', 21E). This is the only example of 'forsooth' with a hyphen in Shakespeare's good quartos and Folio. Compare *The Witch* 279, 1566, 1577.

(2) worsse, worsser ('I am worth no worsse a place', 15E; 'The worsser welcome', 105E). Of the more than two hundred instances of 'worse' and 'worser' in the good quartos and Folio, only two others (F *Lear* 1225E, 1760E) spell with double 's'. Compare *The Witch* 819, 1180, 1405, etc., *Demetrius* 1058, 1776, *Barnavelt* 1593, etc., and also Crane's usual spelling of 'pursse', 'cursse', 'pulsse', etc. For *King Lear* see below, p. 73.

(3) Verb and pronoun hyphened ('Cannot with safetie cast-him', 164E; 'if thou be'st Valiant . . . list-me', 1000E⟨B⟩). Common in Crane manuscripts; also found in Folio 'Crane' texts ('peg-thee', *Tempest* 424C; 'rest-them', *Two Gentlemen* 1214C; 'carry-her', *Merry Wives* 217A; 'auouch-it', *Winter's Tale* 1689B; 'made-me', *ibid.* 1710B). Found in one other Folio text, *2 Henry IV* (for which see Appendix E, p. 165).

(4) Aunciant ('Aunciant, what makes he heere?' 260E; 'Aunciant, conduct them' 465E). So *Demetrius* 1126. This spelling of 'ancient' occurs nowhere else in Shakespeare.

(5) She'l'd ('She'l'd come againe' 494E). The only instance of a pronoun and (wou)ld with double apostrophe in Shakespeare. Compare hee'll'd, you'll'd, I'll'd in *The Witch* (536, 854, 1263; also 857, 917, etc.); you'l'd in *Game* (L) 2077, 2080; *The Duchess of Malfi* (1623), K$_2$^{b}. Compare also the very unusual double apostrophe in thou'd'st ('that such companions thou'd'st vnfold' 2853E⟨B⟩): as is well known, Crane had a habit of multiplying apostrophes needlessly.

(6) Verb and adverb hyphened ('As to throw-out our eyes for braue Othello' 794B). This is a characteristic Crane hyphen (more than three dozen instances in *The Witch*); also found in Folio 'Crane' texts ('Come-on', *Two Gentlemen* 879C; 'Go-too', *Merry Wives* 1384B; 'peere-out' *ibid.* 1921B; 'tyde-vp', *Measure* 323D; 'seal'd-vp' *Winter's Tale* 1307A), and in F *2 Henry IV*. For *2 Henry IV* see Appendix E, pp. 166–7.

(7) Ielouzie ('At least into a Ielouzie so strong' 1084E⟨B⟩). The only other instance in Shakespeare with 'z' occurs in a 'Crane' text, *Merry Wives* 2616B. Compare *The Witch* 371, 772, 1745, etc.; *Barnavelt* 772; *Game* (L) 593 (Ielouzie) where (T) has Iealousie; and 'Leaprouzie' in *Game* (L) 351, 1363.

(8) (doubtlesse) ('This honest Creature (doubtlesse)', 1873B). Not found as a swib elsewhere in the Folio (although 'no doubt' is sometimes bracketed).

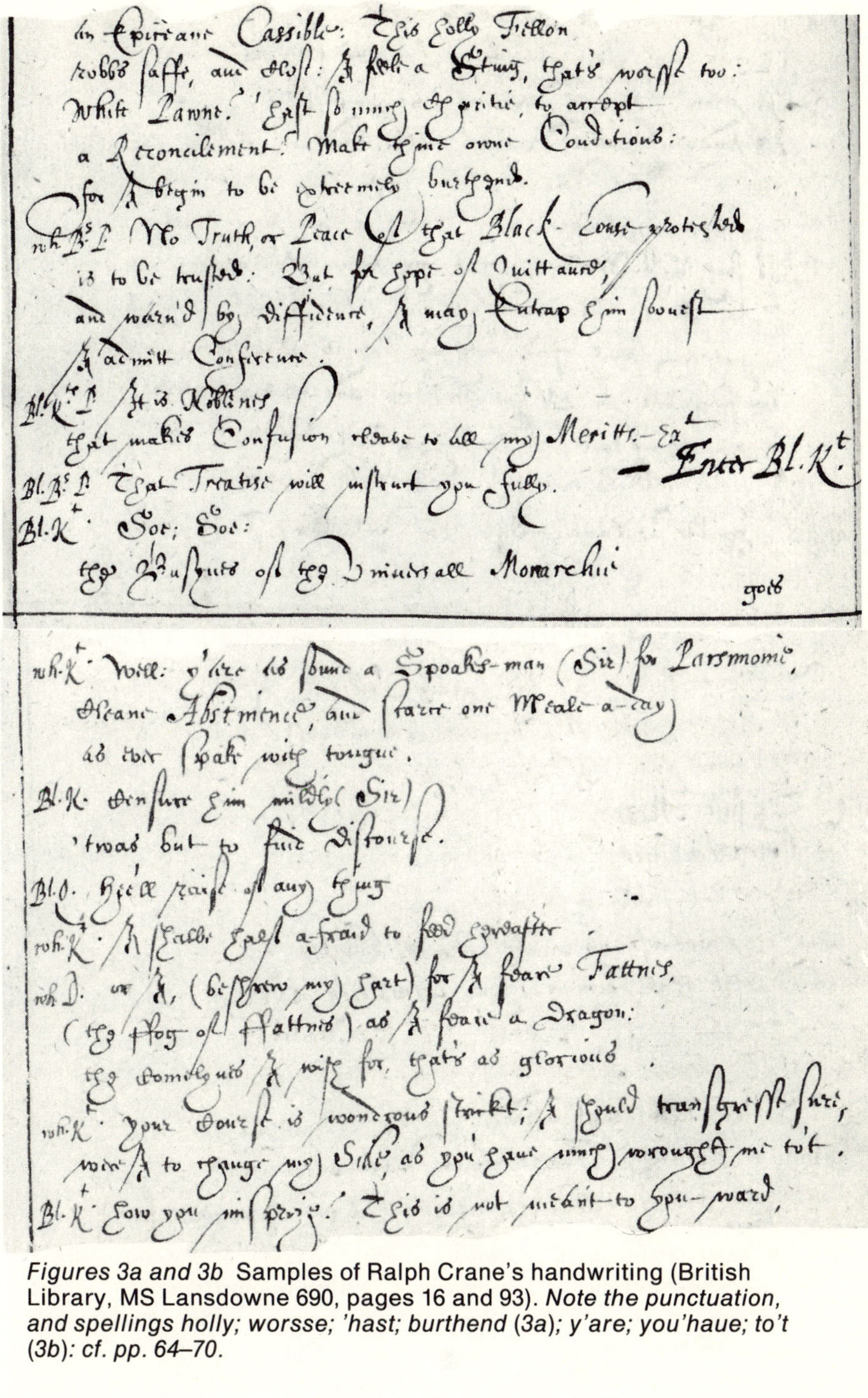

Figures 3a and 3b Samples of Ralph Crane's handwriting (British Library, MS Lansdowne 690, pages 16 and 93). *Note the punctuation, and spellings holly; worsse; 'hast; burthend (3a); y'are; you'haue; to't (3b): cf. pp. 64–70.*

Compare *Game* (L) 118, '(doubtles)', brackets apparently added by Crane, i.e. not present in Middleton's holograph (T); also *Game*, Q3 (a text apparently printed from a Crane transcript), sig. A4b.

(9) 'Saue ('Saue you', 2327B). This form of 'Save' for 'God save' occurs only in 'Crane' texts in the Folio and in *2 Henry IV*: compare *Tempest* 847B; *Two Gentlemen* 74A; *Merry Wives* 1192C; *Measure* 768A. For *2 Henry IV* see Appendix E, p. 166.

(10) quight ('or foredoes me quight' 3237B). Crane's usual spelling: compare *The Witch* 800, 1385, and 'requight' (*Demetrius* 1073); *Game* (L) 591, 1971 (where *Game* [T] reads 'quite' both times). This is an eye-rhyme in F *Othello*; the spelling occurs nowhere else in Shakespeare's quartos or Folio.

These are the more striking 'Crane' spellings in F *Othello*. But many other spellings probably point to Crane as well – for example 'trym'd' ('trym'd in Formes' 54E). Elsewhere in the good quartos and Folio Shakespeare always has 'trim', etc., whereas Crane preferred 'trym' (*Barnavelt* 2751, 2887; *Game* [L] 674, 1620). The spelling 'Willough' (2998, etc.) for 'willow', not used elsewhere by Shakespeare, occurs in Crane (MS. Rawl. poet. 61, fos. 61[a], 62[b]). Again, 'Good-faith' (1179E⟨B⟩) looks like a Crane spelling. This is the only hyphened instance in the Folio, with a close parallel in 'good-sooth' in *2 Henry IV* (1064C), in place of Q *2 Henry IV* 'good faith': as I explain in Appendix E, following others, F *2 Henry IV* is probably also a Crane text. Compare 'good-deed' and 'Good-lucke' in *Winter's Tale* (99A, 1510B), 'good-speed' (*Witch* 657), and Crane's hyphened asseverations, such as 'y'-faith', 'in-troth' (*Witch* 94, 890). Crane's habit of inserting unnecessary hyphens has been amply documented by Howard-Hill.[8]

Many more spellings in F *Othello* are probably significant, being Crane's usual spellings and unusual or very unusual elsewhere. (1) Adjective and noun hyphened, where we would omit the hyphen: 'The gutter'd-Rockes' (831B), 'the felt-Absence' (2343B): cf. *Witch* 267, 285, 1777, 1859. These two F *Othello* readings illustrate another Crane characteristic, hyphened words where the second element begins with a capital letter (so also 're-Lume' 3252B): compare 'dis-Armes', 'vn-Maning' (*Game* [L], 129, 281; Middleton's holograph, T, reads 'disarmes', 'unmanning'); 'a-Wing' (*Demetrius* 346). (2) Adjective and 'one(s)' hyphened: 'Three Great-ones' (12E); 'wise-ones' (917E⟨B⟩); 'Great-ones' (1904B). This hyphen is rare in Shakespeare, but occurs in *Winter's Tale* 2717A, 'blind-ones'; *John*[9] 839B, 'yong-ones'; F *Titus* 885E, 'young-ones'; *Cymbeline* 2093B, 'Rich-ones'. Compare *Game* (L) 147, 1148, where Middleton's holograph (T) omits the hyphen both times; *Demetrius* 312, 2809, 2858, etc. The fact that this hyphen is very unusual in the Folio's 'non-Crane' texts and yet occurs three times in F *Othello* suggests that here, too, Crane's preferred spelling influenced the Folio compositors.

From spelling to punctuation (to which I return in more detail in chapter 11). Crane's punctuation, according to the editors of the MSR *Demetrius*, was 'plentiful and even fussy. . . . His favourite stop was perhaps the colon, which

he uses where other scribes might use a comma, a semicolon, or a full stop'[10] –
or, we should add, where others might use an exclamation or question mark.
Sometimes, I find, Crane chose to write three or more colons in a single verse
line, and this may turn out to be a significant clue as to his presence. Thus –
'for I shall Cursse all now: hate all: for-sweare all:' (*Demetrius* 2225: see also
798, 824, 1200, 1244, etc.); 'goe pray: goe pray: goe pray: we shalbe hangd
all' (*Barnavelt* 932); 'there's six pence more for that: away: keep-close:' (*Witch*
882: cf. also 369, 938, 1330, etc.); 'yes: yes: you doe Marrie:' (*Game* [L], 1440:
Middleton's holograph [T] lacks all three colons). I have noticed the same
peculiarity in four plays in the First Folio:

Thou hast: when was she born? speak: tell me:
(*Tempest* 387)

That profit vs: What hoe: slaue: Caliban:
(*Tempest* 449)

And if it please you, so: if not: why so:
(*Two Gentlemen* 522)

'Tis time: descend: be Stone no more: approach:
(*Winter's Tale* 3307)

Ile fill your Graue vp: stirre: nay, come away:
(*Winter's Tale* 3309)

I know't: I thanke you: you do loue my Lord:
(*Othello* 1601)

I thinke vpon't, I thinke: I smel't: O Villany:
(*Othello* 3476)

The first three Folio plays here are recognised 'Crane' texts: once again F
Othello shares an unusual scribal feature with this family of texts. With *Othello*
3476 compare also 'or the Devill's in't: I thinck: I'll neu'r trust Witch els'
(*Witch* 848). In a modern text we would print 'I think I smell't' at *Othello*
3476; the colon after 'thinke' points to Crane no less than the three colons in a
verse line.

All the suggested 'Crane' spellings and other peculiarities in F *Othello* differ
from their Q counterparts. Q prints Forsooth, worse and worse, cast him and
list me, Auncient and Ancient, Shee'd and thoudst, throw out, Iealousie,
doubtlesse (without brackets), Saue you, quite, trimd, Good faith, guttered
rocks, felt absence, restore (for 're-Lume'), great ones, wise ones, great ones,
and is much more sparing with colons.

To the best of my knowledge none of the 'Crane' spellings listed above
appears elsewhere in the Folio, except in the rare cases indicated. I stress this
because the apprentice compositor, E, shared Crane's habit of peppering
apostrophes in unlikely places, and might be thought responsible for some in

F *Othello*. We can distinguish Crane's and E's apostrophes, I think, by their recurrence in other texts. I assign two instances of 'Reueren'd' on the same page of F *Othello* (TLN 363, 415) to E, because E has the same spelling in F *Romeo* 2457, and indeed had a weakness for inserting an apostrophe between *n* and *d*, as in rin'd (= rind, *Romeo* 1029), grin'd (= grind, *Titus* 2475, 2487). Crane elsewhere spelt 'reverend' without an apostrophe; on the other hand, E spelt 'She'l'd' only in *Othello*, whereas Crane frequently wrote this and related words with two apostrophes. When E's and Crane's spellings can be matched in other texts, I feel fairly confident that we can tell the two men apart in F *Othello* (in some cases, though not in all).

The fate of unusual spellings in printed texts depends, of course, on the compositors. I would expect an inexperienced compositor to be more inclined to follow copy, and an experienced man to correct unusual copy spellings, unless instructed otherwise. Most of the 'Crane' spellings listed above may well have survived only because they were set by the apprentice compositor, E, who – as Hinman has demonstrated – tended 'to follow copy closely'.[11] Even if we accept Howard-Hill's compositor analysis (16 pages set by E, 14 by B) and not Hinman's (6 pages by E, 24 by B), compositor E retained a disproportionate number of 'Crane' spellings: but for the fortunate accident that E was put to work on F *Othello*, we might well have remained ignorant of Ralph Crane's role in the transmission of this text for a few more centuries.

The 'scatter' of Crane spellings in F *Othello* lends some support to the view that unusual spellings will not survive in large numbers in a printed text except in unusual circumstances. This needs to be said, since so many characteristic 'Crane' spellings occur rarely or not at all in F *Othello* – spellings such as those listed on p. 63. As it happens, these spellings are equally rare in other Folio texts thought to be printed from Crane transcripts (*The Tempest*, etc.), so their scarcity in F *Othello* requires no special explanation.

All the same, Crane's distinctive habits leave other traces, and these can throw light on the QF variants in *Othello*. In one of his transcripts of *A Game at Chess* (L) Crane wrote 'hath' some three dozen times where Middleton (T) wrote 'has' or 'ha's'; a similar tendency is clearly visible in Crane's Malone transcript of *Game*, except that there are fewer 'hath' substitutions because this is a shortened version of the play. F *Othello* prints 'hath' for Q's 'has' twenty-two times. A comparison with the QF variants in *Hamlet* and *King Lear* is revealing (these being the two plays that precede *Othello* in the Folio): in F *Hamlet* 'has' or 'ha's' replaces Q2's 'hath' five times (1.1.17, 1.5.130, 3.1.149, 5.1.189, 5.2.154),[12] and there is one reverse change (Q2 has–F hath, 5.2.272). F *King Lear* resembles *Hamlet*, with three Q hath–F has variants (1.2.66, 1.4.101, 5.3.248) and three instances of the reverse (2.2.65, 3.4.53, 166).[13] With *King Lear* Q2 slightly complicates the issue, since F seems to derive in part from Q2, and Q2 sometimes differs from Q1, but this does not change the general picture. The has–hath variants in *Othello* are quite out of line with *Hamlet* and *King Lear*, and strangely similar to the has–hath changes apparently introduced in *Game* (L) by Ralph Crane.

I say 'apparently introduced' because the manuscript from which Crane copied (L) has not survived. He did not copy directly from (T), so a comparison of (L) and (T) could be misleading, especially since a comparison of the two holograph texts of *Game* (T, H) shows that Middleton himself sometimes switched to variant spellings in (H). As it happens, no has–hath variants are found in (T) and Middleton's holograph pages in (H), and it may well be that Middleton's 'unstable' spellings did not extend to this pair of variants.

The has–hath figures in Shakespeare are likely to have been influenced by the dates of plays, by the contexts in which the words are used, and by scribes and compositors. Early plays tend to avoid 'has'; middle-period plays introduce it more often. Despite the fact that variables are involved, it may be significant that the has–hath figures for F *Othello* resemble those for *Measure for Measure*, a 'Crane' text, whereas those for *All's Well* and *Twelfth Night*, two near-contemporary plays, are quite different: F *Othello* has 10, hath 67; *Measure* has 7, hath 71; *All's Well* has 28, hath 53; *Twelfth Night* has 20, hath 35. In the two 'Crane' texts (*Othello*, *Measure*) the has–hath ratio is 1:7 and 1:10, in the other two it is between 1:1 and 1:2. On the other hand, Q *Othello* resembles *All's Well* and *Twelfth Night*, with a very similar ratio. Crane's preference for hath is as visible in these Folio 'Crane' texts as in his transcripts of *A Game at Chess*; Jaggard's compositor, on the contrary, twice changed 'hath' to 'has' in the Pavier reprint of *King Lear* (Gla, L3a), without any obvious reason, such as justification. It should be added that other Folio texts have different has–hath ratios, perhaps influenced by other variables; the curious divergence of Q and F *Othello* nevertheless requires an explanation.[14]

Let us move on to other QF variants in *Othello* where F again introduces Crane's preferred spellings.

(1) *it* changed to '*t*. At least ten instances in *Game* (L); fairly common in F *Othello*, as against Q. For example, 'I humbly thanke you *for't*. / I never knew' (3.1.40, F; *for it* Q).

(2) *the* plus vowel changed to *th'*. At least ten instances in *Game* (L); common in F *Othello*. Example: 'But he (Sir) had *th'*election' (1.1.26, F; *the* Q).

(3) Medial *-d-* changed to *-th-*. Crane changed *burden* and *farder* (T) to *burthen, farther* (*Game*, L, 361, 519, 1290, 1396, etc. Compare 'no *further* conscionable' (*Othello* 2.1.236, F; *farder* Q). This preference for *-th-* forms may explain the QF *murder–murther* variants in *Othello* (4.1.167, 5.1.27, 37, etc.). In all, Q's *murder* and cognates become F *murther* a dozen times, and the reverse change only occurs once (1.2.3, where compositor E first encountered the word).

(4) *a* changed to *on*. Compare the following, in Middleton's *Game* (T) and Crane's transcript (L): 'made that Noyse *a* purpose (T, 651; *on* L); 'set themselues *afire*' (T, 2046; *on fire* L); 'Meate ynough *a conscience*' (T, 2311; *on-conscience* L). Crane preferred the less colloquial *on* to *a*. Now compare the following QF variants in *Othello*: 'Othello, / Is come *on Shore*' (2.1.28, F; *ashore* Q); 'The Riches of the Ship is come *on shore*' (2.1.83, F; *ashore* Q). I believe that other less colloquial F variants may also express Crane's (rather than Shakespeare's)

preference: 'you are Pictures out *of doore*' (2.1.109, F; *adores* Q); 'Or to be naked with her Friend *in bed*' (4.1.3, F; *abed* Q); 'Shore his old thred *in twaine*' (5.2.204, F; *atwane* Q). Perhaps, then, the repeated substitution of F *handkerchief* in place of Q *handkercher* should also be ascribed to Crane?

Comparing these QF variants in *Othello* with similar ones in Q2 and F *Hamlet* one sees that the two F texts often pull in opposite directions, or fail to pull in the same direction: in some cases this may have no significance, in others Crane's preference could explain the *Othello* variants. Why is it that F *Othello* switched from *the* plus vowel to *th'*, whereas F *Hamlet* often switched the other way round (*Hamlet* 2.2.388, 476; 3.1.71, 74; 3.2.34; 5.1.121; 5.2.37, 368, 396)?[15] I return to other possible Crane substitutions later, more complicated ones than some of those listed above: his reduction and elimination of profanity (p. 78), his treatment of stage directions (p. 72), his treatment of other contractions (p. 140). If Crane was indeed the scribe responsible for the F *Othello* manuscript, editors will have to think again about hundreds of QF variants.

*   *   *

Another reason for connecting Crane with the F text of *Othello* must now be mentioned. A list headed 'The Names of the Actors' is printed on the last page, and similar lists are found at the end of four of the Folio's 'Crane' texts – *The Tempest, Two Gentlemen, Measure for Measure* and *The Winter's Tale*. (The fifth 'Crane' text, *Merry Wives*, no doubt fails to provide such a list because the dialogue fills the last page.) In all, seven F plays are followed by a *dramatis personae* list: two occupy complete pages, and were clearly inserted as space-fillers, to occupy pages that would otherwise have had to be blanks. Whether

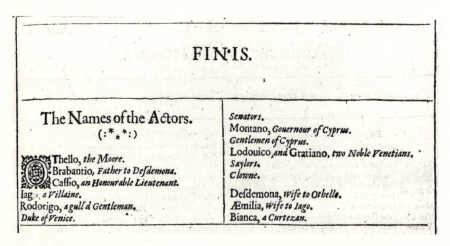

Figure 4 'The Names of the Actors' from the Folio (*reduced in size*)

they were drawn up in the printing house or earlier, the two (*2 Henry IV*, *Timon*) differ from the other five not only in having a page to themselves but also in their headings ('THE ACTORS NAMES', in capitals). The *Othello* list therefore invites comparison with the lists appended to four 'Crane' texts, just as the unusual spellings in F *Othello* relate this text to the same 'Crane' texts.

Characteristically for Crane, the four lists for the Folio comedies differ in little ways from one another, and the *Othello* list also differs from the other four. They are headed 'The Scene, an vn-inhabited Island / Names of the Actors.' (*Tempest*); 'The names of all the Actors.' (*Two Gentlemen*); 'The Scene Vienna. / The names of all the Actors.' (*Measure*); 'The Names of the Actors.' (*Winter's Tale*); 'The Names of the Actors.' (*Othello*). The *Othello* list differs from the other four as follows: (1) it prints the names in roman, not in italics; (2) it places the female names at the end, separated from the males by a space; (3) it prints 'FINIS.' before the list, whereas in the four comedies 'FINIS.' follows the lists; (4) beneath its heading the *Othello* list prints two (unequal) brackets, enclosing two colons, with three asterisks in the middle (see Figure 4) which, for want of a better word, I shall call an embellishment. Nothing like this embellishment can be seen elsewhere in the Folio, though similar ones survive in dramatic manuscripts, as in Middleton's (T) manuscript of *A Game at Chess*, where three asterisks or dots enclosed in brackets are common. The only *dramatis personae* list that I know of in a manuscript written by Crane, in *The Witch*, contains several sets of three asterisks, without brackets or colons, perhaps copied from Middleton's manuscript. Crane, however, also embellished transcripts from other writers with the same three dots or asterisks, as in Rawlinson MS. D301 (title-page), MS. Rawl. poet. 61 (title-page), Harleian MS. 6930, f. 88, and elsewhere: the *Othello* embellishment could yet turn out to be significant.

The fact that 'FINIS.' precedes the *Othello* list suggests that this list was an afterthought. Only fourteen lines of dialogue remained for the last page; arranged in two columns, like the rest of the Folio, these lines fill about one-eighth of the page. To avoid something very like a blank page the list was added and 'FINIS.' was accidentally left where it had already been placed. This hypothesis falls short of proving that the same man was responsible for the F text of *Othello* and for the *dramatis personae* list; Crane, however, seems to be the common factor in the five comedies and in *Othello*, and a *dramatis personae* list follows at the end of five of these six plays, so it is reasonable to assume that Crane supplied all five lists.

Did Crane draw up the lists himself, or copy them from an authoritative manuscript? Two of his lists contain information that was not available in the text of the play as printed: the Duke in *Measure for Measure* is named Vincentio, and Montano in *Othello* is described as '*Gouernour of Cyprus*'. The latter may have been taken from a stage direction in Q *Othello* (2.1.0), '*Enter* Montanio, *Gouernor of* Cypres'. As I explain elsewhere, it was not unusual for Shakespeare to invent names that are not needed, and there are good reasons for thinking that Montano was meant to be the governor of Cyprus.[16] So the possibility that Crane copied his lists (or some of them) from an authorial manuscript cannot be ruled out.

*   *   *

A different kind of evidence concerns the absence from F *Othello* of stage directions for off-stage sounds. Shakespeare's 'good' texts divide into two groups, as Gary Taylor observed.

> All of the printed texts apparently set from Shakespeare's own papers – the good quartos, and the Folio texts of *Comedy*, *All's Well*, *Henry V*, and *Timon* – contain directions for offstage sounds: alarum, chambers, flourish, knock, music, noise, sennet, and trumpet all occur. . . . We must accept that Shakespeare, a deeply professional actor and dramatist, made some notes for sound effects in his own manuscript drafts. Consequently, the complete absence of such directions from *Two Gentlemen*, *Merry Wives*, *Measure for Measure*, *Winter's Tale*, *Cymbeline*, *2 Henry IV*, and *Othello* must result from deliberate scribal excision.[17]

Of the F texts said to be without directions for off-stage sounds, the first four are thought to have been printed from 'Crane' transcripts, and the fifth, *Cymbeline*, has been claimed as a 'Crane' text by Taylor, with some support from the 'swib' evidence supplied in this book.[18] The two remaining texts were not identified by Taylor as 'Crane' copies, but are so identified, with the help of spelling tests and other evidence, again in this book. It follows that the 'deliberate scribal excision' of off-stage sounds may point to one man, Ralph Crane, rather than to a general scribal habit.

In fact, Taylor's statement is not wholly accurate. The F text of *2 Henry IV* reduces Q's directions for off-stage sounds, retaining one. 'Trumpets sound, and the King, and his traine passe ouer the stage' (Q) becomes 'The Trumpets sound . . .' (F); F omits Q's 'Peyto knockes at doore' (E3a), 'Alarum   Enter Falstaffe   excursions' (G3b), 'Retraite' (G4a). *Cymbeline*, moreover, calls for a fairly normal range of off-stage sounds, and cannot be said to illustrate 'the complete absence of such directions': 'Clocke strikes', 'Solemn Musick', 'Solemne Musicke', 'Iupiter descends in Thunder and Lightning' (2.2.51, 4.2.186, 5.4.30, 93). Nevertheless the dearth of off-stage sounds in four Folio 'Crane' texts remains significant, as does the fact that for *Othello*, as for *2 Henry IV*, such directions survive in Q ('A shot', D3b; 'A bell rung', F1a; 'A Trumpet', K1b). The two F texts that I propose as additional Crane texts, *Othello* and *2 Henry IV*, are thus linked with four agreed Crane texts; *Cymbeline*, though not so linked, may be connected with *The Tempest*, another Crane text, where off-stage sounds are likewise recorded generously. Being the first and last plays in the Folio, *The Tempest* and *Cymbeline* could have been given

special treatment. As I see it, though, the case for *Cymbeline* as a Crane text needs further study.

*   *   *

Howard-Hill pointed out (cf. above, p. 63) in his analysis of Crane's scribal habits that the evidence identifying Crane as the scribe responsible for five Folio comedies consists mainly of accidentals – 'marks of elision, parentheses, hyphens and the like'. My list of 'Crane' spellings supports this identification of Crane as a Folio scribe and also depends on accidentals, though not in quite the same way. Howard-Hill concentrated on Crane's usual or favoured spellings ('My object was to identify strong or preferred spellings in different transcripts'[19]), whereas most of my 'Crane' spellings, etc., are best described as occasional, rather than usual, in his work. One or two such occasional spellings would carry little weight on their own. Yet the more unusual ones – For-sooth, worsse, cast-him, Aunciant, She'l'd, throw-out, Ielouzie, (doubtlesse), quight, Good-faith, re-Lume, etc. – taken together with Crane's use of 'swibs' (p. 61), has-hath changes (p. 68), *dramatis personae* lists, colons and other idiosyncrasies, link Crane and F *Othello* in so many ways that it is hard to resist the conclusion that he served as scribe for the F manuscript.

Was he only a scribe? We must keep in mind the possibility that the six or seven Crane transcripts in the First Folio now postulated are not necessarily the end of the story. *Cymbeline* could be another, according to the Oxford editors (see p. 164), and Howard-Hill has now re-opened a related question. Who edited the First Folio? Howard-Hill thinks that detailed supervision of the texts included in the Folio would have been impossible for busy men like Heminges, Condell and the book-keeper of the King's Men.

> On the other hand, there does exist indisputable evidence of an editorial presence in the Folio over some stretch of time, exerted by one who had a documented close connection with the King's Men[20] –

in short, Ralph Crane. By adding *Othello* to the five comedies assigned to Crane we stretch the 'stretch of time' to embrace just about the whole of the First Folio, and the implied question becomes even more interesting: what kind of editorial presence?

Could Crane have been a more senior figure in the Folio's editorial team than others have assumed, one who corrected what less trusted scribes had written and who copied out single pages or scenes that were deemed too untidy or illegible for the printer? We have accepted too readily that the manuscripts that went to the printer were all of a piece,[21] even though we know that some of the surviving dramatic manuscripts of the period were patched (i.e. contained pages that replaced other pages). To illustrate, here is an instance of possible patching in F *King Lear*. This text contains the only (two) 'worsse' spellings in the whole of Shakespeare, apart from F *Othello* (see

p. 64). On the same page as the first 'worsse', F *Lear* press-corrected a difficult passage:

Like Rats oft bite the holly cords a twaine,
Which are t'intrince, t'vnloose:[22]

'holly' was corrected to 'holy'. Now 'holly' (= holy) was a characteristic Crane spelling,[23] and most unusual in Shakespeare. Apart from the corrected word in *King Lear*, more than two hundred entries in the *Concordance* yield only one more instance, in Q *Richard II*, 5.6.49.[24] I imagine that the apprentice compositor E, not recognising the word and nonplussed by the passage in *King Lear*, adopted the copy spelling, as he did in similar circumstances in *Othello* (see p. 68). Again on the same page, numbered 292 in the Folio, just five lines before 'holly', occurs the first of the three Q *has*–F *hath* variants in F *Lear*, which may also reflect Crane's preference for *hath* – so three separate clues seem to point to Crane (worsse, holly, hath). Part of the Folio page's copy, or part of Act 2 scene 2 of *King Lear*, appears to have been written or corrected by Crane, and this raises the possibility that other passages in the same text may also suffer from Crane's scribal or editorial interference.[25]

So what exactly was Crane's role in the First Folio editorial team in 1622–3? If it turns out that he was the man entrusted with the major task of editing *2 Henry IV* from Q and a manuscript, a responsibility far greater than a mere copyist's, and also the man who was later asked to undertake *Othello*, an even more complex editorial venture involving a printed text, Q, and a partly illegible manuscript (see p. 82), Crane must be seen as one of the crucial figures in the preparation of the Folio – and, almost certainly, as part-author of many lines that have passed into literary history as quintessential Shakespeare.

Crane, it is usually said, transcribed manuscripts for four comedies placed at the beginning of the Folio and for a fifth one, *The Winter's Tale*, placed as the last of the comedies. Those who planned the Folio collection may have intended to prepare new transcripts for all the plays, deciding after the first four that this would be a waste of time and money. For all the comedies after the first four they could offer the printer either a clean manuscript or a reasonably good quarto text. Crane had to be recalled because when they reached *The Winter's Tale* no text was available. The prompt-book, at any rate, had gone missing a little later, as we learn from Herbert's office-book licence on 19 August 1623, after the play was printed.[26] Then, it is said, the King's Men managed without Crane, or made use of him in other ways (*The Duchess of Malfi*, one of their plays, was published in 1623 from a Crane transcript).

This narrative may have to be changed in several ways. Can we be certain that Crane merely 'transcribed' the five comedies? Only the Folio version survives of each of the five (and a 'bad' quarto of *Merry Wives*): switching to 'massed entries', Crane certainly tampered with the stage directions. What other editing did he attempt? Did he work from a single manuscript, or was he asked (as, apparently, in the case of *2 Henry IV* and *Othello*) to incorporate readings from a second text? One tends to think of Crane as a simple scribe, humble and faithful, who did as he was told: his transcripts of *A Game at Chess* reveal a somewhat different individual, one who took many liberties, eliminating colloquialisms and profanity, changing words and omitting words, lines and longer passages. The shortened version in the Bodleian Library is quite extraordinary, with a multitude of omissions and, sometimes, lines rewritten to conceal the gaps. In brief, Crane was neither humble nor faithful; he 'improved' his transcripts, as he would see it, a creative or destructive role, depending on one's point of view. He seems to have removed the profanity from *Measure for Measure*, where it all but disappears, and from *2 Henry IV* and *Othello*, and, if so, he did it with his usual inconsistency and editorial high-handedness.

If this alternative narrative comes near the mark it may be asked why Crane was not entrusted with other major editorial duties, in particular the copies for F *Hamlet* and F *King Lear*. Were Heminges and Condell displeased with his work? Probably not: the answer may be that the Folio texts of *Hamlet*, *King Lear* and *Othello*, three plays placed consecutively in the Folio, required much more editorial attention than the first four comedies, and that two or more men worked on the three tragedies, perhaps simultaneously. But Crane might still help out the scribe or editor of *King Lear*, or check through his manuscript when it was completed (see p. 73).

We can say, then, that Crane's role in the preparation of the First Folio appears to have been a significant one, more so than hitherto suspected. At the very least he transcribed five comedies – this is generally agreed – and it may be that be transcribed seven or eight plays in all and even replaced pages in other texts that were illegible or otherwise unsuitable for the printer. The texts that I have claimed for Crane over and above the five comedies – *Othello* and *2 Henry IV* – lack some of the 'Crane' characteristics that have received most publicity, notably 'massed entries', but so do some agreed 'Crane' texts (in print and manuscript); on the other hand, the two have much in common with the five comedies, and the seven texts could be said to form a network of interconnecting threads, just as the five comedies interconnect with Crane's surviving manuscripts. Future students of Crane will have to remember that the textual characteristics of his transcripts – brackets, hyphens, apostrophes, spelling generally, punctuation, massed entries – are never quite the same in two texts, and can come close to disappearing in printed versions.

The case for Crane as the scribe and editor of F *Othello* and F *2 Henry IV* still needs careful scrutiny, and perhaps some of the threads will turn out to be less reliable than I have indicated: once others have tested the evidence, checking up on unusual spellings, swib usage in other texts, and so on, we shall be in a better position to take stock. All that one can safely say at this stage is that a *prima facie* case has been made, and that it rests on the great variety of evidence pointing to Crane, not on any single item. I see it as a working hypothesis, not as an established fact – one that is fascinating in itself, throwing new light (if correct) on the drudgery that preceded the printing of the First Folio, and that, additionally, helps us to understand QF variants in *Othello*, on the assumption that F often derives from quirky Crane spellings that baffled compositors E and B (see p. 68).

Before we leave Crane, one other question still needs to be asked. Despite the distinctiveness of his work, did any other scribe share his writing habits? Could we have become too 'fixated' on Crane, and confused him with another man?

One name springs to mind, a name that has already appeared more than once in this chapter. Comparing Crane's transcripts of *A Game at Chess* with Middleton's holograph (T) one is struck by many unusual spellings shared by the two men. Middleton, like Crane, was associated with the King's Men – wrote *A Game at Chess* and other plays for this company at about the time of the First Folio, and indeed has been credited with the role of reviser or part-author of *Measure for Measure* and *Timon of Athens*.[27] Could Middleton have helped out as scribe or editor of Shakespeare's plays? It is not inconceivable; others have proposed Ben Jonson as the Folio editor, and a dramatist, especially one who will have known Shakespeare personally, would have been the ideal choice if Heminges and Condell needed help. Moreover, Middleton sometimes placed single words in brackets, and the swib count for his holograph text of *A Game at Chess*, 31, strangely resembles that for F *Othello*, 34; also, some of the evidence that I have used to identify Crane derives from Middleton plays (*A Game at Chess*, *The Witch*), and might have been copied by Crane from Middleton. Closer scrutiny discloses, however that Middleton and Crane differed in various ways. All the swib words in Middleton's holograph are vocatives, the great majority being '(Sir)', whereas those in F *Othello* include unusual swib choices – hoa, unbonnetted, doubtless, pish. Many of the spellings that link Crane's Middleton texts with F *Othello* also link F *Othello* with Crane and Fletcher, Webster, etc. (e.g. worsser, verb and pronoun hyphened, She'l'd, verb and adverb hyphened, Ielouzie, trym'd), and 'Aunciant' occurs in Crane's copy of Fletcher's *Demetrius*, not in Middleton. Again, Middleton is unlikely to have changed 'has' to 'hath' in F *Othello*, if we may go by the variants in *A Game at Chess*. Crane, not Middleton, is the common factor, and of course Crane, unlike Middleton, copied out many other play-texts for the King's Men.

A more detailed study of Crane's scribal habits, and in particular of his transcripts of *A Game at Chess*, is now urgently needed. It may yet identify other plays, or parts of plays, in which he had a hand. Such a project will be a *sine qua non* for future editors of Shakespeare, not to mention editors of Middleton, Webster, Fletcher, Massinger and Jonson, a not unimpressive clutch of dramatists.

Chapter 7

Manuscript B

What do we know about the manuscript (B) behind Crane's manuscript (Bb), at two removes from the printed Folio text? It has been said that 'Crane in all his work imposes his own scribal preferences so systematically that he obscures most of the evidence which might identify the kind of manuscript he was himself copying'.[1] 'Systematic', I have tried to show (p. 61), is not the right word for Crane's scribal habits, since his texts differ markedly from each other in their use of massed entries, swib forms, spelling, etc., and within individual texts he also imposed his own preferences inconsistently. That said, it remains true that he obscures much of the evidence which might identify the characteristics of the manuscript he was himself copying. So true, indeed, that I feel less clear about this lost manuscript (B) than others who have described it cautiously or confidently, even though I think I know more about Bb (because this text was not previously attributed to Crane).

The Oxford Shakespeare's *Textual Companion* (1987) summarised its own account of F *Othello* thus: 'F represents a scribal copy of Shakespeare's own revised manuscript of the play', an account signed S.W.W./(G.T.).[2] I take it that this was the view of Stanley Wells, with some contribution from Gary Taylor, and it may well be correct. Taylor's more recent discussion (1993) identified B as a late prompt-book, which is not impossible (Shakespeare's own revised manuscript might have become a prompt-book), yet arrives at this conclusion by way of statements with which I cannot agree.

It is a cornerstone of *Shakespeare Reshaped 1606–1623* (1993) that 'literary transcript' texts, as distinct from prompt-books, did not expurgate profanity.

> Unless we receive very strong evidence to the contrary, we must assume that heavily expurgated Folio texts (like *1* and *2 Henry IV*, and *Othello*), which *might* derive from late prompt-books, indeed *do* derive from late prompt-books. The fact that these texts show signs of having been set from literary transcripts does little to diminish the force of this fiat, for we have no evidence that literary transcripts in this period were purged of their expressive irreverence . . .
>
> Why, after all, should a 'literary' transcript preclude profanity? . . . A

scribe might provide the dignified accoutrements of Latin act- and scene-divisions, the sheen of elaborate punctuation; he might correct the grammar, modernize the spelling. . . . But why should he remove oaths? . . . By removing profanity he would be altering his author's meaning – and doing so in a way which brings his purely literary transcript into unnecessary and uncharacteristic conformity with a merely theatrical expedient.[3]

Taylor underpins these claims with the statement that 'Crane can be seen expurgating a transcript on his own initiative only a single time in a single text – in preparing the King's Men's prompt-book for *Barnavelt*, in 1619'. A footnote explains: 'At l.2425 . . . "vpon my soule" is scribbled over by Crane.'[4] I find, however, that Crane's transcripts of *A Game at Chess* provide other probable instances; and if Crane expurgated his *Game* transcripts this has important consequences for the editor of *Othello*, and for editors of other Folio texts.

Let us compare Crane's Lansdowne transcript of *A Game at Chess* (L) with Middleton's holograph, the Trinity manuscript (T). (1)'what in the Iesuites fingers, by this hand / I'le giue my part now for a parrots feather' (T, 332–3). (L) omits 'by this hand', as again in (2) 'hah? by this hand, most of these are bawdie Epistles' (T, 706), where (L) substitutes 'Anglica' (repeated from 704) for 'hah? by this hand'. It will be noticed that (1) leaves (L) with a short line, and that (2) looks like a clumsy adjustment. (3) 'masse, those are 2 good penniworths' (T, 1886; L omits 'masse'). (4) 'a pox confound thee' (T, 2152) becomes 'mischeif Confound thee' (L). (5) 'light, tis a bawdie Voyce Ile slit the throate on't' (T, 2156) becomes 'this is a Bawdy Pawne, I'll slyt the throat on't' (L). (6) 'Death? præuented?' (T, 2196) becomes 'how? prevented' (L). (7) 'sfoote, this Fat Bishop ha's so squelcht and squeezde mee, so ouerlayde mee' (T, 2408–9) becomes 'This Fat-Bishop, hath so over-layd me, so squelchd, and squeezd me' (L), illustrating expurgation and also Crane's has–hath substitution (see p. 68) and occasional transposition.

Crane's two other manuscripts of *A Game at Chess*, those in the Folger Library (F) and in the Bodleian Library (M), deal with the same passages similarly, but not identically. (1) 'by this hand' (F and M); (2) 'hah, by this light' (F), 'hah? by this hand' (M); (3) 'mas' (F); M omits; (4) 'mischeife' (F); M omits line; (5) F and M omit 'light'; (6) F retains 'death', M reads 'how?'; (7) passage omitted in F and M. In addition, (8) 'blesse mee, threatnens mee' (T 590) becomes 'he threatens Me' in M, whereas 'bless me' remains in L and F.

Crane's treatment of profanity in his *Game* manuscripts may now be compared with interesting examples of purgation in F *Othello* and F *2 Henry IV* (both probably 'Crane' texts: see p. 165). (1) and (2) 'and thither comes this bauble, *by this hand* she fals thus about my neck' (*Othello* 4.1.134–5, Q; F omits 'by this hand'); compare F *2 Henry IV* 2.2.45, where F again loses 'by this hand'; (3) '*bi'the masse* tis morning' (*Othello* 2.3.373, Q; *Introth* F); *2 Henry IV*

2.2.69 'by the masse' Q; 'Looke, looke' F; (4) 'A pox damne you' (*2 Henry IV* 2.4.39, Q; omitted F); (5) 'By this light' (*2 Henry IV* 2.2.65, Q; 'Nay' F); (7) '*Heauen blesse* the Isle of Cypres' (*Othello* 2.2.10, Q; *Blesse* F).

What is noteworthy, I think, is the tendency to fuss with profanity and near-profanity so unsystematically, in the Crane *Game* texts and in F *Othello* and F *2 Henry IV*. We cannot say with absolute finality that Crane purged the *Game* texts, because it is remotely possible that the texts from which he copied were already purged (see p. 69). Middleton, however, almost certainly the 'scribe' of the *Game* text that Crane copied, did not purge his own profanity in (4) to (7), passages that survive in two holograph texts (T and H), though he switched 'light' to 'slid' (5), and 'sfoote' to 'slid' (7).

As it happens, we can compare four groups of Crane texts with alternative texts, and in each case the Crane text purges some (but not all) profanity: (1) Middleton's and Crane's versions of *A Game at Chess*; (2) *The Merry Wives of Windsor*, Q and F ('Crane' text)'; (3) *Demetrius and Enanthe* (Crane) and *The Humorous Lieutenant* (printed in the Folio of 1647); (4) the Folio versions of *2 Henry IV* and *Othello* (now claimed as Crane's) and the earlier Quarto versions. Crane is the common factor, and this persuades me that he took it upon himself to censor profanity, not just 'a single time in a single text' but quite frequently, just as he rewrote and rearranged stage directions, repunctuated, and so on, and also that editors would be unwise to disregard this tendency of his when they consider the purging of the 'Crane' texts in the First Folio.

It may be objected, of course, that the purging of some of the Folio 'Crane' texts seems to have been a more root-and-branch affair than Crane's less intensive purgation of the *Game* transcripts. Three comments spring to mind: (1) that *Game* contains surprisingly little profanity, compared with *Othello* and *2 Henry IV*, so the number of substitutions for profanity is not really significant; (2) that the accepted 'Crane' texts in the First Folio differ in the extent to which their profanity has been purged, as do the three Crane transcripts of *Game*, consequently we must not expect him to be consistent in his treatment of profanity as between his *Game* texts and his Shakespeare texts; (3) that in preparing a text for publication in an expensive Folio Crane may well have taken more care than when he copied a private transcript for a single patron.

Since Taylor insists that, 'unless we receive very strong evidence to the contrary', heavily expurgated Folio texts must be deemed to derive from prompt-books, it will be as well to add that Crane's treatment of profanity is not an isolated case. Greg observed that Richard Hawkins reissued several Beaumont and Fletcher plays

> between 1628 and 1630, and these editions *are* expurgated, although there is no hint of any new contact with the stage. Hawkins also published the second edition of *Othello* in 1630, and it is worth noting that this, like the Folio, is expurgated, though not always in the same manner. There can, therefore, be little question that there existed, some time before 1628, a

purely literary tradition of expurgation, and it is not inconceivable that this may to some extent have affected the Folio.[5]

In fact, other reprints of plays suffered the same good or bad fortune before 1620: the second edition of *Sir John Oldcastle* (1619, apparently printed by William Jaggard) has much in common with Jaggard's Shakespeare Folio, including the curious censoring of 'yea'[6] and substitutions for *Faith, God, 'sblood, Zounds*, etc.

Taylor's theories about expurgation feed into his conviction that many Folio texts were printed from or influenced by 'late prompt-books'. This conviction rests on another assertion that I find hard to believe.

> We can now be reasonably confident that such expurgation was not undertaken by Folio editors or compositors; the alterations must have already been made in the copy supplied to the printer. Nor does it seem likely that Crane himself was copying a private transcript, for if such a transcript existed it might itself have been used as printer's copy; if the owner would not lend it for use by the printer, why should he lend it for use by Crane?

And again:

> If Crane's copy had itself been a literary transcript, it should itself have been suitable for use by the Folio compositors: why bother to pay for another transcription? Logic therefore suggests that Crane's copy was a very particular kind of transcript, the prompt-book itself, which the King's Men may have been loath to let out of their hands.[7]

To answer these questions let us turn to Fredson Bowers. 'The printing of a quarto', said Bowers, 'may be taken as implying the destruction of its manuscript.'[8] The owner of a private transcript – or, for that matter, of foul papers or of an authorial fair copy – would be unwilling to send it to a printer because the printer would mark it, smudge it and return it (if at all) very much the worse for wear. A professional scribe, on the other hand, would not damage the text as he copied it. An owner who valued his manuscript would be strangely short-sighted if he did not realise that it was in his interest to have it copied by a scribe rather than damaged by the printer. And if the scribe chosen happened to be Ralph Crane, he – in his usual, unsystematic way – would censor the text's profanity, and thus the 'late prompt-book' theory becomes unnecessary.

All things considered, I feel uneasy about putting a label to manuscript B, the manuscript of *Othello* copied by Crane. I believe that it may well have been unexpurgated, and that expurgation could have followed in Crane's transcript, Bb. The Willow Song survived in B, Bb and in the Folio, even though it may have disappeared from the acting version, at least for a time (see p. 40). The complete absence from F of music cues and of directions for off-stage noises might be due to Crane, whether or not Crane eliminated such cues and directions as completely as has been claimed (see p. 72). (These cues and/or directions survive in Crane's transcripts of *Barnavelt, Demetrius* and *The Witch*, in the three *Game* transcripts and in *The Tempest*: Crane did not habitually suppress them.) More decisively, if a scribe as experienced as Crane had great difficulty in deciphering B, and frequently misread this text (chapter 8), it would not have been a serviceable prompt-book. The writing, I suggest, was Shakespeare's own (see below). Since Crane sometimes substituted inferior variants where Q must be correct, I deduce that Crane did not have access to the Q manuscript (A): instead, he copied, I shall argue, from another manuscript in the same hand, a far from legible manuscript in which Crane thought he could make out the alternative readings that he selected deliberately, some of them inferior readings. This manuscript, B, I would tentatively identify as the author's not very fair 'fair copy'.

As for manuscript Bb, which I assign to Crane, Bowers threw out a challenge in 1986 that must not be passed over in silence.

> A critic who argues that the Folio version of a quarto play was printed from an independent manuscript and not from a marked-up quarto copy has a peculiar duty to identify the nature of such a spare manuscript that was available for printing in 1622–23. This requirement may have some application to *Hamlet*, but it applies most particularly to *King Lear* and *Othello*.[9]

The 'spare manuscript that was available for printing in 1622–23' is, I believe, a misnomer. Bowers himself saw that the printing of a text implies the destruction of the printer's copy (see above, p. 80): a 'spare manuscript' may have existed – I argue elsewhere that it must have existed (p. 94) – but would not have been 'available for printing', except as parent of the manuscript specially prepared for the use of the printer (Bb, Crane's copy of B).

Chapter 8

Misreading

However many other causes there may be of QF variants in *Othello*, misreading must be one. Graphically related variants are so numerous that misreading must account for most if not all of them. As we have seen (pp. 43 ff.), the Q scribe frequently managed to decipher all but one or two letters of a word; it remains to add that the F scribe encountered similar difficulties, and wrote out a text marred by similar corruptions. In this chapter I argue that the source of the trouble was Shakespeare's own handwriting, which seems to have been far less legible than in the famous three pages of Hand D in *Sir Thomas More*. I believe that Shakespeare wrote the three pages, and that a gap of years must separate Hand D from the composition of *Othello*.[1]

The misreading errors that are common in Shakespeare's texts have been analysed by others, notably by J. Dover Wilson. We can infer from the six signatures and from the three pages in *Sir Thomas More* that Shakespeare wrote in Secretary hand, and letters easily confused in that hand lie at the heart of the problem. I begin with samples of probable misreadings in *Othello*, following 'the commonest misprints in the printed Shakespearian texts' as laid out by Dover Wilson:[2] this will show that much of the misreading in *Othello* closely resembles that in other Shakespearian texts, even though few other texts, if any, rival *Othello* in the frequency of errors ascribable to this cause. Q is always cited first, then F, and variants that are definitely or probably corrupt are marked with an asterisk.

(i) *Minim errors.* In Secretary hand, Dover Wilson explained, 'minim-letters, i.e. letters formed of more or less straight strokes, are *m, n, u i, c, r, w*; and the large number of compositor's errors in words containing such letters prove that he [Shakespeare] must have been more than ordinarily careless in the formation of them, that he did not properly distinguish between the convex and concave forms, and that he often kept no count of his strokes, especially when writing two or more minim-letters in combination'.[3] Examples from *Othello*: 1.1.180 night: *might; 1.3.38 *resterine: re-stem; 1.3.100 maimd: main'd; 1.3.206 more: new; 3.3.152 coniects: conceits; 3.3.331 art: acte; 3.3.358 wide: rude; 3.3.447 time: true; 4.1.258 here: home; 4.2.49 *ram'd: rain'd; 5.1.14 *game: gaine; 5.2.17 once more: One more; 5.2.345 Indian: Iudean.

(ii) *a: minim errors*: 1.3.167 *heate: hint; 2.3.287 pleasure: pleasance; 3.3.60 or: on; 3.3.70 *muttering: mam'ring; 3.3.249 further: farther; 4.1.71 *Coach: Cowch; 5.1.1 Bulke: *Barke; 5.1.107 stirre: stare.

(iii) *e:d errors*: 1.1.29 *be led: be be-leed; 1.3.6. *aym'd: ayme; 2.1.297 euen: eeuen'd ('euend' misread as 'euene' by Q?); 3.3.332 *mindes: Mines; 3.4.66 wiue: Wiu'd; 5.2.125 heard: *heare.

(iv) *e:o errors*: 1.1.53 Those: These; 1.2.29 These: Those; 1.3.83 set: soft; 1.3.146 Doe grow: *Grew; 1.3.270 foyles: seele; 2.3.183 These: Those; 4.1.258 here: home; 4.2.44 those: these; 4.2.47–8 *left . . . left: lost . . . lost⁴; 4.3.20 these: those; 4.3.23 those: these; 5.1.63 those: these; 5.2.201 terrible: horrible.

(v) *o:a errors*: 1.1.47 noughe: naught; 1.1.64 Doues: Dawes; 1.3.134 spake: spoke; 2.1.20 Lords: Laddes; 2.1.48 Pilate: Pylot; 2.1.74 spoke: spake; 2.1.267 cause: course; 2.3.13–14 aclock: o'th'clocke; 3.2.1 Pilate: Pylot; 4.2.80 *hallow: hollow; 4.2.177 dofftst: dafts; 5.2.351 Turband: Turbond; 5.2.359 Spartane: Sparton.

(vi) *t:e errors*: 1.1.47 *noughe: naught; 1.2.46 aboue: about; 1.3.52 *lacke: lack't; 3.3.270 *valt: vale; 4.1.102 conster: *conserue (misreading of 'construe'?); 4.2.53 part: place.

(vii) *t:c errors*: 1.3.107 *youth: vouch; 1.3.250 scorne: storme; 2.1.70 enscerped: ensteep'd; 2.1.226 saciety: Satiety; 2.1. 301 crush: trace; 2.3.303 ingredience: Ingredient; 4.1.127 stor'd: scoar'd.

(viii) *th:y errors*: 1.1.2 you: thou; 3.3.362 you (press-corrected to 'thou'): thou. Perhaps also 1.3.258 which: *why (with t:c confusion). As is well known, *th* could be written like *y* (hence *yat* = that, *you* = thou).

(ix) *h:th errors*: 1.3.148 thence: hence; 1.3.298 her: them; 1.3.392 this: his; 2.1.213 hither: thither; 4.1.276 this: his; 4.2.18 her: their; 4.2.49 he: they; 5.1.60 here: there. Compare (xii), below.

(x) *r errors*: 1.1.164 more: moe;⁵ 1.2.41 *frequent: sequent; 1.3.206 more: new; 1.3.327 ballance: *braine; 2.1.267 cause: course; 2.1.274 trust: *taste; 3.3.331 art: acte; 5.1.1. Bulke: *Barke; 5.1.130 *markes: makes. Compare also (xii), below (final -*r* errors). The letter *r* must have been written indistinctly, perhaps as a single minim stroke or as a twirl. It received little attention from Dover Wilson but caused trouble in both Q and F *Othello*. Not only was *r* confused with other letters, it was sometimes difficult to be sure whether any letter was intended.

(xi) *tilde errors* (the tilde, ~, was the suspension mark for *m* and *n*, usually written above a preceding vowel): 1.1.16 chosen: chose; 1.1.24 toged: *Tongued; 2.1.183 *calmenesse: Calmes (but cf. p. 42); 2.3.229 the: then; 3.3.263 qualities: *Quantities; 4.2.90 forgiuenesse: forgiue vs; 4.2.192 acquittance: acquaintance. Other variants where misreading may be partly to blame include 3.4.178 conuenient: continuate; 5.2.146 iteration: itterance; 5.2.207 reprobation: Reprobance. I assume that imperfections in the paper or other pen strokes were misread as tildes; hence the intrusive *m* or *n* (when wrongly added, not omitted). Compare also final *-n* errors: 3.2.314 stole: stolne (for 'stolen'?); 5.2.161 *know: known, and others above.

(xii) *word endings*: Groups (viii) and (ix) indicate that *h* and *th* were not carefully written, and this is confirmed by other sets of variants.

(1)   He that stirs next, to carue *for* his own rage,
        Holds his soule light:

(2.3.169–70, F; *forth Q)

(2)   Strumpet I come:
        For of my heart, those Charmes thine Eyes, are blotted.

(5.1.34–5, F; Forth Q)

Q misread *for* as *forth*, and F misread *Forth* as *For*. Can we doubt that in Shakespeare's hand the two words were just about indistinguishable, and that *th* was an indeterminate squiggle? That the same might be true of *h* is confirmed by another set of variants.

(3)   *With* such Accomodation and besort
        As leuels with her breeding.

(1.3.239–40, F; *Which Q)

(4)   And it was dyde in Mummey, *which* the Skilfull
        Conseru'd of Maidens hearts.

(3.4.76–7, F; *with . . . Conserues Q)

Q misread *With* as *Which*, and *which* as *with*: a simple *t:c* misreading (cf. vii, above) and a squiggled *h* account for these errors.

These are not the only instances where the same two words are switched around in Q and F.

(5)   And then (Sir) would he gripe, and wring my hand:
        Cry, *oh* sweet Creature: then kisse me hard,

(3.3.423–4, F)

        . . . Cry *out*, sweete creature, and then kisse me hard,

(Q)

(6)   *Out* Strumpet: weep'st thou for him to my face?

(5.2.76, F; O Q)[6]

Finding so many *th* variants in *Othello* (viii, ix, xii), we must ask whether the same cause could be responsible for the play's pervasive *em:them* variants, or for *ha:hath* (2.1.7). At any rate, several of the above groups should be considered together with others where the final letters were not written clearly, a characteristic already noticed (p. 43).

(xiii) *final -r errors*: 1.1.79 *you: your; 94 worse: worsser; 1.2.35 *your: you; 1.3.45 here: he; 2.1.22 *Another: A Noble; 45 *their: the; 56 the: their;

2.3.346 their: the; 3.3.40 you: your; 398 superuisor: *super-vision; 477 as you: at your; 3.4.146 the: their; 5.1.93 you: *your; 5.2.262 *you: your; 297 you: your. Who can doubt in these instances, either that final *r* was unclearly written or that a meaningless pen stroke could look like final *r*? This would be all the more likely if *their* and *there* were written *ther* (as in *Sir Thomas More*, D, 260; *Hamlet*, Q2, 3.4.202; F *Othello* 4.1.63), or if final *r* was written above the line (you^r for your).

(xiv) *final -t errors*: 1.1.2 has: hast; 9 *oft: off; 163 deceiuest: deceaues; 1.2.50 Carrick: Carract; 1.3.52 *lacke: lack't; 108 ouert: *ouer; 2.1.143 *praises: praisest; 274 come into no true *trust *again't*: . . . *taste againe*; 2.3.213 began: began't; 338 *wer't to* renounce his baptisme: *were to . . . ; 3.3.89 *be it as* your fancies teach you: *be as . . . ; 150 *oft* my iealousie / Shapes faults: *of . . . ; 207 their best conscience, / Is not to *leaue* vndone, but *keepe* vnknowne: . . . *leaue't . . . kept*; 3.3.270 *valt: vale; 340 but to *know* a little: . . . *know't*; 3.4.69 loose: loose't; 4.1.60 I mocke you? *no* by Heauen: I mocke you *not*, by Heauen; 4.1.65 Did he *confesse? (confesse it?* F); 4.3.70–1 and vndo't when I had *done it (done* F); 5.2.64 makest: makes. Like final *r*, final *t* could be written above the line.

The knock-on effects of misreading may be visible in some of the variants in list (xiv). At 4.1.60, if either *no* or *not* is a corruption, one of the texts repunctuated as a result of misreading; at 1.1.163–4 and 3.3.109 the misreading of the verb seems to have caused a change of pronoun as well.

(xv) (a) *final -y (or -ie) errors*: 1.1.156, 1.3.116 Sagittar: Sagitary; 1.3.6 the: they; 2.1.41–2 For euery minute is expectancy / Of more *arriuance (Arriuancie* F); 2.1.239 slippery: slipper; 2.3.56 And *the* watch too (*they* F); 3.4.64 lothely: loathed; 4.2.69 O thou blacke weede, *why* art so louely faire (*Who* F). Compare final *-ly* variants: 2.1.234 eminent(ly); 3.3.286 faint(ly); 3.4.81 rash(ly).

(b) *final -y:-e or -y:-ee errors*: 2.1.169 as great a *Flee as Cassio (Fly* F); 2.1.221 *the: thy; 2.3.231–2 which till to night, / I ne're might *see* before (*say* F); 3.3.27–8 rather die, / Then giue *thee cause: away (thy cause away* F); 3.3.135–6 giue *the* worst of *thought*, / The worst of *word (thy . . . thoughts . . . words* F); 3.3.450 Arise blacke vengeance, from *thy hollow Cell (the hollow hell* F); 4.2.48 ff. Had it pleas'd heauen . . . had *he *ram'd* / All *kindes* of sores (*they rain'd * / All *kind* F); 5.1.56 O *my* Leiutenant (*mee* F); 5.2.13 When I haue pluckt *the* rose (*thy* F).

Some quick comments. (xv) (a) I prefer *Sagitary* (F) to *Sagittar* (Q), although both forms were current and both fit in with the metre. The 'dreadfull Sagittary' of *Troilus and Cressida* (Q and F, 5.5.14) supports F. (xv) (b) (4.2.48 ff.) Here *heauen* could be a substitution for *God*[7] – cf. 4.2.143 – so F's *they* looks like a misreading of *he* (see also list [ix]).

(xvi) *final -s errors*: The commonest divergence of Q and F *Othello* was caused by final *-s*: singular versus plural, verbal variants (come–comes), etc. A quick count revealed 101 final *-s* variants, and there are likely to be more. Having noted the misreading of *for: forth, oh:out*, final *-r*, final *-t*, final *-e* and *-y*, and now final *-s* errors, and keeping in mind the many other discrepancies in word endings such as *harlotry:harlot* (4.2.235), and *-ly* variants (p. 85), one is driven to the conclusion that Shakespeare, when he wrote at speed, did not form every letter clearly – indeed, scrawled rather than wrote, and not infrequently left word endings as one or more illegible pen strokes.

(xvii) *word endings again*: In spite of the difficulties experienced by the scribes of Q and F in deciphering Shakespeare's scrawled word endings, we must not ascribe all variant word endings to a single cause. Q's consistent preference for *handkercher* and F's for *handkerchief* (more than two dozen times) may reflect Crane's prejudice against colloquial forms (see p. 69). On the other hand, Q's spelling of the names Montanio (2.1.0 SD, etc.) and Emilla (3.1.41 SD), and possibly Roderigo (for F's Rodorigo), may well be due to Shakespeare's writing; so, possibly, some of the variations between Desdemona and Desdemon.

Here we may pause for a moment to look back at lists (i) to (xvii). It needs to be emphasised, first, that these lists offer samples, not every instance of every kind of misreading. Next, that while a few variants have been entered in more than one list, many more might have been. Again, the reader is asked to return to the discussion of misreading in Q (pp. 41–4): I have not repeated most of the examples cited there, some of which are as extraordinary as any in the play (e.g. 4.1.77 '*ere while, mad* with your griefe' Q; *o're-whelmed* F). Finally, other sources of corruption (such as foul case) no doubt added to the textual confusion, though not on the same scale as misreading.

Even if the F text seems to be less seriously affected, both texts of *Othello* suffer from misreading to an astonishing degree. How can we account for it? At one time I thought that it might have been caused by water damage, perhaps connected with the burning of the Globe in 1613. Water might have smudged or obliterated words as randomly as misreading mars Q and F, and just conceivably might have done so from the first page to the last of a manuscript of twenty-five or so leaves. Except that, as I soon realised, the damage was less random than one's first impression suggested. Water would not have randomly smudged so many word endings. What are the alternatives? The obvious one is that the misreading in *Othello* resulted from difficult and sometimes illegible writing – from a hand that tailed away most frustratingly when it penned word endings (a phenomenon familiar from signatures, including Shakespeare's own signatures).

If, then, we ascribe the frequent misreading that we detect in both Q and F to handwriting, not to the physical condition of one or more manuscripts that came into being some twenty years earlier, this must have been Shakespeare's own handwriting. The scribes who prepared the manuscripts used as copy for Q and F are almost bound to have been two different men, and would not have shared the same scribal characteristics, as do Q and F; they are likely to have been professionals, therefore to have written legibly, perhaps beautifully (as in the case of Ralph Crane). Authors, unlike professional scribes, sometimes write quite illegibly (as in the case of the dramatist Thomas Heywood). Yet if the misreading in Q and F *Othello* points back to the author's illegible handwriting, how does this square with the three pages of Hand D in *Sir Thomas More*, the only surviving specimen of Shakespeare's dramatic composition? The three pages, being really quite easy to read, do not bear out the hypothesis of an illegible hand; in fact, if the three pages date from after 1600, as is sometimes alleged,[8] one could not reasonably claim that the same hand was responsible for the misreading in *Othello*. Like many others I prefer an earlier date – 1593 or 1594 – which would give time, eight years or so, for the writing to become more fluent and, arguably, more illegible. Either the pressures of more and more writing, or perhaps writer's cramp or a nervous disability,[9] could account for the differences between the three pages and the illegibility of the *Othello* manuscripts.[10]

In his analysis of 'The Handwriting of the Three Pages' Maunde Thompson drew attention to a calligraphic eccentricity, the dramatist's 'disposition to play with his pen, to exaggerate pendent curves, and to finish off the final letters of his words in a flourish, more especially as he approaches the end of a line' – a disposition not perhaps unrelated to the problems I have noted in *Othello*.

> But all such flourishes, and also slack formation of curves in the bodies of words which may be almost called flourishes, are not to be counted as merely calligraphic eccentricities; for they may also be the unfortunate causes of misreadings of the letters or words which they affect.[11]

If the tendency 'to play with his pen' and to introduce twirls and flourishes increased between 1593 and 1601–2 (the probable date of *Othello*[12]), this again would have increased the illegibility of Q's and F's authorial manuscripts and the misreading of word endings.

But not only in *Othello*. Very similar difficulties were encountered in the printing of *Hamlet* and *King Lear* and, to a lesser extent, of *Troilus and Cressida*, all plays that date from around 1600 or later. These plays had all been published as quartos before the Folio, yet Heminges and Condell decided in 1623 not to reprint the quartos or (as some think) only to reprint them when heavily corrected. That misreading led to errors in earlier plays cannot be denied; equally it cannot be denied that *Hamlet*, *King Lear* and *Othello* seem to be in a class of their own, as far as misreading is concerned. Whoever ruled that these plays should not be reprinted in the Folio from quickly corrected copies of earlier quartos – as were *A Midsummer Night's Dream*, *The Merchant of Venice* and several more – knew, we must assume, that they needed more editorial attention. This could be because the players possessed a second authorial version, or because they considered the (good) quarto maimed and deformed by misreading or careless workmanship, or for a mixture of such reasons.

The misreading that disfigures Q and F *Othello* seems not to have been an

isolated problem but to reflect a general deterioration in Shakespeare's writing
– confirmed by the misreading in the texts of *Hamlet* and *King Lear* and, most
starkly, in his six signatures. Having emphasised the illegibility of word endings, I must now develop a point already touched upon, that medial letters
were also misread repeatedly. The same combinations could not have been
confused so often without some such explanation (see also [i]–[vii] and [x],
[xi], above).

(xviii) *ea:a errors*: 1.2.68 The wealthy curled *darlings* of our Nation (*Deareling F); 1.3.230 great: graue; 2.1.3–4 I cannot twixt the *hauen* and the mayne /
Descry a saile (*Heauen* F); 3.4.177 I haue this while with *laden thoughts bin
prest (*leaden* F); 5.1.106 Doe you perceiue the *ieastures of her eye (*gastnesse* F);
5.1.107 Nay, an you stirre, we shall *haue more anon (*heare* F). Compare also
Hanmer's attractive emendation at 1.2.75, *waken* for *weaken*(*s*). I deduce that
ea and *a* were not always distinguishable in Shakespeare's hand, a point
corroborated by similar variants in *Hamlet* (Q2 first, then F): 1.2.133 wary:
weary; 1.5.93 hart: heart; 2.2.75 Pollacke: Poleak; 3.1.159 stature: Feature;
5.2.58 defeat: debate. Compare also *King Lear* (Q first, then F): 1.4.246 great:
grac'd; 1.4.275 harke: Heare; 1.4.304 yea: Ha.

Although word endings were a major source of misreading, these and other
medial-letter variants remind us that Shakespeare's writing might tail away,
yet was not much easier to decipher before the word ending. Even the first
letters of a word could be baffling, as here in *Othello*: 2.3.263–4 there is more
offence in that, then in Reputation (*sence* F); 2.3.274–5 so *light*, so drunken
. . . an Officer (*slight* F); 4.1.78 a passion most *vnfitting* such a man (Q
uncorr.; *vnsuting* Q corr.; *resulting F); 4.2.56 To point his slow *vnmouing*
fingers at (*and mouing* F); 4.2.209 Thou hast taken against me a most iust
*conception (*exception* F). That being so, I suspect that a pair of variants
sometimes taken as evidence of editorial sophistication may be due to misreading as well: 2.3.143–4 I'le beate the knaue into a *wicker* bottle (*Twiggen* F).
Here one of the scribes could make out .wi..en or wi..er and guessed the
missing letters.

Next, two of the most curious misreadings in the Folio text. First, 1.3.145
*Antropophague (Q: *Anthropophagie*). This looks like *u*(*v*):*i* confusion, one form of
minim error, as in 1.1.138 this: thus; 2.1.176 Clisterpipes: *Cluster-pipes;
2.3.38 vnfortunate: infortunate; 2.3.220 Thus: This; 2.3.302 vnordinate: inordi-
nate; 5.2.280 infortunate: vnfortunate. I suspect that Q *Anthropophagie* reproduced its copy spelling correctly, for Shakespeare sometimes anglicised Latin
noun endings: compare 'all the *Andronicie*' (*TA*, Q, 2.3.189; so 5.3.131, 176),
or 'Volscies' (*Cor*, F, TLN 241, 460). F's *-ue* ending represents an attempt to
follow the F manuscript, where *-ie* appeared to have two minim strokes – an
error faithfully reproduced.

(xix) Second, F's 'base *Iudean*' (5.2.345; 'base *Indian*' Q), perhaps the most
famous crux in the play. Here the cause of F's error was *e:i* misreading, which
is not uncommon in Shakespeare (though editors have paid little attention to

it). Compare 1.2.17 *Weele: Will; 1.3.124 till: *tell; 143 *hent: hint; 167 *heate: hint; 3.3.453 Aspects: Aspickes; 4.1.77 ere while, mad: o're-whelmed; 5.2.285 Wring: Wrench. One sees in several of these instances, as in Indian: Iudean, that the misreading of *i* or *e* had a knock-on effect, leading to the misreading of letters that are more easily confused (*n* and *u* in Iudean, *a* and *n* in heate). Compare Q2 and F *Hamlet*: 1.2.38 delated: dilated; 2.2.572 *tell: til; 3.1.33 Wee'le: Will; 72 despriz'd: dispriz'd; 3.2.267 *Considerat: Confederate; 4.5.157 *Tell: Till; 5.1.243 desprat: disperate.

* * *

The suggestion that Shakespeare's hand in *Sir Thomas More* misrepresents the illegibility of his writing in later plays, if correct, has momentous implications for his editors. While it is easy to ascribe too many textual corruptions to misreading – as, perhaps, in C.J. Sisson's *New Readings in Shakespeare* (2 vols, Cambridge, 1956), a valuable study of such problems – editors will have to adjust their thinking to a new image of Shakespeare's 'foul papers', and will have to attempt more 'corrective editing' than seemed desirable not many years ago.[13]

(xx) *common QF errors*: So far I have restricted examples of misreading to QF variants, one of each pair belonging to a group of errors repeated elsewhere in *Othello* and, usually, in *Hamlet* and other plays. Having identified such errors, many of them commonplace, we can move on to a related issue, readings where Q and F agree and yet may require emendation. For F sometimes follows Q rather than its manuscript copy (see p. 94) and may therefore follow Q errors: if so, and if misreading is the cause of Q's error, we ought to be able to recover the true reading, aided by our knowledge of frequently confused letters.

(1) Nor to comply with heate, the young affects
     In *my* defunct, and proper satisfaction,
                    (1.3.264–5, Q)

F repeats 'In *my* defunct,'; Capell's emendation, 'In *me* defunct', is supported by (xv) (b), final *-y*:*-e* confusion.

(2) for the loue of his Desdemena [*sic*]: *who* let vs not therefore blame
                    (2.3.14–15, Q; so F)

Abbott (§274) said that the 'inflection of *who* is frequently neglected', citing also 1.2.52 'To who' (Q and F) and 4.2.101 'With who?' (Q and F). Yet more often than not inflected *whom* is used correctly in *Othello*, so a tilde misreading (xi) may explain *whom* printed as *who*. Here it is interesting that QF *who* at 1.2.52 and 4.2.101 was changed to *whom* in two early texts (Q2 and F2), which suggests that uninflected *who* for *whom* was felt to be wrong. Compare also *Hamlet* 3.4.131 To whom (Q2), To who (F).

(3)   Hee'le watch the horolodge a double set,
       If drinke rocke not his *cradle*.
                    (2.3.126–7, Q; *Cradle* F)

The first three editions that I consulted give no help with 'cradle', and I have seen no satisfactory explanation. Perhaps a Q misreading, copied by F (*nodle* misread as *cradle*? i.e. minim and *a:o* confusion; groups [i] and [v]).

(4)   (Saue that they say, the warres must make examples,
       Out of *her* best)
                             (3.3.65–6, Q)

F repeats *her*. Compare (ix), *h:th* confusion – the original MS reading must have been *their* or *ther*.

(5)   *Oth.*   If't be that.
       Iag.   If it be that, or any, *it* was hers,
       It speakes against her, with the other proofes.
                             (3.3.442–4, Q)

F repeats *it*, but many editors prefer Malone's emendation, *that* (i.e. *that* spelt *yt*, misread as *it*. Shakespeare wrote *yt* for *it* in *Sir Thomas More*, D, 126, 134, 135): compare group (viii), *th:y* misreading, and 5.2.118 it (Q), that (F).

(6)   turne thy complexion there,
       Patience *thy* young and rose-lip'd Cherubin,
       I *here* looke grim as Hell
                             (4.2.63–5, Q)

F reads *thou* . . . *heere*. Theobald's emendation, *there* for *here*, is supported by group (ix), *h:th* misreading (but *here* may be correct).

(7)   The poore Soule sat *singing*, by a Sicamour tree
                             (4.3.39, F)

Q omits the Willow Song; Q2 reprinted it from F, but changed *singing* to *sighing*, an emendation generally adopted. It is supported by group (xi), tilde errors, and by *h* misreadings, group (xii).

(8) Returning to final *-s* misreading (xvi), let us note that grammarians defend anomalous *-s* endings, just as they defend uninflected *whom* (2, above); Abbott added that 'though the rhyme and metre establish the fact that Shakespeare used the plural verbal inflection in *s*, yet it ought to be stated that *-s* final in the Folio is often a misprint' (§338). Why only 'in the Folio'? And is it not the case that Shakespeare sometimes bends language for the sake of rhyme and metre, and that such usages need not conform to his normal practice? I suspect that, as with *who:whom*, scores of final *-s* errors survive in the *textus receptus* because editorial inertia prefers the easy option. It is easier to maintain that Shakespeare was lax about grammar than to take appropriate action

once we accept that many final -*s* variants are due to his illegible writing and to a twirl that could be confused with final -*s*.

After all, many final -*s* spellings in Q and F are manifest errors, corrected by all editors. To give a few examples, F – the 'better text', as editors used to say – includes the following: At Rhodes, at Ciprus, and on *others* grounds (1.1.28; *other* Q); The wealthy curled *Deareling* of our Nation (1.2.68; *darlings* Q); And of the Canibals that each *others* eate (1.3.144; *other* Q); I neuer yet did heare: / That the bruized heart was pierc'd through the *eares* (1.3.220; *eare* Q) (here the rhyme supports Q); yet he lookes sadly, / And *praye* the Moore be safe (2.1.33, *prayes* Q). These and other manifest errors suggest that F is not necessarily the better text where final -*s* variants are concerned (whatever the cause of error), and that even when Q and F agree in printing the same 'anomalous' -*s* ending, editors may be justified in treating it as a common error.

Alice Walker identified other QF 'common errors' (see pp. 95ff.), all of which betray themselves by their faulty sense or grammar or metre. If it is agreed that Shakespeare's writing was far less legible than was once assumed, it must follow as the night the day that many more common errors lurk in the *textus receptus*, as a consequence of misreading. For misreading very often produces 'possible' readings – as in groups (i) to (xviii), where the weaker variant would have been accepted by editors had a better variant not survived in the second text. The study of frequently confused letters in *Othello* will, I hope, prompt others to look again at common QF readings that may need to be reconsidered: who knows how many an editorial 'nodle' has been lulled asleep by a 'cradle' (group xx.3)?

Chapter 9

The relationship of the Quarto and Folio texts

Having examined the misreading in Q and F, and concluded that the same kinds of misreading occur in both texts, we naturally ask ourselves whether Q and F both derive, at one remove, from the same authorial manuscript. Not so long ago that would have seemed a perfectly acceptable hypothesis. It may still be defended as a valid hypothesis, though not without qualification. For F *Othello* is one of a number of F texts thought to have been 'influenced' by the Q text of the same play (the others being *Richard III, 2 Henry IV, Troilus and Cressida, King Lear* and *Hamlet*): either F was printed from a copy of Q corrected with the help of a manuscript, or someone 'occasionally consulted' Q while preparing the F copy from a manuscript, or Q influenced F in some other way.

We are particularly indebted to Alice Walker's pioneer studies of almost fifty years ago for the realisation that *Othello* and other F texts were influenced – or shall we say contaminated? – by their Q counterparts. Others had written about individual plays (Greg demonstrated the case for *King Lear*), Miss Walker looked at the general problem. Common errors and common orthographical features suggest that these Q and F texts were connected, though not necessarily in the manner proposed by Miss Walker. She argued that the F texts were printed from Q copies, with corrections written in from a manuscript, and some of the leading textual specialists of the time welcomed her theories: Greg, Bowers, and not a few others.[1] Dissenting or doubtful voices remained, at first, in the minority. J.G. McManaway thought that while Miss Walker's 'challenge cannot be ignored, her explanations will not be widely accepted unless a more detailed study reveals bibliographical dependence of the one text upon the other'.[2] Harold Jenkins, in a masterly point-by-point analysis of Miss Walker's account of the relationship of Q2 and F *Hamlet*, summed up that

> Dr Walker's expert scrutiny of the two texts has revealed, as we have seen, a number of resemblances between them. And when due allowance has been made for those which need not have the significance which she attaches to them, enough remain to make it probable that, in the preparation of F,

some use was made of Q2 . . . . But Dr Walker's theory that the actual copy for the Folio *Hamlet* was a corrected Second Quarto must clearly be rejected.[3]

A broad-fronted attack on Miss Walker's position followed in 1971, in J.K. Walton's *The Quarto Copy for the First Folio of Shakespeare*, an analysis of the 'copy' for fourteen plays printed in the Folio. Walton concluded that the F texts of *2 Henry IV*, *Hamlet* and *Othello* were set from manuscripts; his criticism of Miss Walker's logic, however, did not satisfy all reviewers, and his own method – 'needlessly abstract . . . in parts unattractively magisterial and haughtily contentious' – was described as 'flawed'. Thus Robert K. Turner, whose cool but I think fair review ended: 'On this showing I doubt anyone is going to leap to believe that F *Othello* was set from manuscript, and Walton's conclusions about the nature of the F copy for *2 Henry IV* and *Hamlet* seem to be open to the same kinds of objection.'[4]

Walton's arguments displeased others who nevertheless agreed with some of his conclusions. His method was described by Gary Taylor as 'essentially negative: he has cast doubt on Walker's evidence for printed copy without providing clear positive evidence of his own which would rule out printed copy'.[5] Taylor himself then offered positive evidence by comparing the treatment of 'accidentals' in F texts known to have been printed from Q texts (e.g. *Titus Andronicus* and *Romeo and Juliet*, both printed from Q3) and in those F texts where a Q copy-text is in dispute (e.g. *Hamlet*, *Othello*). He observed that on page dd4 of F *Titus* compositor E retained Q3 punctuation 77 times and only altered it 12 times; on the next page E retained it 126 times and altered it 36 times. 'The same conservative treatment of copy punctuation' persists elsewhere, whenever compositor E worked from printed (Q) copy, whereas on two pages of F *Hamlet* 'the proportion of retained to altered punctuation is 53/82 (pp5) and 65/99 (pp5ᵛ)', which 'demonstrates that E cannot have been setting *Hamlet* from printed copy'.[6]

Taylor noticed that in F *Othello* the use of brackets is significant, though apparently without connecting Ralph Crane with this text.

One particular punctuation variant is virtually sufficient in itself to rule out the use of Q1 as copy for Folio *Othello*. In 44½ pages set from printed copy in *Titus*, *Romeo*, and *Troilus*, Compositor E added only seven pairs of round brackets to his copy. . . . E's work in the Folio, up to quire ss, thus shows a consistent pattern of very sparing additions of round brackets, when his copy is known . . . . But on ss3ᵛ, the first page E set in that quire, and the first page he set in *Othello*, he set *twelve* pairs of brackets not in Q1; on ss4, his next page, he set ten; in the remainder of his work on the play, he set another 49 pairs not in his purported printed copy. Moreover, in the whole of his work in *Antony and Cleopatra* (seven pages), E set only eleven such pairs: the phenomenal increase in *Othello* cannot simply reflect a new preference for this species of punctuation.[7]

The 'brackets' evidence proves that Miss Walker was wrong about Quarto copy, at least as far as F *Othello* is concerned – and, incidentally, confirms my view (p. 68) that the manuscript used as copy for F *Othello* was not in the same hand as the manuscripts used for other F tragedies, with the possible exception of *Cymbeline*.

So brackets bring us back to Ralph Crane. The hypothesis that Crane acted as scribe for the F text of *Othello* may appear to commit me in advance to the view that he wrote out a complete text of the play, rather than to the alternative, that he wrote corrections into a copy of Q. But that need not follow, for Crane's 'swibs' and idiosyncratic spellings might have been written into Q, and none of the evidence presented in chapter 6 points inexorably to the conclusion that Crane transcribed the complete text of *Othello*. I believe, none the less, that he did, and for two reasons. The Crane spellings and swibs are frequently found in lines that did not have to be corrected or inserted in Q (if corrected Q was used as F copy), being identical in the two texts except for some spellings and punctuation. Moreover, since Crane did not adhere rigidly to a single spelling for the words in question, and as often as not himself spelt them as in Q (viz. forsooth, cast him, Auncient, Shee'd, throw out, quite), it would be eccentric to assume that he corrected these spellings in Q to the versions we find in F (for-sooth, cast-him, Aunciant, She'l'd, throw-out, quight) and that he inserted in Q all the brackets that reveal his presence in F (34 swibs, and dozens more). On the other hand, if he wrote out a complete text of the play for the F printer we would expect him to interpolate brackets and his own 'occasional' spellings – exactly as he did in the other transcripts in his hand that still survive.

Dissenting from Miss Walker's theory that F *Othello* was printed from corrected Q, we have still to consider the evidence that led her to this conclusion – the common errors and common orthographical features in Q and F. For even if F was not printed from Q, someone concerned with F might have consulted Q when experiencing difficulties in reading his manuscript copy. That 'someone' is unlikely to have been the F compositors, if I am right about Crane's penning of the 'F manuscript', for Crane's manuscript of *Othello* was no doubt as clearly written as all his professional work. The F compositors would have no difficulty in reading Crane's hand, therefore did not need to consult a more legible text (i.e. Q). It was Crane who experienced difficulties, caused by Shakespeare's illegible writing; I deduce that it was Crane who consulted Q – not necessarily as a short cut, though at times it will have been the easiest option to copy from Q rather than lose time in trying to tease out what Shakespeare had scrawled or might have meant. Indeed, Heminges and Condell could have asked Crane not merely to transcribe Shakespeare's manuscript but to 'edit' it with the help of Q (but cf. p. 101), and, if so, the existence of Q could have slowed down Crane as well as providing him with a short cut whenever Shakespeare's writing defeated him. In either case it follows that when Q and F agree they may both be wrong, and that when F corrects Q it may misread Shakespeare's writing and, again, both texts could be corrupt. Others have come to one or both of these conclusions, based on different views of the provenance and transmission of F's copy. Miss Walker thought that 'we may have fifty or sixty errors common to the two texts [of *Othello*], most of them memorial. Errors of this kind may defy detection.'[8] Radically changing Miss Walker's scenario (viz. introducing Crane and Shakespeare's illegible writing into the story, and rejecting the hypothesis that a corrected Q served as copy for F *Othello*), I still see the editorial implications as discouraging, as did Miss Walker for her own reasons. I think, though, that a clearer understanding of Crane's scribal habits and of the problems created by Shakespeare's writing now puts us in a stronger position editorially: many common QF errors that seemed to 'defy detection' in 1953, when Miss Walker published *Textual Problems*, ought to be less invisible to us if we have made progress in sharpening the textual focus.

What, then, is Miss Walker's evidence for common errors and common orthographical features? Not all of her examples are equally convincing. I have selected some of the best, retaining her layout and explanatory comments. (Line references are changed to key in with Arden 3; to save space I shorten Quarto and Folio to Q and F.)[9]

1.3.43   And prayes you to *beleeue* him (Q)
     And prayes you to *beleeue* him (F)

'Singer's emendation to "relieve" is in accordance with the action taken. The line is otherwise singularly pointless.'

2.1.50–1   Therefore my *hope's* not surfeited to death,
     Stand in bold cure (Q)

     Therefore my *hope's* (not surfetted to death)
     Stand in bold Cure (F)

'The apostrophe is wrong; as the text stands, the word in question can only be taken as a plural noun.'

2.3.214–16 If partiality affin'd, or *league* in office,
     Thou doest deliuer, more or lesse then truth,
     Thou art no souldier (Q)

     If partially Affin'd, or *league* in office,
     Thou dost deliuer more, or lesse then Truth
     Thou art no Souldier (F)

'Pope's "leagu'd" is necessary.'

When she later edited *Othello* for The New Shakespeare, Miss Walker emended other readings common to Q and F that should also be classified as QF 'common errors'.

2.3.163   Haue you forgot all *place of sence*, and duty (Q)

So F, but Hanmer's transposition, 'sense of place', must be correct.

2.3.312–13   the contemplation, marke and *deuotement* of her parts (Q)

So F; Q2 emended to *denotement*, which is accepted by Miss Walker.

2.3.380   My selfe *awhile*, to draw the Moore apart (Q)

So F; Theobald emended to *the while*, accepted by Miss Walker.

3.4.187   Why *who's* is it? (Q; so F)

Editors emend to *whose*.

Next, the orthographical evidence. This involves rare words and familiar ones spelt identically in Q and F.

> There are at least three nonce words in the Quarto and Folio *Othello*: 'moraller' (II, iii, 301), 'probal' (II, iii, 344) and 'exsufflicate' (III, iii, 182), of which two ('probal' and 'exufflicate') appear in identical spellings. It might be argued that their unfamiliarity encouraged copyists and compositors to preserve them as they found them, but this explanation will not account for the identical spelling of more common words which could be spelt in a number of ways. 'Morties' (II, i, 9), i.e. 'mortise', is common to the Quarto and Folio, though half a dozen spellings were possible; 'lushious' (I, iii, 354), as against 'luscious' in the Folio text of *A Midsummer Night's Dream*, is again common to the printed texts; so too is 'Pyoners' (III, iii, 346), as against 'Pioners' in the Folio text of *Henry V* and all three texts of *Hamlet*.[10]

Common errors and common spellings in Q and F are more pervasive than Miss Walker's short but important studies may have suggested, especially if we add in 'false starts' printed erroneously by Q and retained by F (see p. 34). I am therefore disinclined to accept that such instances of QF convergence are due to coincidence or to the survival of authorial spellings. (J.K. Walton[11] dismissed several of Miss Walker's 'common errors' as misreadings; that is, he agreed that the same 'errors' occurred in Q and F, and apparently believed – though he did not spell this out – that they were independent misreadings. He did not see that the more often one claims 'independent' common errors the more likely they are to be connected.) In short, I prefer a compromise solution – that the F scribe consulted Q and adopted some of its readings. The hypothesis that Shakespeare's writing was not easy to read, arrived at for other reasons, adequately accounts for the F scribe's action: he 'occasionally consulted' Q, to save himself time, to benefit from another pair of eyes if the manuscript he worked from was illegible, or because Heminges and Condell told him to do so.

Anyone who feels, as Fredson Bowers did in 1964, that 'Dr Walker's case (though correct) is not nearly so copious or rigorous in its evidence as to make for an acceptable demonstration',[12] should ponder one other kind of evidence – namely, mislineation. Q has a series of short lines on pages 2 and 3, half-lines that later editors run together to give normal pentameters:

> Attending on themselues, / and throwing
> But shewes of seruice on their Lords, /
> Doe well thriue by 'em,
> And when they haue lin'd their coates, /
> Doe themselues homage,
> Those fellowes haue some soule, /
>
> (1.1.50–3, Q)

I have inserted solidi to indicate the 'correct' line endings. Now the last four lines (i.e. two complete pentameters) are divided in F as in Q. In Q it is clear from all the other short lines on pages 2 and 3 that the compositor had to 'lose space' – he had miscalculated in his casting off, and he split single verse lines in two to fill up what would otherwise have remained as white space. In F the same problem did not arise; the lines in question, however, must have been written at the bottom of the first page or near the top of the second page, on leaf one of Shakespeare's manuscript. The first leaf of an old manuscript, more vulnerable than those that follow, could have been damaged; my guess is that manuscript B, Shakespeare's fair copy, was defective at this point, that Crane copied from Q and failed to correct Q's mislineation.

Similar 'lineation' anomalies link the Q and F texts at later points as well.

> *Cas.* Indeede she is a most fresh and delicate creature.
> *Iag.* What an eye she has?
> Me thinkes it sounds a parly of prouocation.
> *Cas.* An inuiting eye, and yet me thinkes right moddest.
>
> (2.3.20–3, Q)

F appears to copy Q in the two middle lines –

> *Iago.* What an eye she ha's?
> Methinkes it sounds a parley to prouocation.

– for this is a prose passage, and the third line should have continued the second, not started on a new line. Here, however, F (unlike Q) divides other lines into two, and F may have needed to 'lose space':

> *Cas.* An inuiting eye:
> And yet me thinkes right modest.
> *Iago.* And when she speakes,
> Is it not an Alarum to Loue?

So it may be a coincidence that Q and F begin a new line after 'What an eye she has'. When we recall the 'common errors' and 'common spellings' in Q and F, however, 'common mislineation' is less likely to be a matter of coincidence, and more likely to have resulted from textual contact. This contact need not mean that F was printed from Q (as Bowers and others believed in 1964) but only that Crane 'occasionally consulted' Q.

*   *   *

We can now return to the question with which I began this chapter. Do Q and F both derive, at one remove, from the same authorial manuscript? A second manuscript in the author's own hand, presumably a fair copy, might account for F's success in so often recovering the 'harder reading', where Q was content with an inferior but not impossible reading. Yet, to look at the question without *parti pris*, we have to concede that Crane's familiarity with Shakespeare's hand, his pride in his 'mystery' and his pole position as a First Folio scribe would lead one to expect a better transcript from him than from the Q scribe, supposing that they copied from the very same manuscript.

The evidence of 'F only' passages is equally inconclusive. While it might be thought that passages cancelled in the Q manuscript (e.g. the Willow Song in 4.3 and 5.2) would not have survived in F if already cancelled when Q was printed in 1622, it is generally agreed that the Folio prints passages in other plays that were meant to be cancelled, and the good quartos of *Love's Labour's Lost* and *Romeo and Juliet* likewise print alternative versions of some speeches, where one of the versions must have been cancelled.[13] Either Shakespeare did not delete the first versions when they were replaced, or cancellations were marked so lightly that the printer – or rather, the printers, for many individuals were involved – did not realise that passages were meant to be cancelled. If the Q and F scribes both copied from the same manuscript, F's success in preserving passages omitted by Q would be in line with other Shakespearian texts: in short, the 'F only' passages do not prove that F derives from a second authorial text.

Several kinds of evidence persuade me that, nevertheless, F probably originated in a second holograph rather than deriving, at one remove, from the foul papers that reached print, at one remove, in the form of Q. First, the alternative passages in which Greg admired 'the Shakespearian quality of both versions' (see above, p. 18). To these I would add the alternative passages that seem to have been written to protect Desdemona (p. 18). After analysing a group of alternative passages, Greg came to the same conclusion several times over: 'It will be noticed ... that in the case of many of the variants Q's reading might very well be the original one, later superseded by the better reading of F'; 'The impression is of deliberate revision in F rather than of corruption in Q'; 'Everything therefore points to F's version having been reached by way of Q's, rather than Q being a corruption of F's.'[14] Do these conclusions really lead on to his summing-up?

> we get a picture of two different scribes struggling with, and at times variously interpreting, much and carelessly altered foul papers – perhaps even of alterations made by the author or with his authority after his draft had been officially copied.[15]

What Greg seems not to have asked himself is this: why did the Q scribe repeatedly choose the earlier alternative reading or passage, and the F scribe the later one, if both worked from the same manuscript? If it was clear to the F scribe that the earlier version had been superseded, why was it not clear to the Q scribe? It would not make sense to argue that the F scribe 'knew the play as it was acted' and was guided by this knowledge, for elsewhere, when he substituted inferior variants, he manifestly depended on what he thought he saw in his manuscript, not on knowledge of the play as acted. So the simplest answer to my questions must be that the Q and F scribes worked from different manuscripts. Only Greg's conviction that Shakespeare did not usually prepare fair copies headed him away from this answer: and, as I have indicated (p. 20), later commentators disagreed with Greg, urging that Shakespeare – like other dramatists of the period – must have written fair copies, occasionally if not invariably.

I am puzzled by Greg's afterthought that variant passages suggest much and carelessly altered foul papers – 'perhaps even . . . alterations made by the author or with his authority after his draft had been officially copied'. The 'officially copied' version, as envisaged by Greg, would be a scribal manuscript: Greg asks us to believe that Shakespeare tinkered with readings in this text that were not corrupt – that is, that Shakespeare changed readings that a scribe had copied correctly. It is not impossible, of course; the changes, however, are mostly quite trivial, and so one asks 'How often did authors revise their own work, introducing trivial improvements, *in scribal copies*?' My impression is that this was not a common occurrence. On the other hand, as I have shown elsewhere,[16] authors commonly changed words and groups of words in the process of copying their own texts. The alternative passages in Q and F in which Greg admired 'the Shakespearian quality of both versions' are best explained, I think, by the hypothesis of two authorial texts, a hypothesis supported by normal professional practice: 'there is no evidence whatever', said Bowers, a statement already quoted (p. 20), 'that an author ever submitted for payment anything but a fair copy'.

The identification of Ralph Crane as the scribe who prepared the manuscript used as copy for F *Othello* introduces another difficulty that Greg did not live to grapple with. Greg postulated one scribal copy, which he defined as the prompt-book (though well aware that this was a thesis vulnerable on several counts: see p. 102). If Crane transcribed the play for the Folio in 1622–3, was there another scribal copy preceding Crane's? What evidence is there for the existence of an earlier scribal copy? Greg's hypothesis needs an earlier scribal copy, one pre-dating Shakespeare's death, if Shakespeare's afterthoughts were written into an 'officially copied' text: yet Crane's transcript accounts for the 'non-Shakespearian' features of F *Othello*, and Occam's razor surely disposes of the earlier scribal copy.

Next, let us consider the implications of F's graphically related but inferior variants: *Tongued* Consuls (1.1.24; *toged* Q); *chances* of vexation (1.1.71; *changes* Q); Officers of *might* (1.1.180; *night* Q); the *braine* of our liues (1.3.327; *ballance* Q); when these *mutabilities* so marshall the way (2.1.259; *mutualities* Q); come into no true *taste* againe (2.1.274; *trust* Q); Would you the *super-vision* grossely gape on? (3.3.398; *superuisor* Q); and many more. Also, the implications of passages where the F scribe seems to have consulted Q, to have adopted Q's wrong punctuation and yet to have switched to an inferior variant:

> When the Blood is made dull with the Act of Sport, there should be *a game* to enflame it, and to giue Satiety a fresh appetite. Louelinesse in fauour, simpathy in yeares, Manners, and Beauties: all which the Moore is defectiue in.
>
> (2.1.224 ff., F; *againe* Q)

F followed Q in punctuating with a stop after appetite, where later editors emend to 'there should be, *again* to inflame it, and to give satiety a fresh *appetite, loveliness* . . .' or the like.[17] Now supposing that Crane had access to the very manuscript previously transcribed for Q, why would he deliberately reject attractive readings like toged, changes, night, balance, mutualities, trust, supervisor, again, etc., which the Q scribe had been able to read in the manuscript, and which Crane would have found repeated in Q? Crane must have felt fairly confident that the words were tongued, chances, might, brain, mutabilities, taste, supervision, a game, etc., before he would switch to these inferior variants, some of which scarcely make sense. Considering how carefully Crane corrected his manuscript from Q in other places, is it not in character that when he encountered strange and implausible readings in his manuscript he would look across at Q, to check how Q dealt with the problem? Yet where the Q scribe read one set of variants, the F scribe thought he saw graphically similar but different words – words much less likely in the context and almost certainly misreadings. While we must not rule out the possibility that some F variants resulted from inadvertence, F departs from Q in so many inferior and also indifferent variants that a second authorial manuscript seems the obvious explanation.

Why, though, would a sensible scribe deliberately choose inferior variants that Shakespeare's editors reject as misreadings? The answer, I think, lies in the attitude of Shakespeare's contemporaries to his language. 'There is an upstart crow, beautified with our feathers, that . . . supposes he is as well able to bombast out a blank verse as the best of you': so Robert Greene, later echoed by Dryden. 'In reading some bombast speeches in *Macbeth*, which are not to be understood, he [Ben Jonson] used to say that it was horror.' Dryden said elsewhere that Shakespeare's style 'is as affected as it is obscure'.[18] These witnesses testify that modern readers are not the first to find Shakespeare's language difficult. Contemporaries and near-contemporaries thought it inflated, obscure and sometimes 'not to be understood'. Of course, others praised Shakespeare's poems as Ovidian and mellifluous; there can be no doubt, though, that his plays are at times linguistically baffling, forcing later editors to write long explanatory notes for which a single word might have sufficed – 'Unexplained.'

Contemporaries recognised that Shakespeare's language could be obscure, and even nonsensical. To quote Jonson again: 'Many times he fell into those things, [which] could not escape laughter.' Shakespeare himself seems to have been aware of such criticisms,[19] and Jonson made it his business to enlighten Shakespeare's colleagues. 'I remember, the players have often mentioned it as an honour to Shakespeare, that in his writing, (whatsoever he penned) he never blotted out line. My answer hath been, would he had blotted a thousand.'

To return to the F text of *Othello*: Heminges and Condell, I suggest, aware that Shakespeare's language and illegible handwriting could cause problems, gave Crane a manuscript to transcribe, a copy of Q to refer to when in doubt, and instructions roughly as follows. 'We need a clearly written manuscript of *Othello* for the printer. Transcribe *this* manuscript. It's not easy to read – if you can make nothing of it, check the passage in *this* printed version [Q], but keep in mind that the printed version is full of errors: it's a badly printed, unauthorised text, and it omits some essential passages. Our manuscript has a much more reliable text. Follow the manuscript, as far as you can, restore all passages omitted from the printed text, and don't worry if you don't understand everything – Shakespeare's language, as we all know, can be convoluted and obscure.' So Crane followed the manuscript, when he thought he could make out what it said, though now and then he followed Q – with some happy and some less happy consequences. He restored passages omitted from Q, and for good measure transcribed from Q some passages not retained by Shakespeare in his fair copy, as well as 'common errors' that reappear in F from Q.

But is it really conceivable that a scribe, knowing of the existence of acceptable alternatives, chose inferior readings, some of them very unlikely indeed? We can say categorically that it is – because precisely the same thing happened when copy for Q2 *Othello*, the second quarto of 1630, was prepared for the printer. Bibliographical links establish that Q2 was printed from a copy of Q hand-corrected by an editor, who deleted many Q readings and inserted in their place F variants – including some of the inferior F variants chosen by Ralph Crane in preference to Q's acceptable readings. Just as Crane, following his instructions, wrote 'super-vision' and not 'superuisor', the Q2 editor, who recognised that F was in many ways a better text than Q, deleted 'superuisor' (and other good Q readings) and substituted 'superuision', directly from F. The 'inferior reading' triumphed not once but twice, in F and in Q2, and probably for the same reasons: Crane and the Q2 editor accepted that Shakespeare had a strange way with words, therefore they both deferred to what they thought was the better text.[20] This must have been a conscious choice on the part of the Q2 editor, and therefore could have been a conscious choice in the case of Ralph Crane as well.

The hypothesis that there were two authorial manuscripts of *Othello*, both frequently misread by transcribers, the second one, F, also revised here and there by the author, remains merely an hypothesis. I have to add that Greg's hypothesis – a single authorial manuscript 'much and carelessly altered' – cannot be dismissed as demonstrably mistaken. But, for the reasons stated, I prefer the alternative. At this point it should be recalled (1) that Greg accepted Miss Walker's theory that F *Othello* was printed from Q; (2) that Greg was unaware of Ralph Crane's presence in F *Othello*; and (3) that Greg was not aware of the fact – I think it may be called a fact – that the holograph text or texts of *Othello* were written in a hand that was far from easy to read. Greg's hypothesis may have been plausible in 1955 when he published it, though there are clear signs that he himself was dissatisfied with it (see below): later findings have shown that he built on shaky foundations, and that his conclusions need to be reconsidered.

Greg thought that the F manuscript was the prompt-book.[21] An authorial copy might certainly become the prompt-book, though hardly one as illegible as the F manuscript must have been, in view of F's misreadings. Greg conceded that it is 'contrary to our experience elsewhere that the cut text [i.e. Q] should derive from foul papers and the full text [i.e. F] from the prompt-book', yet decided that 'it would be extravagant to suppose that if this [F manuscript] was not foul papers it was anything but prompt-copy'. His objections to the extravagance of 'unnecessary' intermediate copies influenced his decision; later studies, however, have indicated that authorial fair copies were not quite as rare as Greg believed.[22] I cannot understand Greg's statement that F's stage directions support the hypothesis of prompt-book origin, for F's give far less help with staging than Q's (see p. 4). F's purgation of profanity no doubt encouraged the notion of a 'theatrical' origin but, as we have seen (p. 78), play-texts were purged in private transcripts and for publication as well as for performance. In my opinion the F manuscript (Bb) and its immediate source (B) both bypassed the theatre: probably B served as copy for the prompt-book, and Bb was prepared as copy for the Folio. To sum up: A (author's foul papers) → B (authorial fair copy) → Bb (Crane's copy, 1622–3, i.e. printer's copy for F) → F. The Quarto had two ancestors: A → Aa (scribal copy) → Q. The Folio had four: A, B, Bb and also Q, which – unhappily for the editor – supplied some F readings that are detectable as common errors and also, we must assume, many more that we cannot now identify.

Chapter 10

Lineation and scansion

Othello Q and F often divide verse lines differently, and editors often rearrange verse lines so that they differ from both Q and F. Are the editors right or wrong? It has now been claimed that editorial lineation in Shakespeare's plays, imposed in the eighteenth century, was 'uncritically perpetuated in almost all editions down to our own day', resulting in a 'metrical mish-mash',[1] as in *Antony and Cleopatra* (2.2.28 ff.):

(1)   *Caes.*   Welcome to Rome.
          Ant.   Thanke you.
          Caes.   Sit.
          Ant.   Sit sir.
          Caes.   Nay then.

(2)   *Caes.*   Welcome to Rome.
          Ant.   Thank you.
          Caes.   Sit.
          Ant.   Sit, sir!
          Caes.   Nay,
      Then —

The F arrangement is shown in (1), and (2) preserves the basic metrical form of the eighteenth century, 'making use of what may be called metrical white space', an innovation in Steevens's edition of 1793 copied by almost all subsequent editors.[2] The editors assume that when Shakespeare's words can be rearranged as iambic pentameters, or as something not too far removed from pentameters, rearranged they must be. Paul Bertram objected that this use of white space imprisoned Shakespeare's dialogue in an Augustan 'metrical corset', and others agreed. When the words refuse to divide readily into pentameters, it was said, would it not be better to return to F's arrangement?

    Now the good quartos and the three pages of *Sir Thomas More* put it beyond dispute that Shakespeare did not employ white space, as above, when he wrote verse dialogue (but cf. p. 122). Yet white space, a 'modern' convention, can be defended in a modernised edition on the same grounds as modern spelling, consistent speech prefixes, interpolated stage directions – they help the modern reader. They help him or her to 'see' and 'hear' the verse, if verse it be.

But is it? The line from *Antony and Cleopatra* would be a strange iambic pentameter, with several stresses in the wrong place. Leaving aside this particular 'line', which is also unusual in dividing into five separate speeches, we must not lose sight of the fact that Shakespeare's versification changed quite astonishingly in the course of his career. From heavily end-stopped and almost monotonously regular iambics in his early plays he moved on to many kinds of metrical innovation, a development that was already well advanced by the time of *Othello*. One such innovation was his increased use of long and short lines, a matter not unrelated to the argument about white space. For example, in Act 1 of *Othello* speeches of two lines or more end with short lines of four to seven syllables 46 times, whereas only 31 end with lines consisting of ten or eleven syllables (i.e. regular iambic pentameters). In Act 1 of *Titus Andronicus*, a much earlier play, only three speeches of two lines or more fail to end with lines of ten or eleven syllables. 'Irregular' (long or short) lines can occur at other points in a speech: I cite these figures only to illustrate, from non-controversial evidence, that 'irregular' lines become more common in Shakespeare's later plays, and then to ask a question. Have editors, aware that Shakespeare grew more relaxed about 'irregular' versification, gone too far along this road, solving textual tangles by postulating even more 'irregular' lines?

Before we can answer this question we must be clear about Shakespeare's normal practices at the time of *Othello*. To begin once more with non-controversial examples: a very large number of words could be lengthened or shortened in pronunciation, and sometimes in writing – notably words with *-en-* or *-er-* syllables (even, heaven, stolen, taken; ever, never, whether, etc.) could drop or keep this syllable, as the metre required. Other words, now usually monosyllables, could be treated as disyllables (dear, fire, hour, and others ending in *-r* or *-re*, preceded by a long vowel or diphthong (Abbott §480).[3] The endings *-ion*, *-ious* and *-io* could count as one or two syllables (jeal[i]ous, Cass[i]o), as could *-ia-* (marriage, Venetian) (Abbott §479), and a very large variety of words could be contracted (§459 ff.). Consequently, many lines in *Othello* that may appear to be long or short to modern readers would not have troubled Shakespeare's contemporaries.

Even after we discount such variable syllables and reinstate seemingly 'irregular' lines as regular, many long and short lines remain in *Othello*. Some can qualify as regular because they contain interjections or interruptions, which are quite normally extra-metrical (§§512, 414).[4]

(1)   Upon malicious bravery dost thou come
         To start my quiet?
    RODERIGO   *Sir, sir, sir* –
    BRABANTIO   But thou must needs be sure
                             (1.1.99 ff.)

(2)   DESDEMONA   Heaven keep that monster from Othello's mind!
EMILIA   *Lady, amen.*
DESDEMONA   I will go seek him. Cassio, walk here about,
                                                                    (3.4.163 ff.)

Hence vocatives and 'profanity' can also be extra-metrical:

(3)   I think this tale would win my daughter too.
Good Brabantio,
Take up this mangled matter at the best:
                                    (1.3.172 ff.)

(4)   *O heaven,* how got she out? O treason of the blood!
                                    (1.1.167)

In *Othello* there are even lines that look like 'double interruptions', where two speakers break in on each other and both complete their own verse line.

(5)   DESDEMONA   But half an hour!
OTHELLO   Being done, there is no pause –
DESDEMONA   But while I say one prayer!
OTHELLO   It is too late.
                                                            (5.2.81 ff.)

This might be printed:

DESDEMONA   But half an hour! But while I say one prayer!
OTHELLO   Being done, there is no pause. It is too late.

Q actually prints Desdemona's line as above, as a single line: 'But halfe an houre, but while I say one prayer.' It could even be that Shakespeare wanted the two actors to speak simultaneously. These lines, though not metrically 'irregular', show how Shakespeare might adapt iambic pentameters for his own local purposes. Again:

(6)   Lend me thy handkerchief.
DESDEMONA   Here, my lord.
OTHELLO   That which I gave you.
DESDEMONA   I have it not about me.
                                    (3.4.52 ff.)

Cambridge 1 prints as a series of short prose speeches, but it is also possible that Shakespeare 'heard' the lines as two acceptable pentameters: '*Oth.* Lend me thy handkerchief. That which I gave you. *Des.* Here, my lord. – I have it not about me.'

   Another kind of irregularity has been called 'the amphibious section' (Abbott §513). 'When a verse consists of two parts uttered by two speakers, the latter part is frequently the former part of the following verse, being, as it were, amphibious'. Thus:

(1)   On most part of their fleet.
         MONTANO   *How? Is this true?*
         3 GENTLEMAN   The Ship is here put in,
                              (2.1.24–5)

(2)   You'd have enough.
         DESDEMONA   *Alas! she has no speech*
         IAGO   In faith, too much!
                              (2.1.102–3)

The italicised half-line is amphibious, being an integral part of two possible verse lines. There are so many amphibious sections in *Othello*[5] that it appears that Shakespeare thought of them as metrically regular.

A further peculiarity may be called the metrical 'echo' line, as when the last line of a speech and the first of the next speech add up to twelve or more syllables, and the second of these short lines echoes the syllable count of the first. Even multiple echoes are possible, as in (4) below.

(1)   And prays you to relieve him.
         DUKE   'Tis certain then for Cyprus
                      (1.3.43–4)

(2)   On the enchafed flood.
         MONTANO   If that the Turkish fleet
                      (2.1.17)

(3)   And fearful to be granted.
         OTHELLO   I will deny thee nothing.
                      (3.3.83)

(4)   Than give thy cause away.
         EMILIA   Madam, here comes my lord.
         CASSIO   Madam, I'll take my leave.
         DESDEMONA   Why, stay and hear me speak.
                      (3.3.28 ff.)

Again, so many 'echo' lines are found in *Othello*[6] that we may consider them normal practice in this play.

For my purposes the important point is that interrupted lines, amphibious sections and arguably echo lines, though apparently 'irregular', show Shakespare to have been alert to the syllable count in his verses. The number of syllables per line, indeed, could have been more significant in his eyes than the iambic rhythm, for, as Abbott observed, he modified this rhythm in so many ways.

From an analysis of several tragic lines of Shakespeare, taken from different plays, I should say that rather less than one of three has the full number of five emphatic accents. About two of three have four, and one out of fifteen has three.[7]

To put it differently, there are many more ten- or eleven-syllable lines in the mature plays of Shakespeare than there are five-stress iambic pentameters; or – the number of syllables per verse line was sometimes Shakespeare's first concern, not a strict adherence to iambic rhythms. If Abbott was right, and even if the syllable count were only of equal importance to the iambic pentameter, we must therefore ask whether editors who have rearranged Shakespeare's verse lines have done so for the right reasons.

One of the great surprises for anyone familiar with traditional texts of *Othello* is that so many long and short lines disappear if the editor chooses to arrange the dialogue in ten- or eleven-syllable lines, Shakespeare's customary measure. In view of the fact that both Q and F are unreliable in their lineation and often disagree with one another, the possibility that Shakespare's verses have been wrongly divided for centuries, and consequently have never been properly 'heard', deserves a little attention. Let us consider two passages from Act 5 scene 2.

(1) (a) Let him confess the truth.

      Oth.   He hath confess'd.
      Des. What, my lord?
      Oth. That he hath used thee.
      Des.   How? unlawfully?
      Oth. Ay.
      Des. He will not say so.
      Oth.   No, his mouth is stopp'd;
Honest Iago hath ta'en order for't.
      Des. O, my fear interprets! what, is he dead?
      Oth. Had all his hairs been lives, my great revenge
Had stomach for them all.
      Des. Alas, he is betray'd, and I undone!
               (Cambridge 1, lines 68–75)

(b)   Let him confess the truth.

OTHELLO   He hath confessed.
DESDEMONA What, my lord?
OTHELLO   That he hath – ud's death! – used thee.
DESDEMONA How? unlawfully?
OTHELLO   Ay.
DESDEMONA   He will not say so.

OTHELLO   No, his mouth is stopped. Honest Iago
    Hath ta'en order for't.
DESDEMONA   O, my fear interprets!
    What, is he dead?
OTHELLO   Had all his hairs been lives
    My great revenge had stomach for them all.
DESDEMONA   Alas, he is betrayed, and I undone.
                        (Arden 3)

Version (a) is the 'traditional' one, its lineation followed by Cambridge 2 and 3 and by other editors. Yet it contains three lines that hang loose from the metrical norm ('What, my lord?', 'Ay' and 'Had stomach for them all'), and it simply omits an instance of 'profanity', Q's *vds death*, whereas the same editors elsewhere restore Q's profanity. Version (b), on the other hand, can claim to be metrically regular and, apart from restoring *vds death* (omitted by F), has not added to or subtracted from the QF texts, except by choosing variants from one or the other.

It may be urged that in this instance the difference between the two versions is not huge – indeed, might not be noticed in the theatre. Two points need to be made: first, that this is not an isolated passage, and that the issue is the editor's sense of a metrical norm, which can have a knock-on effect in many other passages. Second, that there must be a difference, however fleetingly heard, when the line-division is changed.

(2) (a)   Sweet Desdemona! O sweet mistress, speak!
        Des.   A guiltless death I die.
        Emil.   O, who hath done this deed?
        Des.   Nobody; I myself. Farewell:
    Commend me to my kind lord: O, farewell!
           (Cambridge 1, lines 120–3)

    (b)   Sweet Desdemona, O sweet mistress, speak!
    DESDEMONA   A guiltless death I die.
    EMILIA   O, who hath done
    This deed?
    DESDEMONA   Nobody. I myself. Farewell.
    Commend me to my kind lord – O, farewell!
                     (Arden 3)

Here version (a) has three short lines, version (b) is regular. Even if we think of the second short line in (a) as an 'echo' of the first, (a) departs from the metrical norm and (b) observes it. And should it be objected that (b) has a strange line ending ('done / This deed?'), one could answer that Emilia finds herself in a strange situation and fumbles for words: she cannot call it a murder, with Desdemona still alive, so it is not unnatural if she hesitates very slightly on 'this' and 'deed'. This particular line division ('done / This deed?') was actually introduced by Capell in the eighteenth century, was copied by a few editors but, such is the herd instinct of the majority, has not won a place in the *textus receptus*.

The essential difference between Cambridge 1, the traditional text, and Arden 3 is this: Cambridge 1 frequently departs from the metrical norm, whereas Arden 3 prefers to arrange the dialogue in ten- or eleven-syllable lines wherever this seems possible. As we have seen in (2) (b), there may be some argument whether or not the Arden 3 lineation is in fact 'possible'. The familiarity of some of the passages in question will perhaps interfere with one's judgement, as in the case of 'O that this too too solid [or 'sullied'] flesh would melt'. This is a difficulty; it should be remembered, however, that to change Shakespeare's lineation is a less drastic step than to emend his words, especially when the change brings his lineation into conformity with his regular measure instead of fracturing it.

We must not pretend that we are dealing with a simple choice between right and wrong. The presence of long and short prose passages in *Othello* is a complicating factor, as is Shakespeare's habit of fudging the difference between them as he prepares to switch from prose to verse, or from verse to prose.

(1)   The Moor! I know his trumpet!
CASSIO   'Tis truly so.
DESDEMONA   Let's meet him and receive him.
CASSIO   Lo, where he comes!
                                                            (2.1.178 ff.)

(2)   Welcome, Iago, we must to the watch.
                        (2.3.12)

(3)   Here at the door, I pray you call them in.
                        (2.3.43)

(4)   'Fore God, they have given me a rouse already.
                        (2.3.61)

(5)   To th'platform, masters, come, let's set the watch.
                        (2.3.116)

Passage (1) follows prose and leads into verse: Cambridge 1 prints as prose, Arden 3 as verse, and both are defensible. Passages (2)–(5) also fall between prose and verse, and could be either: looking like rhythmic prose or prosaic verse, they ease the transition from one to the other. Shakespeare, I take it, wanted to minimise the difference between verse and prose at these points, and here it scarcely matters which of the two the editor prefers.

On the other hand, it matters greatly that editors and readers should understand the consequences of believing in a 'stress-based' as against a 'syllabic' verse line. Those who think stress and verse feet all important have been in the ascendant for some time,[8] and are responsible for a text that, I think, seriously misrepresents the rhythms of Shakespeare's verse. While the 'syllabic' principle cannot solve every problem of versification in *Othello*, the alternative is to allow the verse to break down repeatedly even when the verse measure can and should be defended.

(1) (a)　　*Oth.*　Fire and brimstone!
　　　　　Des.　My lord?
　　　　　Oth.　Are you wise?
　　　　　　(Cambridge 1, 4.1.233)

　　(b)　OTHELLO Fire and brimstone!
　　　　DESDEMONA　　　　　　　　My lord?
　　　　OTHELLO　　　　　　　　　　　　Are you wise?
　　　　　　　　　　　　　　　　　　　(Arden 3)

(2) (a)　And makes men mad.
　　　　　Emil.　Cassio, my lord, hath kill'd a young Venetian
　　　Call'd Roderigo.
　　　　　Oth.　　　　Roderigo kill'd!
　　　And Cassio kill'd!
　　　　　Emil.　　　　No, Cassio is not kill'd.
　　　　　Oth.　Not Cassio kill'd! then murder's out of tune,
　　　And sweet revenge grows harsh.
　　　　　Des.　O falsely, falsely murder'd!
　　　　　　　　　　　　(Cambridge 1, 5.2.110–15)

　　(b)　　And makes men mad.
　　　　EMILIA　　　　　　　Cassio, my lord, hath killed
　　　　　A young Venetian, called Roderigo.
　　　　OTHELLO Roderigo killed? and Cassio killed?
　　　　EMILIA No, Cassio is not killed.
　　　　OTHELLO　　　　　　　Not Cassio killed?
　　　　　Then murder's out of tune, and sweet revenge
　　　　　Grows harsh.
　　　　DESDEMONA　O falsely, falsely murdered!
　　　　　　　　　　　　　　　　　(Arden 3)

Passages (1) and (2) are embedded in verse and fit in comfortably as verse, as long as we remember that 'Fire' in (1) could be a disyllable and that the *-ian* and *-io* of *Venetian* and *Cassio* in (2) could sound or slur over the 'i' (cf. p. 104). Cambridge 1 and similar editions allow the verse to break down quite unnecessarily in both passages, three times in passage (2).

*　　*　　*

The problem of metrical 'irregularity' in *Othello* also seems to be much more pervasive than it really is because Jaggard's compositors, as we have seen in the reprinted 'Pavier' quartos of 1619 (p. 52), did not always follow their copy when dealing with contractions or 'contractable' words. They shortened or lengthened such forms – for example, in *King Lear* (1619), as follows: Happely > Haply 91,[9] thar't > thou art 497, into't > into it 538, on's > of his 566, for't > for it 584, it'h > in the 607, at'h > on thy 608, i'st > is it 719, shees > she is 758, side's > side his 765, gainst > against 813, you'l > you will 971, Byt'h > By the 1112, too'th > to the 1265, thoud'st > thou wouldst 1569, toward > to 2005, ouer > ore 2158, speakest > speakst 2287, tha're > they are 2401, and so on. Repeated instances of the same change are not here recorded; each one cited, it will be noticed, involves – or appears to involve – a change in the number of syllables, usually adding a syllable, although the reverse also happens. This means that when the same compositor(s) set another play – let us say *Othello* – an 'irregular' verse line, one that can be made regular by introducing or lengthening contractions, may need to be emended according to the known habits of the compositor[10] and, of course, of the author.

What contractions did Shakespeare habitually use? We can find out from the early quartos and from *Sir Thomas More*. It is important to distinguish texts written and, if possible, printed before *Othello* from Folio texts because contractions were in a transition phase at the turn of the century, and Folio contractions could be post-Shakespearian. To begin with some quartos printed up to and including the year 1604, the following contractions are common, and are probably all pre-Shakespearian: weele, Tis, Ile, lets, Here's, shees, sheel, th', ore, wheres, byth, fallst, nere, thats, ist, ene (= e'en), twas, tother, Theile, twill, toote (= to it), twere, youle, yfaith, Heele (all from *Romeo and Juliet*, Q2). Less common: thou'se (= thou shalt), ont (= of it), ast (= as it) (also *Romeo and Juliet*). In other early quartos we may note to's (to us), a'the (of the), i'th (in the), by th'weeke, ant (of it), th'other (*Love's Labour's Lost*, 1598); warn't (warrant), in's (in his), hate (have it), S'hath (she has), within's (within these), ber (by our), neer's (near us), tha'r (they are), th'owt (thou will), Woo't (wouldst), thou'lt (thou wilt), all's (all his), for's (for his), Ift (if it), th'art (thou art) (*Hamlet*, 1604–5). Some were colloquial contractions, others were in general use: clearly their occurrence in plays depended on a number of variables, including genre and the social rank of speakers. The three 'Shakespearian' pages of *Sir Thomas More* contain some less familiar contractions, yet differ from the quartos only to the extent that the quartos differ from one another: we encounter whats, tis, thipp (the hip), letts, weele, byth, thart (thou art), tane (ta'en), tooth (to the), thats, thappostle, twere, gainst, youle, thoffendor, thers.

A.C. Partridge dealt at length with contractions in *Orthography in Shakespeare and Elizabethan Drama* (1964). I agree with much of what he wrote, and readers will find his documentation useful. More needs to be said, however, about the contraction of auxiliary verbs.

(1) *I'm*. Partridge noted *Ime* and *I'me* in the play *Woodstock*, adding '*O.E.D.* has no example of this contraction until Cowley's *Mistress*, 1647. The normal orthography before 1600 is found in *Woodstock* 282 "*I am* sweld more plump than erst I was", the licence of elision or slurring being assumed by the actor' (p. 37). In fact, *I'm* is not uncommon in the Shakespeare Folio ('For I haue seene more yeeres I'me sure then yee', *Julius Caesar* TLN 2117; cf. *Timon* TLN 1088, 1152, 1371,[11] etc.). We may take it that elision or slurring was also intended in *Othello*:

> *I am* glad on't: / 'Tis a worthy Gouernour.
>   (2.1.30: usually treated as one line)

> He thought 'twas Witchcraft. / But *I am* much too blame:
>   (3.3.214: usually treated as one line)

> To prey at Fortune. Haply, for *I am* blacke,
>   (3.3.267)

> *I am* most vnhappy in the losse of it.
>   (3.4.103)[12]

(2) As is well known, many contracted forms first appear around the turn of the century – first appear *in writing*. But there can be little doubt that before 1600 these forms were part of the spoken language. The auxiliary *'ve* (= have) is a good example: according to the *Oxford English Dictionary* (Have: 2a, d) this contraction is recorded in the eighteenth and nineteenth centuries. Yet there are so many instances in Shakespeare where the scansion points to monosyllabic *I've, we've, you've, they've* that it surely follows that the contracted forms, even if not yet in common use in the written language, must have been familiar in speech.

Here are some from *Othello* (F).

> Doe well thriue by them, / And when *they haue* lin'd their Coates
>   (1.1.52: usually treated as one line)

> *I haue* charg'd thee not to haunt about my doores:
>   (1.1.95)

> My Seruices, which *I haue* done the Signorie
>   (1.2.18)

> *I haue* found great loue among'st them. Oh my Sweete,
>   (2.1.204)

> *You haue* knowne him long, and be you well assur'd
>   (3.3.11)

To your owne person. Nay, when *I haue* a suite
                    (3.3.80)

Yes, *you haue* seene *Cassio*, and she together.
                    (4.2.3)

And yet she'le kneele, and pray: *I haue* seene her do't
                    (4.2.23)

We haue done our course: there's money for your paines:
                    (4.2.95)

I haue laid those Sheetes you bad me on the bed.
                    (4.3.20)

Will not go from my mind: *I haue* much to do,
                    (4.3.29)

I haue heard it said so. O these Men, these men!
                    (4.3.59)

I haue rub'd this yong Quat almost to the sense
                    (5.1.11)

That can thy Light re-Lume. / When *I haue* pluck'd thy Rose,
                    (5.2.13: usually treated as one line)

Oh, are you come, *Iago*: *you haue* done well,
                    (5.2.165)

Vpon a Soldiers Thigh. *I haue* seene the day,
                    (5.2.259)

I haue made my way through more impediments
                    (5.2.261)

I haue done the State some seruice, and they know't:
                    (5.2.337)

There are other passages, of course, where *I have*, etc., need two syllables, and it may be that the uncontracted form will be preferred by some readers in some of the lines quoted above. Nevertheless, the number of metrically curious or irregular lines that remains, should *I have*, etc., always be heard as disyllabic, calls for an explanation: I mean the long lines (e.g. 1.2.18, 5.2.13) and lines that stress the third syllable. And the simplest explanation is that the *'ve* forms were already available, in the spoken if not generally in the written language.[13]

It must now be added that the *Oxford English Dictionary* erred by a considerable margin, as so often, in its dating of the *'ve* forms. For, though not found in Shakespeare's early good quartos, they occur in the Folio. In *Henry VIII* (I'ue, th'haue, th'haue, y'haue, Y'haue, W'have: TLN 476, 588, 741, 1329, 3329, 3453; in *Hamlet*, where Q2's 'I haue seene' and 'I haue done' became F's 'I'ue seene' and 'I'ue done' (TLN 3080, 3678); in *Timon* (ye'haue, Y'haue: TLN 368, 2292); in *Antony and Cleopatra* (Y'haue: TLN 1304, 1361); and no doubt elsewhere. Indeed the good Quarto of *Troilus and Cressida* (printed 1609 by G. Eld, written close to *Othello*) includes 'th'haue' (F4[a]), and the *Sonnets* (printed 1609, also by Eld) include 'y'haue' (120.6). Although some of these contracted forms could have been substituted by scribes or compositors, their presence shows that these contractions were known, and the fact that they were not standardised as *I've, you've*, etc., suggests that they were also fairly new, at any rate in the written language. Leaving aside Shakespeare, other writers in the early seventeenth century used the same contractions (see p. 115), so Shakespeare's editors really ought to take them into account.

(3) The same is true of *'d* contractions (I'd, we'd, you'd, he'd, she'd, they'd). They are absent from the early quartos, though not from *Troilus and Cressida* (1609: yow'd, youd, Ide: F2[a], F4[a], I3[b]) or from *Othello* (1622: Shee'd, You'd, I'de: TLN 494, 871, 1793, 1893, 2354, 3352, 3417, 3592). Other lines in *Othello* might therefore be printed with the contracted forms. I quote from the Folio.

> I had thought t'haue yerk'd him here vnder the Ribbes.
>
>   (1.2.5)

> I had rather to adopt a Child, then get it.
>
>   (1.3.192)

> I had rather haue this tongue cut from my mouth
>
>   (2.3.217)

> I did not thinke he had bin acquainted with hir.
>
>   (3.3.99)

> And not their Appetites? I had rather be a Toad,
>
>   (3.3.274)

> Beleeue me, I had rather haue lost my purse
>
>   (3.4.25)

> (As like enough it will) I would haue it coppied:
>
>   (3.4.190)

> What if I had said, I had seene him do you wrong?
>
>   (4.1.24)

> Oh good my Lord, I would speake a word with you.
>
>   (5.2.89)

Again, editors are left with long lines (3.3.99, 4.1.24) and strangely placed stresses unless they contract *had* and *would* to 'd. Contract *had* to 'd? Some authorities claim that *I'd, you'd*, etc., in Shakespeare are always abbreviations for *I would, you would*, not for *I had, you had*.[14] But 'd for *had* occurs in Middleton (*Game*, T, 20, 251), and also in Crane (*Game*, L, *ibid.*) in the form *they'had*, which signifies elision, so Shakespeare, their contemporary, could have intended the same contraction, even if he wrote the full form *I had*. His many verse lines scanning *I'd*, at any rate, point to this conclusion.

Much of the seemingly irregular metre of *Othello* turns out to be regular once we introduce contractions that were beginning to appear at the time, in the spoken and later in the written language. We are entitled to do this, or rather we are duty-bound to consider the possibility, for several reasons. First, compositors switched contracted and uncontracted forms, not least Jaggard's compositor B, who set much of *Othello*; consequently editors ought to consider a switch in reverse. Second, we also know that other writers switched contracted and uncontracted forms.

In 1965, when I drew attention to the instabilities in Shakespeare's texts, the two holograph versions of Middleton's *A Game at Chess* illustrated the point that some authors frequently substitute indifferent variants in copying out their own work. A modern editor may not think of contracted and uncontracted forms of the same word as indifferent variants, but Middleton evidently did, and Shakespeare's editors would benefit from a study of Middleton's two holographs. In these extracts, taken from the recent Malone Society edition,[15] the Bridgewater–Huntington copy (H) is cited first, then the Trinity manuscript (T); I have added italics.

(1)   how much *ha's* wrongd mee, I'me ashamde hee blushes not;
                                  (1868; *hee has* T)

(2)   if I might councell you You *neuer should* speake
                          (1878; *should nere* T)

(3)   yes, at your feares, at *th'* Ignorance of youre power,
                              (1900; *the* T)

(4)   *I'me* quit wth you now for my discouerye
                          (1931; *I am* T)

(5)   that *sufferdst* him through blinde Lust to bee led
                          (1942; *sufferedst* T)

(6)   *You haue* enricht my Knowledge, (Royall Sir)
                          (2006; *y'aue* T)

(7)   or exercize *th'*ould Romane paynfull-Idlenes
                          (2013; *the* T)

(8)   enclose some Creekes *a'th* Sea, as Sergius Crata did
                          (2022; *of the* T)

(9)   some of youre whitehouse Gurmundizers, *espetiallie*
                              (2045; *spetially* T)

(10)   Huldrick Bishop of Ausburge *ins* Epistle
                              (2148; *in his* T)

(11)   Serpents and Adders those names to bee *knowen* by
                              (2160; *knowne* T)

(12)   the Secretst poyson; *I'me* an Archdissembler, (Sir)
                              (2162; *I am* T)

(13)   whose worths not *knowne* but to the skilfull Lapidarie
                              (2173; *knowen* T)

(14)   *I'me* not so easilye mou'de when I'me once sett
                              (2226; *I am* T)

Although only about 400 lines in H are in Middleton's hand and generalisation
could be dangerous, H seems to prefer colloquial contractions and T spells out
uncontracted forms, perhaps a conscious policy. Yet the reverse also happens
(2, 6, 9), and I suspect that *knowne* and *knowen* (11, 13) disclose what really
matters: the variants I have listed, which appear to make a difference of a
syllable, were not 'heard' by Middleton as we hear them. The longer written
form was meant to be slurred or contracted, the shorter form lengthened, as
and when the metre required it. As far as Middleton was concerned, the
contracted and uncontracted forms were interchangeable.

The same can be said of Ralph Crane, who transcribed three separate
copies of *A Game at Chess* which can be compared with Middleton's holographs.
Here are a few samples from one of the three, Lansdowne MS. 690 (cited as
L); the first extract is always from the Trinity MS. (T, holograph), and
variants are in italics.

(1)   in theire iust order readie to goe *to it*
                              (59; *to't* L)

(2)   I *ne're* see that face but my pittie rizes,
                              (103; *neuer* L)

(3)   disarmes youre Soule *e'en* in the heate of battayle,
                              (129; *even* L)

(4)   *to the* Father Generall, so are designes
                              (169; *to th'* L)

(5)   *I'ue* bragd lesse
                              (380; I *haue* L)

(6)   were in my Diocesse, *Ide* soone change his whitenes,
                              (1350; *I would* L)

These examples illustrate Crane's tendency to switch from contracted to uncontracted forms (*Iue* > *I haue*, *Ide* > *I would*), and to switch other words in the opposite direction (*it* > *'t, to the* > *to th'*). As we shall see, these and similar changes distinguish some of the commonest F *Othello* variants from Q, some of which also appear to go against the metre – a not uninteresting fact if, as I have argued, Crane transcribed the manuscript for F *Othello*. In Crane's eyes these various forms were interchangeable, as in Middleton's.

If Jaggard's compositors, Middleton and Crane all exhibit 'instability' in their treatment of contractions, it would be surprising if Shakespeare differed – he, after all, seems to have surpassed most contemporaries in 'unstable' spelling. He was capable of writing 'moor . . . more . . . moore' in one line, and 'Shreiff . . . shreef . . . shreeve . . . Shreiue . . . Shreue' in five consecutive lines in *Sir Thomas More* (Addition D, lines 168, 164–8), and would be predisposed to regard contracted and uncontracted forms as interchangeable. Consider, now, two verse lines from the Quarto of *Richard II* (1.1.110, 2.1.90):

> Thomas of Norfolke what saist thou to this?
> Thou now a dying sayest thou flatterest me.

Would anyone seriously propose that *saist* and *sayest* should be pronounced differently? Or that 1.3.180 from the same play is short of a syllable?

> Sweare by the duty that y'owe to God,

And what are we to make of *mightest* and *mightst* in *Romeo and Juliet* Q2 (3.3.68, a single verse line printed as two)?

> Then mightest thou speake, / Then mightst thou teare thy hayre,

Consider, again, two lines from the *Sonnets* (1609).

> Nor shall death brag thou wandr'st in his shade
> (18.11)

> And age in loue, loues not t'haue yeares told.
> (138.12)

Even if scribes and compositors introduced some contracted or uncontracted forms that are clearly wrong, there are so many, spread over so many different texts, that we may safely deduce that Shakespeare himself was often responsible. Does that mean that in a modernised text we should break with the QF tradition, lengthening or shortening *I've, I have* and the like whenever the metre warrants it? On the assumption that compositors and scribes should be blamed, and also Shakespeare himself, because he didn't care?

We may note in passing that editors of *Othello* quite happily break with *either* Q *or* F when the sense or scansion seems to require it, so to depart from *both* Q *and* F is not as bold a step as may at first appear, since F was clearly influenced by Q and indeed even copies Q's errors (see p. 95). Both Q and F are often wrong, separately, in their scansion or treatment of contractions, as in (1) and (2) below, and it follows that they will sometimes be wrong together.

(1)   You see this Fellow, that is gone before,
       He's a Souldier, fit to stand by *Caesar*,
                        (2.3.117–18, F; *He is* Q)

(2)   The Towne will rise. Fie, fie, Lieutenant,
       You'le be asham'd for euer.
                        (2.3.158–9, F)

       The Towne will rise, *godswill* Leiutenant, *hold*,
       You will be sham'd for euer.
                        (Q; my italics).

(3)   My Wife must moue for *Cassio* to her Mistris:
       Ile set her on *my selfe, a while*, to draw the Moor apart,
                        (2.3.378–80, F; . . . I'le set her on. | *My selfe a*
                        while, to draw the Moore apart, Q)

These are three passages from the same scene. In (1) editors prefer Q, which preserves the iambic rhythm, as against F (which wrongly contracts *He's*); in (3) Q and F are both thought to be corrupt (editors emend: 'I'll set her on. | Myself, the while, to draw the Moor apart . . .'). In (2) F tones down profanity (*godswill*), as elsewhere; loses *hold* (which is metrically necessary); and apparently introduces a contraction (*You'le* for *You will*), and therefore changed *sham'd* to *asham'd*, to preserve the rhythm. F, supposedly the 'better text', is frequently emended by traditional editors from Q, and emended even when it agrees with Q (Cambridge 1 departs from F in (1), (2) and (3)): that being so, the same editors can scarcely object if we emend other passages on similar principles.

'Emend' is actually too strong a term: Arden 3 *rearranges* lineation and spelling, it *interprets* the QF words, it does not substitute entirely different words. And this is not a wanton or unlicensed rearrangement, since it takes into account the known habits of Shakespeare's compositors, of Ralph Crane and, in so far as we can deduce them from the good quartos and *Sir Thomas More*, of Shakespeare himself. To answer, now, the question at the end of the second-last paragraph: yes, we must seriously consider breaking with the lineation and contractions of Q and F – always stressing that locally the difference will be slight, while at the same time the cumulative effect will be significant.

It goes without saying that the more often an editor throws in his hand and decides 'it doesn't look like verse, it must be prose', the more often he will be inclined to repeat this evasion. A witness who is careless with the truth will be thought untrustworthy, and a text thought to be careless about versification may well suffer in the same way: after some time the editor will too readily give up on versification. Such a defeatist attitude can do harm, not only locally but also to the 'character' of the text as a whole.

Having discussed passages that are traditionally printed as prose but can be defended as verse, I now want to look at other instances in which the 'character' of the language of *Othello* requires us to think again about lineation and metre.

(1)   I thinke my Wife be honest, and thinke she is not:
      I thinke that thou art iust, and thinke thou art not:
                      (3.3.387–8, F; not in Q)

F has a long line, which could be made 'regular' by contracting 'she is' to 'she's': if we choose to contract, the echo in the next line necessitates a second contraction (thou'rt). Even if there were no long line, we may well think it more appropriate to stress *not*, the final word in each line, rather than *is* and *art* (*she's* was a common contraction; *thou'rt* also occurs later in F *Othello*, 5.2.170).

(2)   Oh thou weed:
      Who art so louely faire, and smell'st so sweete,
      That the Sense akes at thee,
      Would thou had'st neuer bin borne.
                      (4.2.68–70, F)

Line 70 had to be divided in F because it was too long, as a single line, for F's verse measure. Later editors make it a single twelve-syllable line, as in Cambridge 1:

   That the sense aches at thee, would thou hadst ne'er been born!

– introducing a contraction (*never* > *ne'er*). Is there a case, then, for introducing two contractions?

   That the sense aches at thee, would thou'dst ne'er been born!

Compare *King Lear*, where *thou hadst* was printed *thou'dst*: 'And thou hadst beene set i'th'Stockes for that question, thoud'st well deseru'd it' (2.4.64–5, F). At a less climactic moment the consonant clutter of 'would thou'dst ne'er been born!' might be thought unacceptable. Here it compels Othello to spit out his words and emotions, not inappropriately, and it converts a long line into one that is regular.

(3)   No, Heauens fore-fend I would not kill thy Soule.
      Des. Talke you of killing?
      Oth. I, I do.
      Des. Then Heauen haue mercy on mee.
      Oth. Amen, with all my heart.
      Des. If you say, I hope you will not kill me.
                      (5.2.32–5, F)

This is printed as in F by 'traditional' editors, such as Cambridge 1 and 2. Cambridge 3 rearranges the short lines.

DESDEMONA   Talk you of killing?
OTHELLO   Ay, I do.
DESDEMONA   Then heaven
      Have mercy on me!
OTHELLO   Amen, with all my heart.

The Cambridge 3 editor, Norman Sanders, saw that the short lines were not meant to be prose. Shortly thereafter, though, he follows F (and Cambridge 1 and 2):

(4)   To this extremity. Thy Husband knew it all.
           Æmil.   My Husband?
           Oth.   Thy Husband.
           Æmil.   That she was false to Wedlocke?
           Oth.   I, with *Cassio*: had she bin true,
       If Heauen would make me such another world, . . .
                                   (5.2.137–40, F)

Alternatively, editors could rearrange (as in Arden 3):

       To this extremity. Thy husband knew it all.
   EMILIA   My husband?
   OTHELLO   Thy husband.
   EMILIA   That she was false?
       To wedlock?
   OTHELLO   Ay, with Cassio. Had she been true, . . .

In both (3) and (4) editors who re-line as verse introduce a new emphasis: 'Then heaven / Have mercy on me!' differs from 'Then heaven have mercy on me!', inserting a slight pause after 'heaven' (which could mean that 'Have mercy on me!' appeals to heaven *and* to Othello). The rearrangement in (4), bringing with it a slightly heavier pause, and in effect dividing one question into two, may seem to be a more drastic 'emendation', but is it really? Once we recall that the QF punctuation (and particularly F's) has little or no authority, and that Shakespeare never indicates the line division of verse lines divided into three or more speeches, the all-important fact must be that both (3) and (4) are preceded and followed by verse and themselves divide into unexceptional verse. Editors have failed to print (3) and (4) as verse, I suspect, not because there are good reasons for not doing so but because they suffer from a contagious disease known as editorial inertia.

All the more curious, then, that editors who cannot bring themselves to print (1) to (4) as verse none the less print verse lines such as the following.

(5)   The Moore replies,
    That he you hurt is of great Fame in Cyprus,
    And great Affinitie: and that in wholsome Wisedome
    He might not but refuse you. But he protests he loues you
                            (3.1.45–9, F)

(6)   She was a Charmer, and could almost read
    The thoughts of people. She told her, while she kept it,
    'Twould make her Amiable, and subdue my Father
    Intirely to her loue: But if she lost it,
                            (3.4.59–62, F)

Cambridge 1–3 copy F's lineation. Whether or not I am correct in suggesting that 'And great Affinitie' (5) should be considered a deletion in the manuscript that was printed in error (see p. 37), which would give this passage a 'regular' syllable count, the fact is that the same editors think (5) and (6) acceptable as verse, but not the rearranged verse lines of (1) to (4)! Perhaps, though, this is not so very curious after all, for it could be said that there is consistency behind this inconsistency – again, editorial inertia. Many editors retain F's lineation in (5) and (6), there is safety in numbers, so why bother to ask whether it is consistent to hold that Shakespeare could have written (5) and (6) and at the same time to repudiate (1) to (4) as unsatisfactory iambic pentameters?

   We can dispose of this uncomfortable question by stressing that the versification of *Othello*, though much more 'regular' than Cambridge 1 and many modern texts would lead one to believe, was nevertheless experimental and variable. Shakespeare was at the height of his powers; he knew that his colleagues, the actors, would not trip up on metrically unusual lines: I am willing to believe that he enjoyed innovation, including metrical innovation, and that he delighted in bending and stretching his metre.

(7)   He hath a dayly beauty in his life,
    That makes me vgly: and besides, the Moore
    May vnfold me to him: there stand I in much perill
                            (5.1.19–21, F)

Is the last line metrically irregular? Not if syllables are contracted or slurred, as they often have to be in the theatre: 'May ûnfold me tô hîm' or 'May 'nfold me to'm, there stand I in much peril'. The line can count as a 'regular' iambic pentameter: it is unusual, to be sure – like so much else in *Othello* – and shows how innovative and elastic Shakespeare's metre may be, at this stage of his career. Sceptics should compare *A Game at Chess*, Q3, where the half-line 'Ide teare 'em from my heart' (T, 1382) appears as 'Il'd teare 'm from my heart': Q3 here has 'regular' metre, and proves that -*m* could be a non-syllabic contraction. Similarly Q3 'strike 'm groueling' (1952; T: 'em).

*   *   *

The suggestion that Ralph Crane prepared the manuscript used as copy for F *Othello*, and the inference drawn from Crane's transcripts of *A Game at Chess* that he might introduce or cancel elisions, gives editors more freedom than they have dared to claim in the past. It remains true, however, that F's lineation errs less frequently, and less calamitously, than Q's and should be retained whenever the syllable count supports it.

Before I try to show how radically we may have to depart from 'traditional' texts in order to return to the lineation probably intended by Shakespeare, I must question a statement quoted in the opening paragraph of this chapter. 'Metrical white space' was not invented in the eighteenth century, even if refined then and imposed more systematically on play-texts than ever before. A verse line involving three speeches or parts of speeches might not be immediately recognisable as verse in a text dating from Shakespeare's lifetime: but one involving two speeches should have presented no problems to an experienced reader.

> To bring me to him.
> *Officer.* 'Tis true most worthy Signior,
> The Dukes in Counsell, and your Noble selfe,
> I am sure is sent for.
> *Bra.* How? The Duke in Counsell?
>
> (1.2.91–3, F)

The second element that completes the verse line may not be indented to start one space beyond the end of the previous speech, as in modern texts; nevertheless, Shakespeare and his first readers knew, as assuredly as we know it today, that such half-lines, taken together, form iambic pentameters. Metrical 'white space' is visible at the end of each half-line (although some dramatists, including Ben Jonson, wrote the second half-line on the same line as the first half-line, visually marking the completeness of the pentameter in a different way).

This may seem all too obvious. If so, consider the second and third speech in *Othello*, as printed in two influential editions.

> (1)   *Ia.* But you'l not heare me: If euer I did dream
> Of such a matter, abhorre me.
> *Rodo.* Thou told'st me,
> Thou did'st hold him in thy hate.
> *Iago.* Despise me
> If I do not. Three Great-ones of the Cittie,
>
> (F)

> (2)   *Iago.* Sblood, but you will not hear me:
> If ever I did dream of such a matter,
> Abhor me.
> *Rod.* Thou told'st me thou didst hold him in thy hate.

Iago.   Despise me, if I do not. Three great ones of the city,
                                                        (Cambridge 1)

Cambridge 1 follows the lineation of Q, except that in Q 'Abhor me' was tagged on at the end of the preceding line. As a result Cambridge 1 prints three metrically irregular lines in a total of five – extraordinary, at the very beginning of a verse play. F, more trustworthy than Q in lineation (though by no means always so), prints four 'regular' pentameters, clearly marked by white spaces; one, the third, appears to put its stresses on the wrong syllables ('Thou didst hold him in thy hate. Despise me' – viz. three stressed and seven unstressed syllables), yet can be read differently if delivered very fast, as is necessary in this heated exchange.

Of such a matter, abhor me! – Thou told'st me
Thou didst hold him in thy hate! – Despise me
If I do not!

I assume that 'Sblood' stood at one stage in the F text but can be discounted metrically, like other expletives (see p. 105). Why, then, print three irregular lines out of five, rather than five regular lines, which is what the Folio clearly directs?

For very similar scansion, with just a single strong stress in a verse line, compare

O fie upon thee, strumpet!
                                    I am no strumpet
But of life as honest as you, that thus
Abuse me.
                    As I? Foh, fie upon thee!
                    (Arden 3, 5.1.121–3)

This is another heated exchange, and can be scanned

O fie upon thee, strumpet!
                                    I'm no strumpet
But of life as honest as you, that thus
Abuse me.
                    As I? Foh, fie upon thee!

These passages show, perhaps more clearly than any others in the play, the fundamental difference between a 'syllabic' and a 'stress-based' verse line. The Cambridge 1 lineation ('Arranged as by Steevens (1793)') was perpetuated by Cambridge 2 and 3, by Arden 2, Riverside and many more. World, world, O world! Thy strange mutations make us hate thee . . .

*   *   *

Much depends, then, on the editor's lineation. And lineation depends, in many instances, on elision, since the editor can make lines metrically regular by adjusting contractable syllables – printing *I am* as *I'm*, or *I'm* as *I am*. We now reach a question (I have been circling around it) that can no longer be avoided: should editors adjust contractable syllables in this way? Is it defensible? Is it necessary?

Trained actors instinctively run together or separate syllables when they feel that this is required by the metre. And untrained readers? Should the editor 'adjust', for their benefit? In *Othello* this would involve changing a very large number of readings (I have picked out and commented on only a few representative passages). The day will come, I think, when editors of modernised texts may make these changes, perhaps as a matter of course. After all, such an editor wants to help the modern reader; if he tidies speech prefixes and stage directions, and 'translates' the language from Elizabethan to modern English, he could be accused of half-hearted or inconsistent modernisation should he refuse to give similar help with scansion – that is, with the speaking of the verse.

The day may come, but has not yet come. The suggestion that scribes and compositors and Shakespeare himself often treated *I am* and *I'm* and all contractable combinations as interchangeable, either longer or shorter, will have to be scrutinised by others before we can act upon it. The textual implications are too far-reaching; before we 'adjust' scores of readings in *Othello*, and in other plays where the same principles apply, we had better be sure of our ground. Would it be reasonable to say 'I've done the state some service, and they know it' (5.2.337; QF: 'I haue done the State some seruice, and they know't')? Will the world be grateful? The verdict, of course, cannot be given in isolation. All the other lines in which *I have* scans more smoothly as *I've* will have to be taken into account (see p. 112), and also the *I have–I've* preferences of Ralph Crane, of the Q and F compositors, and of Shakespeare himself, as far as we can ascertain them. Then, if adjustment still seems reasonable, the time will have come for thinking more precisely on the event (or th'event).

On the face of it, 'adjustment' seems necessary, for the benefit of beginners and for the sake of consistent modernisation. But there are also disadvantages. What of the large number of other words that could be monosyllabic or dissyllabic (see p. 104, and add common words such as devil, evil, power, spirit, etc.), and indeed all the variable syllables listed by Abbott (§459–92)? Should the editor mark *every* elision? Would that not be to swim against the current of 'modern spelling', by multiplying quaint words such as giv'n, heav'n, pow'r etc.? It is a further difficulty that both Q and F mark some but not all possible elisions of many words.

(1)   E[u]en on the instant.
      Othello.   What is the matter, thinke you?
                  (1.2.38, F)

(2)   And it is still it selfe.
      Duke.   Why? What's the matter?
                (1.3.59, F)

'What is the matter' and 'What's the matter' is a question that echoes through the play. In (1) Q has 'What's the matter' and F would be hypermetrical if 'What is' counts as two syllables. Quite clearly, neither Shakespeare nor his scribes and compositors aimed at consistency in this kind of detail. Should the editor accept the reading of his chosen text? If he prefers to adjust, where will adjustment end?

An even stronger argument against marking some or all elisions in a modern-spelling text runs as follows. (1) No one knows exactly how Shakespeare's verse was spoken. 'Contractable' syllables might count as one syllable or as none or, if slurred, as something in between. (2) While Shakespeare is said to have 'instructed' his actors in their parts,[16] he no doubt listened to their views as well and accepted, like every man of the theatre, that there are many possible ways of speaking a verse line, with different pauses and stresses, different pitch and speed of delivery. Elision is just one of many variables, and would have to remain adjustable (rather than editorially 'adjusted', i.e. firmly fixed) in the light of all the others. (3) Even if modern readers stumble when they first encounter some of Shakespeare's seemingly irregular verse lines, it is better to force them to scan for themselves, thus driving home the point that Shakespeare's scansion should be considered more variable than a printed page normally suggests. Naturally the editor must warn readers that they have this freedom and this responsibility. (4) Should the editor take it upon himself to mark all possible elisions, or all that will convert a seemingly irregular verse line into one that would count as regular, he could easily go too far. Do we wish to put the verse into a metrical strait-jacket, imposing a monotonous regularity on every line? Are we certain that this is what Shakespeare wanted?

The editor of Arden 3, steering or drifting as indicated in the previous paragraphs, adopts a *laissez-faire* policy, yet thinks it right to take some decisions into his own hands. *Othello*, in Arden 3, follows F as control text but accepts Q readings, especially where 'contractable' words are concerned, when Q gives regular metre and F fails in this respect. Again, if the syllable count, language and context justify it, *Othello* breaks with 'copy-cat' editing by printing as verse passages traditionally printed as prose. These decisions bring surprises in the lineation of some of the most familiar speeches in the play. They depend on assumptions laid out and defended in this chapter, which I shall restate. (1) Verse and prose are often very much alike in the play, deliberately so. (2) Though some 'pentameters' are scarcely iambic, the preceding and following lines indicate that verse is intended. (3) In such lines the syllable count rather than the iambic rhythm is the decisive factor. (4) Accepting the ten- and eleven-syllable line as the play's standard measure, we find that *Othello* contains a much smaller number of long and short lines, and many more regular verse lines, than are printed in other editions. (5) We find, also, that both Q and F often preserve 'regular' verse lines even when they go off the rails in their lineation. This is reassuring, for it suggests that mislined passages suffer from superficial wounds that can be cured and, after almost four hundred years, can still be made 'perfect of their limbs'.

Chapter 11

Punctuation

If, as suggested in the previous chapter, the metre and line division of *Othello* need to be carefully reconsidered, the same is true of the play's punctuation. Not because every generation uses or misuses punctuation in its own way, but because later editions have been much influenced by the Folio, and the Folio punctuation for *Othello* is so often demonstrably erroneous.

How faithfully did Jaggard's compositors follow the punctuation in their copy? The attentive reader may recall two seemingly different views: D.F. McKenzie found 'some 715 changes' in the punctuation of a reprinted play,[1] and Gary Taylor counted twelve punctuation changes on one Folio page of a reprinted play[2] which, if a representative page, would yield a total of 264 for the play. McKenzie, of course, examined one of the 'Pavier' quartos of 1619, while Taylor chose a later text, one set by another compositor, the apprentice E. The two different figures should not surprise us, since compositor E is known to have followed copy more closely than did more experienced men: they illustrate an inevitable divergence, one to be expected in any printing house, and the only surprising thing is that E, who was inclined to be conservative, introduced so many changes.

The figures supplied by McKenzie and Taylor only tell us how faithfully Jaggard's men followed *printed* copy. It is more than likely that when they set from a manuscript they changed the punctuation even more drastically. If, however, they set from a manuscript prepared by Ralph Crane we can be certain that the author's punctuation will have been changed beyond recognition before the compositors ever clapped eyes on it. Crane had firm views about textual accidentals – spelling, punctuation, capitalisation, etc. – and did not hesitate to 'improve' a text when he transcribed it. Shakespeare's autograph texts, it is generally agreed, were very lightly punctuated, as in the good quartos and in Hand D of *Sir Thomas More*;[3] the heavy punctuation of F *Othello* can be confidently assigned to Crane and compositors B and E – which is another way of saying that it inspires no confidence whatsoever.

Since we have figures for punctuation changes made by compositors B and E, let us add some equally arresting figures for Ralph Crane. Taking just the first hundred lines of Act 1 scene 1 of *A Game at Chess*, and comparing them in

Middleton's holograph (T) and Crane's Lansdowne transcript (L), we observe the following differences: (1) Crane's changes in punctuation, 52; (2) Crane's added punctuation, 54; (3) identical punctuation, 20. For the first hundred lines of Act 2: (1) changes, 51; (2) added, 50; (3) identical, 36. For the first hundred lines of Act 3: (1) changes, 59; (2) added, 41; (3) identical, 21. These should be taken as approximate figures, for several reasons: Crane's colon and semicolon are often indistinguishable, as are his question and exclamation marks; because of the fineness of Crane's pen strokes, some commas and stops do not appear on microfilm (I used the original in the British Library), and some are not easy to distinguish from imperfections in the paper. My count includes commas, stops, colons, semicolons, question and exclamation marks, dashes and brackets (a pair of brackets counted as one). The 'retained' punctuation consists largely of commas; Crane added and changed to heavier punctuation, especially colons. He also introduced many apostrophes and some hyphens (not included in my count).

Except for his distinctive brackets, Crane's punctuation is not easy to differentiate from that of the Folio compositors, and, as we have seen (p. 60), even Crane's brackets are not always a reliable indicator of his presence. A glance at his transcripts of *The Witch, Barnavelt* and *Demetrius* immediately confirms that Crane shared the Folio compositors' inclination to punctuate heavily, including their partiality for colons. Whether such similarities should be ascribed to Crane's 'editorial' presence in the Folio (see p. 73) or to a change of fashion as between Shakespeare's 'good' texts (most of which were written and/or printed in the 1590s) and the various 'Crane' transcripts and the First Folio (all of which cluster close to the year 1623), it is at present impossible to say. We can say, though, that Crane and the Folio compositors will have superimposed completely inauthentic layers of punctuation on Shakespeare's manuscript of *Othello* and that, even if we cannot distinguish Crane's from that of the compositors, we should take all Folio punctuation with a pinch of salt, especially all heavy punctuation.

The same warning applies to Q *Othello*. Being the last of the good quartos, its punctuation is heavier than that of its predecessors and, we have to repeat, the more heavy the less confidence-inspiring. At least some of its colons must derive from the Q manuscript, though not therefore from Shakespeare.

(1)   Twould make her amiable, and subdue my father
       Intirely to her loue: But if she lost it

                                (3.4.61–2)

Line 62 was accidentally printed twice, as the last line of sheet H and as the first of sheet I: we may assume that the colon stood in the manuscript. (2) Again, if I am right in thinking that the Q scribe rather than the Q compositor had difficulties in deciphering illegible writing, and misread 'thee' and 'thy' (p. 85, group [xv] [b]), it follows that the Q scribe inserted a colon after 'cause':

For thy solliciter shall rather die,
Then giue *thee cause: away.*
> (3.3.27–8; *thy cause away.* F)

More heavily punctuated than earlier good quartos, Q must be post-autho-rial in much of its pointing. Either the Q scribe or the compositor – again it hardly matters that we cannot always tell them apart – or, more probably, both scribe and compositor, added to Shakespeare's light punctuation, with the result that Q can look as 'post-Shakespearian' as F.

(a)   That's not amisse:
But yet keepe time in all; will you withdraw?
Now will I question Cassio of Bianca;
A huswife that by selling her desires,
Buys her selfe bread and cloathes: it is a Creature,
That dotes on Cassio: as tis the strumpets plague
To beguile many, and be beguild by one,
He, when he heares of her, cannot refraine
From the excesse of laughter: here he comes:
> (4.1.92 ff., Q)

(b)   That's not amisse,
But yet keepe time in all: will you withdraw?
Now will I question Cassio of Bianca,
A Huswife that by selling her desires
Buyes her selfe Bread, and Cloath. It is a Creature
That dotes on Cassio, (as 'tis the Strumpets plague
To be-guile many, and be be-guil'd by one)
He, when he heares of her, cannot restraine
From the excesse of Laughter. Heere he comes.
> (F)

The Folio, however, is more consistently 'heavy' in punctuation, whereas Q sometimes intersperses lightly pointed passages or speeches and a surprising number of dashes (see p. 46): it appears that each printed text inherited or created special problems.

The Q and F texts are alike in interpolating punctuation where it is not needed. First, some Q errors:

(1) (a) 'I will tell *thee, this* Desdemona is directly in loue with him' (2.1.216 ff.; *thee this:* F); (b) 'there should be againe to inflame it, and giue saciety a fresh appetite. Louelines in fauour' (2.1.225 ff.; F copied the stop after *appetite*, modern editors emend QF [see p. 100]); (c) 'I haue rubd this young gnat almost to the sense, / And he grows *angry now*: whether he kill Cassio' (5.1.11–12; *angry. Now* F). In such passages we see the scribe or compositor, puzzled by an underpunctuated text, inserting a comma, stop and colon in the wrong

place. (d) At other times Q fails to insert punctuation, probably again because the A or Aa manuscript was underpunctuated: 'Ha you stor'd *me well.*' (4.1.127; *me? Well* F).

(2) F deserves more attention, having had a more harmful effect on subsequent editions. Intrusive punctuation again reveals that the scribe or a compositor, dissatisfied by a lightly pointed text, officiously interpolated commas, etc., in the wrong places.

(a) *Intrusive commas*

(1)   Let vs be coniunctiue in our reuenge, against him
                                    (1.3.368–9)

(2)   Must bring this monstrous Birth, to the worlds light
                                    (1.3.403)

(3)   It giues me wonder great, as my content
                                    (2.1.181)

(4)   Iago, is most honest:
          (2.3.6)

(5)   And would, in Action glorious, I had lost
                                    (2.3.182)

(6)   Th'immortall Ioues dread Clamours, counterfet,
                                    (3.3.359)

(b) *Intrusive semi-colons and colons*[4]

(1)   Vnlesse the Bookish Theoricke:
          Wherein the Tongued Consuls can propose
                                    (1.1.23 ff.)

(2)   You shall marke
          Many a dutious and knee-crooking knaue;
          That (doting on his owne obsequious bondage)
                                    (1.1.43 ff.)

(3)   I haue't: it is engendred: Hell, and Night,
          Must bring this monstrous Birth, to the worlds light.
                                    (1.3.403)

(4)   I am not bound to that: All Slaues are free:
                                    (3.3.138)

(5)   *Oth.*   I gaue her such a one: 'twas my first gift.
          Iago.   I know not that: but such a Handkerchiefe
                                    (3.3.439–40)

(6)   To the felt-Absence: now I feele a Cause:
                                    (3.4.182)

The degree to which F's scribe or compositor misunderstood the text, and made matters worse by adding punctuation, sometimes emerges from Q, as in 4 (above), where Q reads 'I am not bound to that all slaues are free to,'.

(c) *Intrusive stops and question marks*[5]

(1)   It is a iudgement main'd, and most imperfect.
      That will confesse Perfection so could erre
$$(1.3.100-1)$$

(2)   I pray you heare her speake?
$$(1.3.175)$$

(3)   hath to night Carrows'd.
      Potations, pottle-deepe; and he's to watch.
$$(2.3.50-1)$$

(4)   I am sorry to heare this?
$$(3.3.347)$$

Some erroneous punctuation marks may be ascribed to 'foul case', but quite often one sees that a simple misunderstanding explains it − as when sentences beginning with 'Why' or 'What' are changed into questions.

(5)   *Duke.*   Why at her Fathers?
$$(1.3.241)$$

(6)   Why? But you are now well enough: how came you thus recouered?
$$(2.3.289-90)$$

(7)   What man? 'Tis a night of Reuels
$$(2.3.40)$$

Compare Q:

(5)   *Du.*   If you please, bee't at her fathers.

(6)   Why, but you are now well enough . . .

(7)   What man, tis a night of Reuells

   Although future editors may prefer Q's punctuation as more authentic than F's, generations of editors have regarded the Folio as the 'better text' and, when in doubt, have chosen to follow it. One of the differences between the two texts is that F is much more positive, imposing stops that rule out all readings except one, whereas Q sometimes omits punctuation, as Shakespeare evidently did, leaving open a choice of readings. The two versions of (b) (4) (p. 130) reveal how disastrously the more positive method can go astray, and the benefits of not tampering with punctuation. F's officiousness may misrepresent the author's intention even when it produces possible punctuation, since often there are other possibilities: the fact that F has chosen one gives editors the comfortable feeling that it must be the right one, which is far from certain. When we learn that F's punctuation was imposed by Ralph Crane, who punctuated in his own idiosyncratic way, and by the Folio compositors, who are known to have changed punctuation in hundreds of readings per play, we cannot be optimistic about F's faithfulness to the author's original copy; moreover, common QF errors in punctuation, as in placing a stop after *appetite* (2.1.226 ff., p. 100 above), warn us to be cautious even when F agrees with Q. Or, to put it less timidly: editors should mistrust all F punctuation whenever a possible alternative suggests itself.

Quite apart from manifest errors, there are more than enough reasons for mistrusting F's punctuation. Too many different agents had a hand in it – is this not perhaps a case of irretrievable corruption? Not so: we can go back to Shakespeare's own papers, on the assumption that they contained very little pointing – we can strip away F's punctuation, leaving only the words, and then we can cast around for other possibilities.

(1)   *Oth.*   Peace and be still
        Desd.   I will so what's the matter
                    (5.2.46–7)

F punctuates 'I will so:', Q has 'I will, so,' which suggests that F divides the line in the wrong place. Desdemona overcomes her agitation, forcing herself to sit still, and then asks Othello to go on: 'I will. So: what's the matter?'

(2)   *Oth.*   What hath he said
        Iag.   Why that he did I know not what he did
        Oth.   What what
        Iag.   Lie
        Oth.   With her
        Iag.   With her on her what you will
                    (4.1.31 ff.)

Line 32 was printed '*Iago.* Why, that he did: I know not what he did.' (F), and '*Iag.* Faith that he did – I know not what he did.' (Q). Now the stop after 'did' could signify an interruption, as after 'Lye' and often elsewhere. In this instance both Q and F may have missed an opportunity to insert a necessary stop, where Shakespeare's 'underpunctuated' line requires it. Iago plays his usual game, hinting and not completing his thought, as in the tantalising 'Lye.' and at 3.3.34 ff., 93 ff.; line 32 could therefore be printed 'Faith, that he did – I know not what. He did –' (he breaks off, implying not that he doesn't know, but that he cannot bring himself to say what Cassio did).

(3)   We must not now displease him
        Emil.   I would you had never seen him
        Desd.   So would not I my love doth so approve him
                    (4.3.15–17)

Line 16 begins 'I, would you' (F) and 'I would you' (Q). Remembering that
'ay' was commonly spelt 'I', we may ask whether F's comma signals a heavier
stop – '*Emil.* Ay. – Would you had never seen him!' (a 'double take' by
Emilia, who first agrees, then vigorously changes tack. Orally these alternatives might be almost indistinguishable).

(4)   *Oth.*   Amen to that sweet powers
          I cannot speak enough of this content
          It stops me here it is too much of joy
                         (2.1.193–5)

Both Q and F print 'I cannot speake enough of this content', and editors have
followed this punctuation. Since Q and F add intrusive stops and also omit
necessary stops, we ought to consider an alternative to l. 194 – 'I cannot
speak. Enough of this content!' (picking up l. 181, 'It gives me wonder great
as my content', and l. 189). Whatever 'speak enough of' may mean, the
alternative seems to me at least equally plausible and, in view of the shaky
basis of QF punctuation, no less 'authoritative'. Editors should warn readers
of the existence of such concealed alternatives, instead of treating Q and F as
sacrosanct. In many cases the finality of print will appear to 'privilege' the
editor's choice even though he or she feels no corresponding certainty.

Whether accepted or not, these examples illustrate the possible consequences
of Shakespeare's light punctuation: either a scribe or compositor might
add stops in the wrong place, or stops were not clearly marked where they
should have been had the Folio's system of punctuation been applied consistently. Shakespeare's own punctuation (and to some extent Q's) could not
mislead in quite the same way, since it held out no promise of consistency.
But unfortunately F's detailed and heavy punctuation may impress readers
as definitive, even though – as is evident from its many errors – it has no
authority whatever and, all too often, ought to be rejected as unintelligent
guessing.

Comparing Shakespeare's light punctuation with the Folio and all subsequent editions, we can go one step further. All systematically applied grammatical punctuation must mislead, by pre-empting choices: not only because a
scribe, compositor or editor may choose badly but because, in the act of
choosing, he eliminates the possibility of other options, whereas Shakespeare,
writing scripts for actors, preferred not do so. Consider this exchange:

   Bra.   Thou art a Villaine.
   Iago.   You are a Senator.
              (1.1.116, F)

Q's punctuation is identical. In a modern-spelling edition I am tempted to
print 'You are – a senator!' or '*You* are . . . a senator!' Yet this pointing could
be criticised for excluding other equally attractive possibilities: '*You* . . . are a
senator!' or '*You* are a . . . senator!' Four words, three possible pauses, several

possible intonations: Shakespeare left these things open, the Folio and later editions usually incline the other way.

Tidy grammatical punctuation imposes a structure on Shakespeare's dramatic dialogue that, I suspect, was never intended. Just as ordinary conversation includes unfinished sentences, clauses that hang loose from the grammatical structure and non-verbal elements, Shakespeare's dialogue often breaks away from 'correct' grammar, and an editor who wishes to help readers by adding punctuation – as in the Folio and its derivatives – actually changes Shakespeare's language qualitatively, pegging down its free flow or its unexpected jumps from one thing to another, making it proceed instead in too orderly a fashion. Exactly like 'amphibious' half-lines that belong metrically with either the preceding or the following half-line (see p. 106), some groups of words are free-floating in the grammar of theatre language.

(1)   I would not haue your free, and Noble Nature,
       Out of selfe-Bounty, be abus'd: Looke too't:
       I know our Country disposition well:
                    (3.3.202–4, F)

Q has 'Out of selfe-bounty be abus'd, looke to't:'. Some editors follow Q, linking 'look to't' to what goes before; others connect it with the next line – 'Out of self-bounty be abused; look to't:', or persist with two heavy stops, as in F. Yet another possibility, in the theatre if not in a modern printed text, is that 'look to't' is part of 203 *and* of 204, lightly linked to both rather than firmly disconnected from both.

(2)   Why, there's no remedie.
       'Tis the cursse of Seruice;
       Preferment goes by Letter, and affection,
                    (1.1.34 ff., F)

Q has 'But there's no remedy, / Tis the curse of seruice, /' and, I believe, more accurately reflects the author's manuscript. F's heavy punctuation disjoins ''tis the curse of service'; Q's light punctuation has the opposite effect.

Modern punctuation, like the Folio's, misrepresents the fluidity of Shakespeare's dramatic dialogue. He lived at a time when English punctuation was not standardised, any more than English spelling, and he was more free than later writers to innovate. Hooking one clause or sentence into or onto another can be as much a personal idiosyncrasy as a writer's imagery, and Shakespeare's individualism is as unmistakable here as in all the other arts of language. His dramatic speakers jump from one thought to another without always explaining how, and the audience has to fill in what is missing (just as it has to tease out unspoken motives).

The Folio's heavy punctuation fills in these ellipses visually; a colon can thus have the force of a conjunction (and, therefore, because, for example), although editors may assign to it the force of a 'disjunction'.

(1)   After some time, to abuse Othello's eares,
      That he is too familiar with his wife:
      He hath a person, and a smooth dispose
      To be suspected: fram'd to make women false
                              (1.3.394–7, F)

(2)   I kist thee, ere I kill'd thee: No way but this,
      Killing my selfe, to dye vpon a kisse
                              (5.2.356–7, F)

We may fill in as follows: (1) . . . [this is plausible because] he has a person and an insinuating disposition that invites suspicion [because so obviously] framed to make women false; (2) I kissed thee before I killed thee, [therefore there is] no way but this. Whatever its shortcomings, such a paraphrase indicates that very often Shakespeare's language was responsible for the Folio's colons, even if his hand did not write them.

Our difficulties with Shakespeare's punctuation all trace back to the first 'consumers' for whose use his texts were prepared. His own foul papers and fair copies were intended for his colleagues, actors who needed 'performance scripts'; the Folio texts were revised, at considerable expense, as a set of 'reading texts' for the general public. In an ideal world one would like to see modern performance scripts as lightly pointed as the good quartos, or entirely without punctuation, for the benefit of modern actors; in the less than ideal world of 'modernised texts' we have to put up with some punctuation, but should warn purchasers that many editorial decisions must remain doubtful, and that the very existence of punctuation in modern texts is regrettable, if not indeed reprehensible.[6]

Chapter 12

Some conclusions

The new information contained in this book has prompted guesses and arguments of various hues, sometimes supporting what others have said and sometimes, it may be thought, merely bold or reckless. Cross-references to earlier or later chapters have shown, I hope, that most of the arguments interlock with evidence presented elsewhere. What seems possible at one point may become probable in the light of later information. I propose, next, to reassess some of the arguments that have gone before, noting how they hang together and also how they may contradict one another. Finally, having outlined some of the strengths and weaknesses of *The Texts of 'Othello'*, I shall consider the implications for an editor of the play, not least for the editor of Arden 3. These implications could apply to other plays as well: if, as I believe, we now know more about the pre-printing history of F *Othello* than about that of any other F text, we can begin to speculate about F's editorial procedures, which are likely to have been similar to those adopted for other F texts, and perhaps not only 'Crane' texts.

INDIFFERENT VARIANTS

I have touched on 'indifferent variants' in several chapters without firmly grasping this nettle, a major irritation for all editors of two-text plays. When the two texts offer alternatives of equal merit, readings not significantly different and both acceptable, these are described as indifferent variants (either because the editor cannot honestly express a preference, or because it matters very little which he chooses). Examples from *Othello* include: these–those, the–that, singular plural, tense changes or, from Act 1 scene 1, you will–you'l 4, chosen–chose 16, the–th' 26, Christian–Christen'd 29, But–Why 34, be all–all be 42, does–doth 60, you are–y'are 85, worse–worsser 94, etc. Editors normally solve this problem by declaring one of the two texts to be 'the better text' and simply following the better text whenever they encounter indifferent variants – a solution not unlike that of editors of classical texts who follow the most trustworthy manuscript when 'the judgement is helpless'. In the words of A.E. Housman:

Since we have found P the most trustworthy MS. in places where its fidelity can be tested, we infer that it is also the most trustworthy in places where no test can be applied . . . . A critic therefore, when he employs this method of trusting the best MS., employs it in the same spirit of gloomy resignation with which a man lies down on a stretcher when he has broken both his legs.[1]

The notion of a 'better text' brings its own problems, however, as W. W. Greg explained.

> to say that one text contains twice as many errors as another tells us next to nothing about their relative accuracy, unless we also know the frequency of variation . . . . Even if there were on an average one *variant* in every blank-verse line (of about eight words), the texts would still have respectively 96 and 92 per cent of the *words* correct, and their relative accuracy would not be in the ratio of 2:1 but of 24:23, which is after all pretty close.[2]

Editors who reject 170 readings from F *Othello* and 500 from Q (as they used to do, in round numbers) should not call F 'the better text' but, more accurately, 'the very slightly better text'. Once we add that some of Q's rejected readings may well be not corruptions but authorial in origin, replaced in F by authorial revision, the notion of a 'better text' becomes even more dubious.

Before we lie down on Housman's stretcher, imagining that we have not a leg to stand on, let us attend to another group of indifferent variants, one discussed in an earlier chapter (p. 69): Q it, F 't; Q the, F th'; Q murder, F murther; Q ashore, abed, atwane, etc., F on shore, in bed, in twain; Q has, F hath (22 instances). These are indifferent variants, no less so than the–that, singular–plural, and in these cases I am tempted to follow the supposedly inferior text, Q, since there are good reasons for thinking that F's variants were substituted by the F scribe, Ralph Crane.

Crane's arrival on the scene as a not wholly negligible factor in the transmission of F *Othello* discredits the notion of the 'better text' even more, if that is possible, in so far as the supposedly 'better text', F, turns out to be particularly untrustworthy in some of its indifferent variants and in its punctuation, two areas where editors have traditionally preferred F to Q. To pin down a fallacy that has had a long innings in textual theory and editorial practice: the evidence of 'substantive' variants, even should it point decisively to one manuscript or printed version as the better text, is not always relevant when the editor has to choose between indifferent variants, because substantive and indifferent variants were not necessarily copied with the same fidelity.[3]

How should we proceed? We know next to nothing about the scribe or scribes responsible for Q *Othello*. And, since compositor studies have concentrated on a limited range of spelling tests, we have scarcely made a start on a closely related problem, the treatment of indifferent variants by compositors, yet this could be the way forward. Take these QF variants from *Othello* (Q cited first):

(1)   For when my outward action *does* demonstrate
                                    (1.1.60; *doth* F)

(2)   Zounds sir *you are* robd
                    (1.1.85; *y'are* F)

(3)   What will I doe *thinkest* thou?
                    (1.3.304; *think'st* F)

(4)   continue her loue *vnto* the Moore
                        (1.3.343; *to* F)

(5)   *Ye* men of Cypres, let her haue your knees
                                (2.1.84; *You* F)

(6)   *An* you'll come to supper . . . *an* you will not
                            (4.1.157–8; *If . . . if* F)

(7)   If any wretch *ha* put this in your head
                            (4.2.15; *haue* F)

Most of these indifferent variants occur many times in *Othello*, and in other Shakespeare plays, and they are only a fraction of the total that needs investigation. The Folio variants, usually adopted by editors in preference to Q's, being the readings of 'the better text', may well be compositorial substitutions – or so I suspect from the substitution of identical variants in the Pavier quartos of 1619, most of which were straight reprints and came from the same printing house as the Folio.[4]

(1) *does* > *doth*: compare *Lear* 996, 2032; *Pericles* 1.2.44, 4.3.29; *Yorkshire Tragedy* 2.144.
(2) *you are* > *y'are*: compare *3 Henry VI* 1.1.108; *Oldcastle* 3.157, 4.104, 7.196, 16.28, 18.1; *Merchant of Venice* 5.1.151.
(3) *-est* > *st*: compare *Lear* 154, 2287, 2335; *3 Henry VI* 1.1.116, 2.1.24, 5.1.77.
(4) *vnto* > *to*: compare *2 Henry VI* 1.3.21; *Oldcastle* 14.40, 15.32.
(5) *ye* > *you*: compare *Pericles* 4.2.120; *Henry V* 2.2.104; *Oldcastle* 6.22, 7.53, 11.93, 12.17, 13.8, 22.40, 80.
(6) *and* > *if*: compare *Merry Wives* 1.4.19, 26; 2.2.131; 3.5.6, 13; *Lear* 622, 988, 1156, 2460; *3 Henry VI* 4.6.12, 5.1.46; *Merchant of Venice* 2.4.11.
(7) *ha* > *haue*: compare *Pericles* 4.6.61; *Merry Wives* 2.1.56; also *a* > *haue* (*Henry V* 2.2.79).

Some such substitutions look like modernisation (*an* > *if*), yet others switch to the less 'modern' form (*does* > *doth*). When we learn that the same texts sometimes reverse their substitutions, a different explanation suggests itself.

(5b) *you* > *ye*: compare *Pericles* 1.2.35; *2 Henry VI* 3.2.70, 4.2.60, 63; *3 Henry VI* 2.2.104, 4.4.3; *Oldcastle* 2.144, 3.169, 4.71, 4.89, 14.3.

In at least some cases these variants seem to signify not a compositorial preference but compositorial indifference; that is, the compositors thought of the 'variants' as alternative spellings of the same word, like *do–doe* or *battell–battaile*, even though the change might appear to involve a syllabic difference (*you are: y'are, -est: 'st*). The same conclusion can be drawn when closely related variants are reversed, as in *King Lear* (1619), where *hath* becomes *has* (1708, 2985) but *does* becomes *doth* (996, 2032).

Nevertheless, compositors and texts do suffer from preferences, as well as indifference. *King Lear* (1619), a reprint, introduces a number of indifferent variants that are related to similar substitutions in the First Folio. Abbreviations were expanded, as compared with *King Lear* (1608), as follows:[5]

Compositor changes (1619)

(1) Pronoun and auxiliary verb (e.g. *you'l* > *you will*): 497, 971, 1569, 2401, 3048. (2) Preposition and 'the' (e.g. *it'h* > *in the*): 607, 608, 916, 1113(2), 1114, 1265, 1629, 1810, 2249, 2452, 2773.
(3) *'s* > *his* (e.g. *on's* > *on his*): 565, 765, 828.
(4) *'t* > *it* (e.g. *into't* > *into it*): 538, 584, 1005, 1018, 1124, 1125, 1550, 1576, 1815, 2564.

Despite a few indications to the contrary (*does* > *doth*, *-est* > *'st*), the main thrust of the substitutions in *King Lear* (1619) is away from the old-fashioned or colloquial towards the more modern or formal, as also in other changes such as (5) *a* > *he* (525, 766, 1705, 1992) and (6) *and* > *if* (see p. 53).

The preferences of F *Othello* go in the opposite direction from *King Lear* for (1) to (4), compared with Q *Othello*, or are less clear-cut.

F *Othello* preferences

(1) Pronoun and auxiliary verb shortened (e.g. *you will* > *you'l*): 1.1.4, 85; 2.3.151, 159; 3.3.121, 126, 221, 228; 3.4.16; 4.1.89; 5.2.37, 170. Reverse (*Ile* > *I will*): 1.1.181; 1.2.48; 1.3.241; 2.1.102; 3.3.301; 3.4.22, 190; 4.2.135, 201; 5.2.89.
(2) Preposition and 'the' shortened (e.g. *to the* > *toth'*): 1.1.37; 1.3.280; 2.1.139; 2.3.116, 161; 3.1.4; 3.3.316; 3.4.82; 4.2.7, 146; 4.3.6, 66, 79, 83; 5.1.62.
(3) *his* shortened to *'s* (*in his* > *in's*): 5.2.62.
(4) *it* shortened to *'t* (e.g. *believe it* > *believe't*): 2.1.284, 286; 2.3.6; 3.1.40; 3.3.283, 318; 3.4.33, 79, 82, 87, 108, 170; 4.2.130; 4.3.7, 66, 76; 5.2.227. Reverse (*'t* > *it*): 2.3.192; 3.3.442; 4.1.142.

We must remember, of course, that F *Othello* was not a reprint, like *King Lear* (1619), and that the treatment of (1)–(4) in F *Othello* involved others apart from the F compositors. If the argument of chapter 6 is correct, it involved Ralph Crane – and Crane's (L) text of *A Game at Chess* introduced some of the (1)–(4) changes that distinguish F *Othello* from *King Lear* (1619), when (L) is compared with Middleton's manuscript of *A Game at Chess* (T). The symbol > signifies a change from (T) to (L).

Crane's preferences

(2) Preposition and 'the' shortened (e.g. *to the* > *toth'*): 169, 550, 597, 640, 750, 886, 1053, 1136, 1165 and many more.

(3) *in his* > *in's* 2347; *of us* > *on's* 1448.

(4) *it* shortened to *'t*: 59, 542, 603, 606, 1343, 1353, 1685, 1716, 1798, 1875, 2269. Reverse change (*'t* > *it*): 442; 1317 and 1043 *t'ad* > *it had* is not quite the same, since we are dealing elsewhere with unstressed final (*i*)*t*.

As for (1), the changes in F *Othello* almost all involve the pronouns *you* or *thou* (*you will* > *you'l*, *you are* > *y'are*, *thou art* > *thou'rt*), with two instances of *they are* > *they're* (3.3.126, 3.4.16). The reverse changes almost all involve the pronoun *I* (*I'll* > *I will*, *I'd* > *I would*), with two exceptions: *you'd* > *you would* 2.1.102, *he'll* > *he will* 3.3.301. In *King Lear* (1619) the pronoun-related changes go the other way: *thar't* > *thou art* 497, *you'l* > *you will* 971, *thoud'st* > *thou wouldst* 1569, *You're* > *You are* 3048. Crane, like F *Othello*, changed *I'd* > *I would* (or *I'would*), 84, 1068, 1350, 1382, and also lengthened *I'm* > *I am*, *I'd* > *I had* , *I've* > *I have*. Unlike F *Othello*, Crane did not shorten all *you* + auxiliary verb forms, but he often inserted apostrophes, no doubt intending the same effect: *youre* > *y'are* 655; *you are* > *you'ar* 1685; *you haue* > *you'haue* 295, etc. Crane's changes here are less unambiguous than elsewhere because he was inconsistent with apostrophes and because Middleton himself often used the shortened form.

I do not anticipate that readers bombarded with variant readings from the 'Pavier' quartos and Crane manuscripts will feel grateful, or will want me to rush to emend the text of *Othello* by eliminating indifferent variants apparently interpolated by Crane or by the Folio compositors. We have not yet arrived at the editors' Promised Land, where all is sweetness and light; on the other hand, I hope that we have at least reached what Fuller called 'a Pisgah Sight', a glimpse of future opportunities. Identifying the preferred spellings of Crane and the Folio compositors one sees that a very large number of indifferent variants in F *Othello* could well be post-Shakespearian. In some cases we may even think that we know what went wrong.

(1)   *Duke.*   Why at her Fathers?
        Bra.   *I will* not haue it so.
                 (1.3.241, F; *Ile* Q)

(2)   *You would* haue enough.
        Des.   Alas: she ha's no speech.
                 (2.1.102, F; *You'd* Q)

(3)   The Towne will rise. Fie, fie Lieutenant,
      You'le be asham'd for euer.
            (2.3.158–9, F; *You will be sham'd* Q)

(4)   'Tis monstrous: Iago, who *began't?*
            (2.3.213, F; *began?* Q)

(5)   Is't lost? Is't gon? Speak, *is't out o'th'way?*
            (3.4.82, F; *is it out o'the way?* Q)

(6)   Haue not deuis'd this Slander: *I will* be hang'd else.
                  (4.2.135, F; *I'le* Q)

In (1), either Crane or the compositor could have changed *Ile* to *I will*; in (2), Q *You'd* > F *You would* looks like a compositor's substitution. As for (3), it is tempting to suggest that Crane changed *You will* to *You'le*, then patched the metre by switching from *sham'd* to *asham'd*. (He made similar verbal adjustments in the Malone manuscript of *A Game at Chess*, a version that omitted dozens of short passages and tinkered with words to avoid puzzling transitions.) The short line (4) could be explained as resulting from an original *it*, shortened to *'t* by Crane and accidentally omitted by Q. The short line (5) may include two Crane abbreviations, *it* > *'t* and *o'the* > *o'th'*. The long line (6) could be attributed to either Crane or the compositor.

But this will not do. We really know far too little about the treatment of indifferent variants by Jaggard's compositors in other Folio plays to be ready for hard conclusions. Others will have to assess the new evidence, and this will need time. All that we can safely say at this early stage[6] is that, first, some scribes and compositors seem to have switched around many of the indifferent variants that, as it happens, are also a prominent feature of the texts of *Othello* (and of several other plays), and that, second, F *Othello* probably suffered more from such textual 'instability' than Q, because of the interference of Ralph Crane and of F's compositors.

Understandably, Crane and the compositors would have chosen a less incriminating word. An editor, almost four centuries later, may regret what they did, whereas they saw their role as constructive: they tidied the text, updated it, converting a messy play-house script into a reading text fit for an expensive Folio – and if changes such as *you will* > *you'le* or *to the* > *to'th* appear to damage the metre, that was not their intention. The modern editor, however, aware that the scribes and compositors of both Q and F carelessly changed the lineation of many speeches, will be a little more critical, since indifferent variants that introduce syllabic changes confirm that metrical considerations were not given a high priority.

The six passages cited on pp. 140–1 illustrate how the metre can be affected by alterations that we may tentatively assign to the preferences of a scribe or compositor, the result being long or short lines and / or misplaced stresses. Yet the 'constructive interference' of scribes and compositors – to use a more neutral expression – has an even more pervasive effect on the language of the play in scores of readings.

(1)   It were a tedious difficulty, I thinke,
      To bring *them* to that Prospect: Damne *them* then,
                    (3.3.400–1, F; *em, em* Q)

(2)   Nor I neither, by this Heauenly light:
      I might *doo't* as well *i'th'* darke.
                    (4.3.65–6, F; *doe it, in the* Q)

(3)   By Heauen I saw my Handkerchiefe *in's* hand.
                    (5.2.62, F; *in his* Q)

The differences may be slight, but deserve some attention. (2) F's abbreviations speed up the line. We have to ask whether the line is a rapier-thrust, or a lingering over and savouring of a smutty joke. (3) F's *in's* involves the virtual disappearance of *his*. I prefer the staggered rhythm of Q, spelling out the accusation by dwelling distinctly on each word ('in-his-hand!'). As I would be the first to admit, these differences are to some extent subjective, (1) in particular, but each of the three examples must be judged in the light of the more general shift from *em, 't, i'th', in's* to *them, it, in the* and *in his* in the Folio, in Crane transcripts and in the work of Jaggard's compositors in other texts. Moreover, the differences between *em* and *them*, etc., are not wholly trivial: if one reads aloud, or thinks of an actor trying out these lines, it will be clearer that F changes the texture of the play's language. Taken together with F's heavy punctuation, which has the same effect (see p. 134), F's indifferent variants are by no means as trivial collectively as they may seem to be individually.

THE 'BETTER TEXT'?

The argument seems to be steering to the conclusion that Q is the 'better text', an outcome that fills me with misgivings. Why so? After all, having stated the case against Q's publisher and printer as forcefully as I could (chapter 3), I deferred to the evidence that places the Q text in a more favourable light – its Shakespearian spellings and stage directions, its printing of 'false starts' and 'first thoughts' that might survive in a text deriving from foul papers but not in one that was a memorial reconstruction, and its misreading errors that point back (like F's) to an often illegible text in Shakespeare's hand, a text in which it was easy to confuse some letters, especially final letters that are not normally confused in Secretary hand (chapter 4 and Appendix C; chapter 8). So why not accept Q as the better text? For two reasons: first, because Q has more than its fair share of textual corruption (mishearing, textual dislocation and omission, mislineation); second, because the very notion of a 'better text', once taken for granted, needs to be looked at more closely.

To begin with the first: by 'more than its fair share' I mean in comparison with other foul-paper texts such as *Love's Labour's Lost* Q1, *Romeo and Juliet* Q2, *Hamlet* Q2, and the like. The differences between these texts, published in the period 1598–1604, and Q *Othello* may be attributed in part to the later date of the latter: by 1622 a more 'modern' textual presentation was deemed necessary (hence the act division and heavier punctuation in Q *Othello*). Further, if a scribal transcript came between the foul papers of *Othello* and Q, as seems to be widely thought, or if the foul papers were exceptionally untidy and illegible, one or both could produce an additional stratum of errors. The many kinds of corruption in Q do not rule out the theory of foul-paper provenance – some, indeed, may support it – but I still find them worrying. At the start of the chapter I promised to look back at weaknesses in this account of the texts of *Othello*: the principal one is my sense that Q, though apparently very close to Shakespeare's own papers, has not yet yielded up all its secrets.

As for the 'better text', I am just as reluctant to award this title to Q as to F. Having seen that scribes and compositors can be more trustworthy in one textual department than in another, I would divide the honours as follows: F *Othello* is more reliable with 'substantive' variants and verse lineation, and less reliable with at least some indifferent variants, punctuation, stage directions and profanity. Does that mean that editors should follow F in their choice of substantive variants and lineation, and otherwise follow Q? They may in future wish to lean in these directions, but no hard-and-fast rule is at present acceptable – for the simple reason that both Q and F are often manifestly corrupt in the department in which they impress us, in general, as the more trustworthy. The editor must feel free to emend F's substantive and Q's indifferent variants, though perhaps less free than used to be the case.

If I am correct in saying that F *Othello* is more reliable than Q with substantive variants, we must not lose sight of the fact that F miscorrected many substantive variants (see p. 100) – that is, Crane seems to have misread Shakespeare's manuscript, and preferred what he thought were manuscript readings to Q's better variants. It follows, I think, that Crane will have misread indifferent variants as well. An editor might nevertheless argue that just as Crane's miscorrections of substantive readings are outnumbered by the 'true' readings that he recovered, his indifferent variants will include more 'true' readings than misreadings. The analogy is not entirely sound, though, since Crane and F's compositors deliberately re-spelled so many indifferent variants. The editor finds himself in a no-win situation.

The editor's lot will be even more difficult if he believes, as I do, that some of the variants in *Othello* are authorial in origin. For an author's substitutions can involve the very words that are switched around by inattentive scribes and compositors – and, for all we know, may equally result from carelessness. On the other hand, the author may decide in full consciousness that he prefers *these* to *those*, *the* to *that*, or that one of the play's most sublime speeches can be improved:

> when I haue pluckt *the* rose,
> I cannot giue it vitall growth againe,
> It *must needes* wither; I'le smell *it* on the tree,
> *A* balmy breath, that *doth* almost perswade
> Iustice *her selfe* to breake her sword $_\wedge$ *once* more,
>
> (5.2.13–17, Q)

When I haue pluck'd *thy* Rose,
I cannot giue it vitall growth againe,
It *needs must* wither. Ile smell *thee* on the Tree.
Oh Balmy breath, that *dost* almost perswade
Iustice $_\wedge$ to breake her Sword. *One* more, *one* more:

(F)

It is clear that some of Q's variants stand or fall together (*the* and *it*, *A* and *doth*), as do F's equivalent variants (*thy* and *thee*, *Oh* and *dost*), but less clear who made these changes. The author? Someone else? Those who believe, as I do, that the texts of *Othello* transmit authorial second thoughts and much corruption will have to learn to live with a third possibility, that the eight variants in these four-and-a-half lines could include authorial afterthoughts as well as corruptions – an editorial witches' brew.

A CONFLATED TEXT?

The 'revision' of Shakespeare's plays has become a gold-rush, with more and more speculators jostling or encouraging each other – many more than I expected thirty years ago when, a lone lorn creature, I tried to persuade the world of the instability of Shakespeare's texts.[7] Carried away by this later enthusiasm, I think that I went too far in 1982, comparing the revision of *Othello* with that of *King Lear* (see p. 10). Whatever the fate of *King Lear*, Shakespeare seems not to have revised *Othello* by adding longer passages; on the other hand, the argument that Q and F reflect two authorial strains in some shorter passages has been reanimated by the new evidence pointing to Q's closeness to Shakespeare's own papers. How, then, should editors present the texts of *Othello* – in a single 'conflated' text, or as two quite distinct versions of the play?

Of late, the older practice of conflation has been dismissed as obsolete. It would be, if different versions of the *Prelude* or *Hyperion* were at issue. Where Shakespeare's divergent Q and F texts are concerned, we have to grapple with an entirely different problem, for authorial revision is only a hypothesis, not a certainty, whereas widespread corruption in one or both texts is an undeniable fact. In *King Lear*, the foremost candidate in the queue of Shakespeare's supposedly revised plays, the relationship of revision to corruption, a crucial question, has not so far been dealt with satisfactorily:[8] it would not be too difficult to show that at least some of the 'revision' could qualify no less readily as corruption. Yet even should one accept *King Lear* as definitely revised, must conflation of the two texts therefore cease? The editorial policy of 'little or no conflation' adopted by The Oxford Shakespeare would not have pleased A.E. Housman.

> Q contains many readings which are obviously nonsensical or inadequate, and the chief problem for an editor is the extent to which it should be corrected by reference to F. Naturally, we have retained Q wherever we could make defensible sense of it.[9]

This is the policy of The Oxford Shakespeare. Editors of classical texts used to write in similar vein, and Housman had no patience with them.

> To believe that wherever a best [text] gives possible readings it gives true readings, and that only where it gives impossible readings does it give false readings, is to believe that an incompetent editor is the darling of Providence, which has given its angels charge over him lest at any time his sloth and folly should produce their natural results and incur their appropriate penalty. Chance and the common course of nature will not bring it to pass that the readings of a [text] are right wherever they are possible and impossible wherever they are wrong: that needs divine intervention.[10]

To retain either Q or F *King Lear* 'wherever we could make defensible sense of it' is to invite disaster. It would mean, in texts as corrupt as *King Lear* or *Othello*, that a very large number of 'possible readings' would be given the status of 'true readings' and, even worse, that a very large number of corrupt readings would masquerade as the milk of the word.

As I see it, an editor who believes in the revision of *King Lear* must still come to terms with Q and F corruption, and consequently will want to conflate now and then, if not as much as in the past. Editors who argue for small-scale revision in *Othello*, and who accept that misreading accounts for large-scale corruption, cannot sensibly refuse to conflate – the alternative being to achieve a small good at the cost of an all-corroding evil. When the same kind of textual variation can be traced back repeatedly to the same cause, as with so much of the misreading in *Othello*, we may safely rule out 'revision' at these points and correct one text from the other. How could we refuse to do so when all editors, similarly aware of the cause of QF divergence, reinstate the profanity in F *Othello* from Q?

An editor of *Othello*, if he believes that Q and F transmit some revision and much corruption, will have to conflate – though not necessarily as in the *textus receptus*. The extent to which he conflates will depend on his view of the transmission of each text. Should he think Q more faithful to the foul papers than F was faithful to Shakespeare's fair copy (chiefly because of Ralph Crane's textual 'interference'), this ought to affect editorial policy. For a conflating editor, however, another question must come first: even if it seems wrong to describe either Q or F as 'the better text', which of the two should he choose as parent text,[11] the basis of a conflated text?

Here I have to confess to a failure of nerve. 'Video meliora, proboque;/ Deteriora sequor': I see and approve better things, and follow worse. The arguments of this book drive me to a conclusion that I did not anticipate, namely that the reliability of F *Othello* has been overrated and that Q's has been underrated – am I not honour-bound to choose Q as parent text? Not, I think, at this point in time. As already stated, others will have to weigh the new evidence concerning Ralph Crane and Jaggard's compositors, the authorial fair copy, misreading, etc., before we proceed to change the 'received text' of *Othello* in scores of lines. Having already introduced more changes than any modern editor in the play's lineation and punctuation, I feel that, for the time being, I have done enough, or too much. To echo Dr Johnson, 'I am almost frighted at my own temerity.' When others have reviewed the textual situation and dispelled uncertainties, I may want to re-edit *Othello* with Q as parent text. To echo St Augustine, 'Let me live chaste, Lord! but not yet.'

Ripeness is all.

FUTURE EDITIONS

Aware of so many uncertainties, an editor would be dishonest if he suggested that the textual problems of *Othello* have been solved. Yet any new version of the play, whether in old or modern spelling, tacitly claims precisely this, and a special authority because, as general editors like to say, 'the text of each play has been freshly edited'.

Add a prestigious series title, such as The Oxford Shakespeare or The Cambridge Shakespeare or – best of all – The Arden Shakespeare, and ninety-nine readers out of a hundred will assume that the text they have bought is unadulterated Shakespeare, 'well of English undefiled'. Some editors may actually want their readers to think so, even though they themselves must know that all editions of *Othello*, including their own, almost certainly print hundreds of words or forms of words that Shakespeare did not write.

Because of the number and variety of textual problems that remain unsolved, any new edition of *Othello* will give a false impression unless the editor states as emphatically as he can that readers should not be deceived by the apparent finality of print. If it is the 'series policy' – as in the case of The Arden Shakespeare – not to indicate accented syllables or all elisions but to leave such matters to the reader, it will be as well to list some of the consequences. (1) The spelling of words will not necessarily reveal the number of syllables intended by Shakespeare. (a) A large stock of English words had an adjustable syllable (see above, p. 104); heav[e]n, pow[e]r, etc.; so too, Cass[i]o, Rod[e]rigo and other foreign names. (b) A pronoun and auxiliary verb may have to be expanded (*I'm > I am*) or contracted (*I have > I've*), because scribes, compositors and perhaps Shakespeare himself sometimes used these forms interchangeably (p. 115). (c) Other contractions, such as *th'*, *'t*, *'s*, if retained from the parent text, as they usually are in Arden 3, may be scribal or compositorial in origin and may have to be pronounced *the*, *it*, *is*; the reverse change may also be necessary.

(2) Partly as a consequence of (1), editors cannot always know whether a speech or passage should be printed as prose or verse. Arden 3 *Othello* introduces verse lineation quite often where other modern editions prefer prose (chapter 10, and p. 107). No editor should be too dogmatic about these differences, since Shakespeare himself seems not to have wanted a strict distinction between prose and verse in some passages, especially in passages of abrupt transition.

Readers should be left in no doubt about other editorial decisions that could arguably have had a different outcome. (3) Most of the punctuation in Q and F must be post-Shakespearian. In a modern-spelling edition all the punctuation, whether or not it derives from Q or F, should be regarded as merely a matter of opinion, not as authorial, fixed and final. (4) Some, at least, of F's indifferent variants look like scribal or compositorial substitutions (p. 141). This is not to say that Q's indifferent variants should always be chosen instead of F's, but it serves to warn us that, in the present state of ignorance, editors have no satisfactory procedures for dealing with a problem that, in *Othello* alone, involves hundreds of readings. (5) With 'substantive' variants (such as *knauerie–brauery*, 1.1.99, or *might–night*, 1.1.180) one would like to think that, after almost four centuries, all problems are solved and that good sense has prevailed. A glance from one edition to another reveals, however, that editors, even if they know nothing else, still know how to disagree: most editors print some substantive variants that the majority of other editors rejects. We have not yet reached a consensus, therefore readers should be on their guard even where substantive variants are concerned.

Readers of *Othello* have to be even more vigilant than readers of single-text plays (such as *The Tempest* or *Macbeth*), for two special reasons. (6) The two texts of the play contain 'common errors', corrupt readings in Q that were copied in F (see p. 94). The combined authority of Q and F, once taken as almost a guarantee of correctness, needs to be treated with caution. Editors now emend a number of 'common errors', those that fail to make sense or betray themselves in some other way; we have to accept that many more common errors still survive in our edited texts, simply because they are not self-evidently corrupt. A reader who can think of new procedures for identifying hitherto undetected common errors will be a public benefactor. (7) At least some of F's variant passages look like authorial revision, rather than Q corruptions put right in F (see pp. 16ff.). If F incorporates some revision, however little, it is likely to include other authorial afterthoughts that are less obvious and, indeed, not necessarily improvements (e.g. these > those, tense changes and other indifferent variants). Again, we need new procedures, to distinguish authorial revision from corruption.

(8) Stage directions, if added by editors, are now usually placed in square

brackets, as in Arden 3, thus warning readers that such directions have less authority than those reprinted from Q or F. But how much 'authority' should we attach to Q and F stage directions? And to those added by editors? We know from surviving dramatic manuscripts that stage directions were commonly written in the right-hand margin, at approximately the correct point. Editors therefore move stage directions up or down when a printed text (or a manuscript, if one exists) fails to place them precisely where the dialogue requires.[12] The precise placing, however, can be a matter of dispute. More important, Elizabethan play-texts may provide a complete account of entrances and exits – in fact this is quite rare – yet usually offer much less guidance concerning props and 'stage business' than we would like. At the start of the final scene, Q *Othello* reads '*Enter* Othello *with a light*', while F has '*Enter Othello, and Desdemona in her bed*': each text omits an essential prop. Towards the end of Act 3 scene 3, Q reads '*he kneeles*' (a misplaced stage direction, printed opposite Iago's 'Pray be content', which implies that it refers to Iago, even though it must refer to Othello); a few lines on, Q reads 'Iago *kneeles.*' F omits both directions, and neither Q nor F indicates when the two men stand up again. Sometimes the dialogue fills us in on stage business, as at 4.2.153 ('Here I kneel': there is no stage direction), but more often than not we are left to our own devices. How far from Iago and Cassio should Othello stand in the eavesdropping scene (4.1.94 ff.)? Should Othello appear on the upper stage or the main stage at 5.1.27? Even if the editor tries to help by inserting a specific stage direction, readers should be warned that production problems can be solved in many ways, and that 'editorial' stage directions are likely to be even more untrustworthy than edited dialogue. In short, readers should feel free to imagine the stage business that they think appropriate: the staging of *Othello*, like so much else in the Q and F texts, calls for vigilant readers who distrust all editors – readers no less intelligent than Mrs Quickly, who realised at last that she had been put upon. 'I have borne, and borne, and borne, and have been fubbed off, and fubbed off, and fubbed off ... There is no honesty in such dealing, unless the poor reader should be made an ass and a beast, to bear every knave's wrong!'

*   *   *

This may sound like an excessively pessimistic conclusion. I prefer to think of it as realistic: some editors save themselves trouble by simply pilfering from their predecessors, some editions are better than others. Readers of Shakespeare have been fubbed off by copy-cat editors, and by editors who have not examined the texts in sufficient detail. But, as I have tried to show in this final chapter, conscientious editors can also do great harm, unintentionally, by backing the wrong textual theory and excluding dozens or even hundreds of authentic readings. The decision to prepare a conflated text (or not), the choice of Q or F as parent text, could have disastrous consequences, substituting the words of scribes or compositors for the words of Shakespeare. Consequently readers should always keep an eye on the textual notes, just in case the editor has chosen badly. Honest editors would admit, I think, that very often the choice of one variant as against another is more open to question than the black and white of print and paper may suggest. The words of the play, though not writ in water, still require patient textual scrutiny from future editors, and from all self-respecting, non-passive readers.

Appendices

APPENDIX A: SHAKESPEARE'S 'FOUL PAPERS'

Throughout much of this century it has been taken for granted that Shakespeare gave his company the 'unblotted papers' of his plays, written in his own hand; that the company kept these holographs and, when it decided to publish a play, gave the printer these papers rather than the scribal fair copy, which normally became the prompt-book. A.W. Pollard, R.B. McKerrow and W.W. Greg were responsible for this 'orthodoxy', which I questioned thirty years ago. It has now been questioned again by Paul Werstine.[1]

Werstine argues that whereas categories such as 'foul papers' and 'memorial reconstruction' seem to have 'always been with us', in fact 'both are of comparatively recent origin'; also, that in the seventeenth century 'foul' or rough sheets referred to incomplete copies of plays, not to foul papers as defined by Greg ('the text substantially in the form the author intended it to assume . . . but too untidy to be used by the prompter'). Does it follow that Elizabethan–Jacobean acting companies did not know or possess 'foul papers' as defined by Greg?

Before we turn to acting companies it should be stressed that 'foul' papers, sheets, etc., was a term in general use, and not confined to the theatre. In Webster's *The Devil's Law-Case* (1623), when an advocate tears up his brief ('some four score sheets of paper', which had taken four nights to copy), Sanitonella declares 'I must make shift / With the foul copy', and produces it.[2] A Dr Petty, accused in the House of Commons in 1659 of not surrendering the originals of certain documents, 'informed the House that the particulars in his hands were foul books and papers, out of which those he had returned were extracted'.[3] Accordingly Edward Knight's note in a transcript of Fletcher's *Bonduca* that 'this hath been transcribed from the foul papers of the author's, which were found',[4] need not refer to a category of 'dramatic manuscripts' as familiar then as were prompt-books, but might be a non-technical term, as in the case of Webster and Dr Petty. Yet unless we are to assume that dramatists could write plays so effortlessly and cleanly that no fair copies were required, foul papers must have existed, whatever the technical term used at the time.

Werstine thinks that in seventeenth-century usage foul papers would be frag-
mentary and incomplete; perhaps so, in some instances, but Webster and Dr
Petty do not support this view, and in other examples that I have collected[5]
'foul' refers more often to the roughness of the text than to its incompleteness.
This confirms Greg's definition, not Werstine's, though fair copies might of
course add passages not found in the foul papers, or for that matter might
omit passages.

Werstine does not believe that the actors feared theft. 'Since there is no
evidence (that I know of) that a theatrical manuscript was ever stolen from
Shakespeare's company, the fear of theft that Pollard projects upon the company seems groundless.' Compare, however, (1) the Lord Chamberlain's letter
(quoted above, p. 25: 'Playes . . . lately stollen or gotten from them [the
players] by indirect meanes'); (2) Heminges and Condell in the First Folio
('you were abus'd with diuerse stolne, and surreptitious copies'). As is corroborated by (3) the 'blocking' and 'staying' of plays in the Stationers' Register,
and by subsequent publications, the fear of theft was not entirely groundless. I
have argued[6] that some dramatists did not sell their plays lock, stock and
barrel to the actors, retaining copies of their play-texts and in some cases the
right to publish: none the less an author like Shakespeare, with no permanent
home in London, might still prefer to leave his papers at the theatre for safe
keeping, or with the company's business manager, and this could explain how
Heminges and Condell were later able to print so many 'foul paper' texts in
the First Folio.

Werstine thinks that 'no "good" quarto has ever been shown to have been
set from "foul papers" because the marks that have been used to identify "foul
papers" as printer's copy are also to be found in extant "prompt-books"'. To
which one might reply that these 'marks' appear in different texts in more or
less profusion and in different combinations; some 'marks' no doubt passed
from the author's papers into scribal copies, but that is not to say that texts
cannot be distinguished when one considers *all* the marks of each text, not just
one or two kinds.

It is difficult not to sympathise with Werstine's complaint that 'the current
rigidified hierarchy of the "good"/"bad" quartos has come oppressively to
limit negotiation in Shakespeare textual criticism', which means (I suppose)
that every text has its own history and should not be equated with any other
text, however superficially similar. And it may well be that 'foul paper' texts
were printed, in some or most cases, from a scribal copy, not directly from the
foul papers, as Pollard, McKerrow and Greg assumed. Yet 'foul papers' remains an indispensable concept, even if the term was not used in the
seventeenth-century theatre as Pollard, etc., came to use it (i.e. for a class of
dramatic manuscript); and I believe that the textual characteristics of foul
papers, as described by Pollard, McKerrow and Greg, are still of interest to
editors, as long as we remember that scribes, compositors and Shakespeare
himself were all, textually speaking, 'infirm of purpose'.

APPENDIX B: THOMAS WALKLEY AND JOHN EVERARD (CONTINUED)

Describing the lawsuit between Thomas Walkley and Dr John Everard in chapter 3, I said that the details could be checked in Appendix B. Walkley's bill of complaint and Everard's answer are both partly illegible: the ink has faded, and one of the parchments is also badly mutilated. A summary of the two documents follows in modern spelling, mostly in the words of the original: square brackets are used for passages where I have had to resort to guessing or have added comments, pointed brackets for words or letters that are partly visible.

(1) *Walkley* v. *Everard*: the bill of complaint[1]

Thomas Walkley, citizen and stationer now is and by the space of seven [years] hath been a free man of London and free of the Company of Stationers, and during all the same time hath used and exercised the trade, art and faculty of stationer ... And whereas Sir Michael Everard, late of < ... > Iones in the county of Middlesex, knight, deceased, did in his life-time write a treatise touching military discipline and did entitle it *Bellona's Embrion*; and afterwards, in or about the month of September in the year of the reign of our sovereign lord King James which now is over England the twentieth, he, the said Sir Michael [made his will] and made his wife, the Lady Margaret Everard, his sole executrix and shortly after died. She, desiring the general good of the weal public, and that the treatise might be known to posterity, about the month of December, in the year of the King's reign the twentieth, had conference with Mr Doctor Everard, sometimes preacher at the parish church of St Martin in the Fields in the county of Middlesex and late kinsman to the said Sir Michael, touching the printing and setting forth of the treatise. Dr Everard undertook to make it fit for the press and likewise to cause it to be imprinted at his own charge. But unable to perform [his promise], within a short time after he did come and fly unto your orator [i.e. Walkley], as he had done many times before ... [They agreed on an impression of 750 books] ... moiety of the same, and the other half or moiety to be to the use and behoof of the said Dr Everard ... < Lady Marg > aret, having notice hereof, ... did most willingly embrace and entertain [the agreement] ... and delivered unto Dr Everard < fou > rtie pounds ... but with this caution, that the said Dr Everard and your orator should become [?bound] in several bonds for ... performance and finishing thereof. [Three bonds were signed, to the value of £200, for the finishing of the impression within a certain time. In the January following] Walkley procured a printer with paper and other necessary items, and Dr Everard did at several times after deliver to Walkley part of the treatise. Walkley spent £30 on the cost of printing, demanded this sum from Dr Everard but could never have it. Weary both with laying out his money and bestowing his endeavours upon such dilatory satisfaction he [?refused] to proceed any further till he received some security for his indemnity. Dr Everard afterwards, that is on or about the 9th October 1623 came to a new agreement with Walkley. Walkley was to finish the impression of 750 books at his own charge, one [?half] thereof to his own use, and Walkley should give Dr Everard £5; and Dr Everard, being then Rector of the parish of Wilby, Northants, should make a lease of the rectory to Walkley for one year next ensuing. Walkley continued with the printing till towards Easter 1624, when Dr Everard had delivered so much of the treatise as made 60 sheets in folio, 750 times, the printing of which has cost Walkley at least £60. But now so it is, Dr Everard not only detains all the . . . which have been paid to him, amounting to £67, but now since Easter, since the printing of the 60 sheets, Dr Everard hath utterly denied to deliver to Walkley any more of the treatise, although he detaineth as much or more of the residue thereof. So Walkley cannot proceed or make an end of the said work. And after the lease was made to Walkley, and before he could get possession, the rectory was sequestered to the King's Majesty because of the non-payment of the first fruits.

Walkley, for all his labour and expenses, is in continual fear and danger of arrest . . .

*   *   *

Dr Everard's answer to the bill of complaint covers the same events and, as one would expect, disagrees about much of the detail. I omit common ground, and summarise in modern spelling.

(2) *Walkley* v. *Everard*: the answer[2]

. . . . Walkley, at the earnest entreaty of Lady Margaret Everard, agreed with Everard that if he [Everard] would undertake the care of perusing and reviewing [the manuscript], he would deliver to Lady Margaret 20 of the said books perfected and imprinted. Everard, together with John Nanton, stood bound to her but [?she] would also give £20 to Everard towards his satisfaction. Yet the business could not be brought to pass according to the intention and desire of Everard . . . It was agreed that 750 copies should be printed by one Bernard Alsop, 100 to be printed on large crown paper and the other 650 . . . at the only cost and charge of the defendant and that then Lady Margaret should receive 20 perfect books . . . Walkley should have the other 315 books to his own proper use . . . Then Walkley and Everard became jointly bound to Lady Margaret in a bond . . . deliver into Walkley's hands £9, which Everard had received of Lady Margaret to buy paper . . . And after Everard had paid 20/- for the licensing of the copy of the said book . . . . paid £5 to Alsop, as by the accounts of the said Alsop may appear . . . Everard being imprisoned in the Gatehouse, Westminster, for debt about March 1622 [i.e. 1623 New Style?], and his lecture at St Martin's in the Fields where he was preacher being at the same time by the Great Seal of England taken away from him, he, Everard, being utterly disabled thereby to proceed with the impression of the book . . . that they would for a time have patience with him . . . Walkley brought one

Thomas Snoden a printer ... finding that Alsop had already printed 38 sheets, Everard, Snoden and Walkley advised and cast up what sums of money they owed Alsop in arrears to finish the impression. [It was £45.] Everard, being Rector of the parish church of Wilby, Northants, gave Walkley a lease of it for one year, so that Walkley would have security for the sum of £50. Walkley was to have half the books, and seemed well content. But Everard [believed] that Walkley would not be of sufficient ability to perform the impression, knowing him to be indebted to several persons ... Walkley meant nothing but fraud and deceit, to cozen Everard of the fruits of his rectory ... now in the hands of the executors of Lady Margaret ... Walkley asked to speak to Everard privately and, weeping tears, told him that unless he [Everard] would be bound to him he [Walkley] would be utterly undone. [Walkley wanted to make over the lease to George Humble in return for a bond for £100.] Walkley and Everard came to a new agreement with several articles, viz. That I Thomas Walkley shall at my own proper costs and charges finish the impression of that book ... That Walkley gives Everard a bond for £200 for the performance of the articles ... That the book begun to be printed by Alsop should have a frontispiece cut in brass and imprinted according to Everard's device ... Walkley never performed any of these articles ... [Walkley was preoccupied with another book] which he called his *Nero*, and neglected to set *Bellona's Embrion* to the press ... Everard sent more copy to Snoden; when he went to Snoden's house he found why the treatise had not gone forwards for half a year. Only 7 or 8 sheets had been printed [by Snoden], because Walkley was already indebted to Snoden for great sums of money for [other] work Snoden had done for him. Therefore Snoden would work no more ... Everard asked for an entire copy of all the sheets; Snoden said he could have a copy of the sheets he [Snoden] had printed ... [Walkley was arrested about three years past by George Humble on an action for £100.] Walkley entreated Everard to come to him, where by prayers and tears he prevailed on him and a brother of his, on a bond of £200 penalty whereby he bound himself to Everard to save him harmless against George Humble ... Walkley protested with horrible oaths that he had paid all arrears, but Snoden said he had not observed the articles ...

*   *   *

Because of gaps in the texts the charges and countercharges of the two men are not as clear as one would like (and it should be noted that the dots between sentences may indicate short or lengthy omissions); the heading and end of both the parchments I found impossible to read, yet the motives of the two litigants are visible enough. Walkley claims that he has invested large sums in the printing of *Bellona's Embrion* and will be ruined unless Everard gives him the rest of the manuscript; Everard replies that Walkley is so heavily in debt to others that he would not be able to finance the printing of the rest of the book, and reveals in passing that Walkley's financial problems have gone on for at least three years.

Among the Orders and Decrees of the Court of Chancery there are several concerned with '*Walkley* v. *Everard*', and they confirm some of the crucial dates. Most of them concentrate on the rectory of Wilby.[3] On 15 July 1624 Walkley asked for a sequestration of the profits of the rectory, stating that his lease of the rectory would end on 9 October next: if he was not relieved he would be utterly remediless, having received no profit by the lease. On 20 August Everard replied that Walkley's scandalous bill is full of untruths; by reason of his debts and other engagements he (Everard) fears to be taken in execution for a debt of Walkley's for £100, Walkley having combined with Everard's creditor to have him arrested for debt; Everard asks for a supersedeas for the discharge of the sequestration. On 13 September an Order referred to *Bellona's Embrion*:

> And whereas it was also alleged that the plaintiff together with the defendant Everard had entered into divers bonds to the Lady Everard conditioned for printing of a book within a time limited and the plaintiff having to his great charge printed part thereof could not get the residue of the papers out of the defendant Everard's hands whereby to finish the said impression and so stood liable to the said bonds and had been lately arrested thereupon. Therefore it was desired that the said defendant might be ordered to deliver the said papers to the plaintiff. It is therefore ordered that a day till the next general seal be given to the said defendant either to deliver the said papers or to show good cause why he should not deliver the same to the plaintiff as is desired.[4]

Some additional information is available from other sources. Sir Michael Everard made his will on 28 April 1621, when about to go overseas, and probate was granted to Lady Margaret, his widow, on 25 September 1622.[5] Lady Margaret made her own will at Flushing on 12 September 1622, probate being granted on 17 February 1622/3.[6] In her will she referred to her husband's treatise:

> Item I giue unto docter Euerard my [most *deleted*] worthy cosen tow of my husbands bookes himselfe chosing amongst them and doe earnestly recommend into his care the publishing of my husbands studies I would not haue any thinge change least It may change the conceate especaly of the < . . . > military part nor of the deuine part but with a serious consideration.[7]

One would like to know why Dr Everard ceased to be considered 'most worthy'. Had his negotiations with Walkley dragged on for some time? Walkley registered the treatise on 14 February 162 ⅔, presumably after Lady Everard's death.

Thomas Walkley. A Booke Called BELLONA's *Embrion* by Sir *Michaell*

Euerard knight, published after his Decease by his Cosen German *John Euerard* Doctor in Divinity . . . vj^d

(Arber, *Transcript*, IV.91)

*   *   *

Next, some notes on John Everard's career and personality.

(1) From *The Dictionary of National Biography*: John Everard (1575?–1650?), educated at Clare College, Cambridge (BA 1600, MA 1607, DD 1619). Reader at St Martin's-in-the-Fields, London, before 1618; in January 1618 censured by the Bishop of London 'and compelled to publicly apologise to the lord mayor and aldermen for slandering them in a sermon'. Imprisoned in the Gatehouse, March 1621, for preaching against the Spanish marriage. Still in prison in September, when he petitioned the king to release him, 'promising not to repeat his offence'. Did not keep his promise, imprisoned again in August 1622 and at later dates, for the same cause. Each time 'some lord or other' begged his pardon: released, he again 'took up his text on the unlawfulness of matching with idolaters'. The king noticed, and said 'What is this Dr Ever-out? his name shall be Dr Never-out.' Everard's 'great powers of preaching drew large congregations, and when, being appointed chaplain to Lord Holland . . . he left St Martin's for Kensington, his audiences were fashionable and aristocratic'.

(2) To this account we may add the following. (a) According to the list of rectors at Wilby, Everard was the incumbent from 1622 to 1625. (b) Everard's signature is reproduced (in the facsimile for Giles Fletcher) in Peter Beal's *Index of English Literary Manuscripts* (I, 2, facsimile XIV). (c) *DNB* mentions 'three manuscripts by Everard' in Cambridge University Library (actually three translations bound together, one dated 1628, another 1638: MS. Dd-12-68). The same library has two leaves (four pages) of verses by Everard, Latin and English, with the heading 'Bacchus'. The English verses, in the first person, describe the poet reeling home in the early hours fortified by Bacchus, and thus able to defy 'my thundress'. Even if not autobiographical, these not untalented verses throw some light on Everard's sense of humour (Add. 2615–33):

> If I reel home, when Chanticleer
> Proclaims the Mattins to be near,
> My Thundress peaceably obeys mee;
> For if to passion once she raise me,
> The De'il abit she can out:scold me,
> I make the house to hot to hold me: . . .

More directly relevant, so far as his dispute with Walkley is concerned, one wonders whether Everard's statement that he was imprisoned in the Gatehouse for debt (see p. 153) could have been economical with the truth, as his more serious offence will have been his preaching against the Spanish marriage, for which he was certainly incarcerated. Again, at a time when pluralism was the accepted practice, did Everard surrender the rectory of Wilby voluntarily, or was he forced out in 1625? Did he leave St Martin's for Kensington, as *DNB* put it, or was he deprived of St Martin's 'by the Great Seal of England', as he himself said in his answer to Walkley (above, p. 153)?

(3) What comes through clearly, from all we know about Everard, is this: he preached against the Lord Mayor and Aldermen, and repeatedly against the Crown; he fell out with his publisher, and probably lost one or two livings. A difficult man? When he died a colleague praised him as meek and amiable, gracious in all his behaviour and 'ready to pardon and pray for his enemies'.[8] Perhaps so, at the end of his life, but not necessarily in the 1620s. Whatever Walkley's shortcomings, my guess is that Everard had his faults as well: Walkley may have cut corners, and perhaps lied when he got into difficulties, but Everard's testimony is not self-evidently reliable. If *Bellona's Embrion* ever surfaces again, which is by no means impossible, we may be able to judge the two men more accurately. For the time being I would adjudicate between them as follows: Everard seems to have been a determined opponent, one who might not hesitate to bend the facts to discredit Walkley; on the other hand, Walkley's other books and their printing history, and his close association with Nicholas Okes, bear out Everard's account of him.[9]

*   *   *

Next, a note on Walkley's epistle to the reader, printed in Q *Othello*. This epistle must be seen as one of a series. (1) *A King and No King* (1619), Walkley's dedication to Sir Henry Nevill: 'I present, or rather returne to your view, that which formerly hath been received from you, hereby effecting what you did desire.' (2) *Philaster*, Q2 (1622), Walkley to the Reader: '*Philaster*, and *Arethusa* his love, have laine so long a bleeding, by reason of some dangerous and gaping wounds, which they received in the first Impression . . . Although they were hurt neither by me, nor the Printer; yet I . . . have adventured to bind up their wounds.' (3) *The Pursuit of . . . Lazarillo* (1622): Walkley 'dedicateth this strangely recouered Continuation' (see above, p. 25). (4) *Othello* (1622), Walkley to the Reader: 'the Author being dead, I thought good to take that piece of worke vpon mee', therefore 'I haue ventered to print this Play.' In each case Walkley hints that he acquired the text in a roundabout or unconventional way – not an admission of guilt, yet a self-vindication that just concedes that others might want to ask questions. Placed in the context of the various plays that reached print in dubious circumstances (above, pp. 24–5), many of them apparently published by Walkley, the epistles and dedications significantly fail to identify the 'others', yet Walkley must have known that acting companies, as well as authors, claimed to have rights in play-texts.

*   *   *

In Johnson's *Shakespeare* of 1765, the first two editions of *Othello* are described as '1. Quarto, – Preface by Thomas Walkely. 2. 1622. N.O. for Thomas Walkely' (VIII, 318). Johnson repeated, in an 'Appendix to Vol. VIII', '1. Othello, *William Shakespeare, no date, Thomas Walkely*. 2. D°. William Shakespeare, 1622, N.O. for Thomas Walkely.' This looks like misinformation (Johnson did not claim to possess 1, or to have collated it): no copy of Q without the date is now known. Or is it possible that Walkley first issued Q without a date, or that he published two editions, as Johnson believed, one of which has perished?

APPENDIX C: 'SHAKESPEARIAN' SPELLINGS IN Q *OTHELLO*

Although Q *Othello* contains many obvious misprints, and many spellings that may appear to be misprints, many of its 'odd' spellings are actually Shakespearian – that is, they occur elsewhere in the canon. This suggests that the manuscript from which Q was printed could have been Shakespeare's own papers, or a copy close to his papers (see p. 34). The list that follows was compiled with the help of *The Harvard Concordance to Shakespeare* by Marvin Spevack. Line references in the *Concordance* are to *The Riverside Shakespeare*: to avoid confusion all line references to Shakespare's plays in this appendix, except for one play, repeat those in the *Concordance*. The exception is *Othello*, where I cite Arden 3.

Each entry is arranged as follows. (1) The word, in its original spelling, from Q *Othello*; (2) an asterisk, in some cases, to indicate that the spelling is common elsewhere in Shakespeare; (3) if necessary, the modern spelling equivalent in brackets; (4) line reference from Arden 3; (5) line references to – usually – three other plays or poems where substantially the same spelling is found; (6) a number, in some cases, to indicate how many instances of the word and of close cognates are cited in the *Concordance*. For (5) I use 'good' quartos and the Shakespearian pages of *Sir Thomas More* (*STM*: from the Malone Society edition prepared by W.W. Greg, 1911, reprinted 1961, pp. 73–8) in preference to Folio texts, in so far as there is a choice. Q and F identify the relevant Quarto and Folio texts: when I do not indicate a Q or F source it can be assumed that the 'earliest good text' is meant. In a few instances the actual spelling of these Q and F texts follows the line reference in brackets.

accumilate (3.3.373): *Son* 117.10 (4 recorded).
affoordeth (1.3.115): *STM* IIC 133; *RJ* 3.1.60; *1H4* 3.2.78.
ake(s) (3.4.147): *VA* 875, *RJ* (Q2) 2.5.26; *Ham* (Q2) 5.1.93.
approoued (1.3.78): *Son* 42.8; *MA* 4.1.44; *Ham* 1.1.29.
atchieu'd (2.1.61): *MV* 3.2.208; *R2* 2.1.254; *Ham* 1.4.21.
attone (4.1.232): *2H4* (Q) 4.1.219 (attonement); *Cor* 4.6.73; *Tim* 5.4.58.

battaile (1.3.88): *Luc* 1438; *1H4* (Q) 3.2.105; *TC* (Q) 3.2.28.

Battell (1.1.22): *VA* 99; *MND* 5.1.44; *1H4* 4.3.13.

beastiall (2.3.260): *R3* (F) 3.5.81 (beastiall); *Ham* 4.4.40 (bestiall) (3 recorded).

beleeue* (2.1.247): *LLL* 1.1.159; *RJ* 1.4.14; *Ham* 3.1.128.

boord (aboord) (3.3.24): *LLL* 2.1.218; *MA* 2.1.143; *Ham* 4.6.18.

boulster (3.3.402): *TS* 4.1.201 (2 recorded).

cald (= called) (1.2.44): *RJ* 1.3.101; *R2* 4.1.143; *Ham* 1.4.84.

catieffe (= caitiff) (5.2.316): *RJ* 5.1.52 (Catiffe) (14 recorded).

cease (= seize) (4.2.38): *R2* 2.1.209; *3H6* 4.8.52; *AC* 3.11.47.

Cittadell (2.1.94, 208, 281): *AW* 4.1.56 (Citadell), *AC* 4.14.4 (Cittadell) (7 recorded, 5 in *Oth*).

Citty* (1.1.7): *Tit* 1.1.26; *MV* 3.3.30; *Tim* 5.4.19.

clime (= climb) (2.1.185): *LLL* 1.1.200; *Tit* 2.1.1; *TC* (Q) 1.3.129.

Coffe (4.2.29): *LLL* 5.2.922; *RJ* 3.1.25; *MND* 2.1.54.

comming (3.3.40): *MV* 3.1.100; *R2* 2.2.11; *Ham* 1.1.123.

controule (5.2.263): *Son* 58.2, 107.3, 125.14; *Cor* 3.1.161.

coppied (3.4.190): *Son* 11.14 (coppy); *H5* 3.1.24; *Ham* 1.5.101.

Countrey* (1.3.98): *STM* IIC 6; *Luc* 1838; *LLL* 1.2.117.

Crocadile (4.1.245): *Ham* 5.1.276 (5 recorded).

dam (= damn) (3.3.478): *CE* 4.3.53; *MV* 1.1.98; *JC* 4.1.6.

demy (= demi) (5.2.298): *MV* 3.2.115; *R2* 2.1.42; *Ham* 4.7.87.

desteny (3.3.279): *MV* 2.1.15, 2.2.62; *TC* (Q) 5.1.64.

Deuesting (2.3.177): *H5* 2.4.78 (3 recorded).

deuided (1.3.181): *Son* 46.2; *1H4* 2.3.32; *Ham* 1.1.76.

ecchoes (3.3.109): *TS* 1 Ind. 26; *Tit* 2.2.6; *RJ* 2.2.161.

Epithites (1.1.13): *LLL* 4.2.88 (epythithes); *MA* 5.2.66 (epithite) (6 recorded).

extacy (4.1.80): *Ham* 2.1.99, 3.1.160, 3.4.74 and 138 (all 'extacie', elsewhere 'extasie').

extreame (5.2.344): *LLL* 5.2.740; *1H4* 1.3.31; *TC* (Q) 4.2.102.

eyd (= eyed) (3.3.168): *TA* 5.1.44 (wall-eyd); *R2* 2.2.19 (eyde); *Son* 104.2 (eyde).

So much for the first five letters of the alphabet. To save space, I now omit (5), line references to three other plays or poems, except when these are of special interest, positively or negatively. Readers may take it, however, that in each case at least three identical or very nearly identical spellings have been located, unless I state the contrary.

(vn)fould (5.1.21); ghesse (= guess) (3.3.148); grones (5.1.42); groser (= grosser) (3.3.223); herraldry (3.4.47); Honny (2.1.203): *Ham* 3.1.156; *Luc* 836, 840 (Honnie); humaine (3.3.264); hye (= high) (4.1.186): *AW* 1.1.220; *AC* 1.5.49, 4.15.43 ('hie' is more common); Ilanders (3.3.284): [Iland] *Luc* 1740;

H5 3.7.140; *TC* (Q) 3.1.154; Intire(ly) (3.4.62); Isebrookes (= ice brook's?) (5.2.251): [ise etc.] *LLL* 5.2.912 (Isacles); *MV* 2.1.5 (ysicles); *H5* 3.5.23 (Isyckles); Kitchin* (2.1.110); Lethergie (4.1.53): *2H4* 1.2.112; *TC* (Q) 5.1.19 (lethergies) (7 recorded); lyer (= liar) (5.2.127): *MND* 5.1.435; *Ham* 2.2.118; *RJ* 1.2.91 (liers); lowd* (2.1.149); Lyon (2.3.271); mandat (4.1.259): *Ham* 3.4.204 (4 recorded); mannage 2.3.211; mary (= marry, exclam.) (4.1.88); meerly (1.3.335); merrits (3.3.190); mistris* (2.3.48); moouing (1.3.136); musique (2.1.199); musition (4.1.185); peece* (= piece) (3.1.24); Physition (1.3.311); pitty* (1.3.169); politique (3.3.13); prooue* (3.3.264); prophane (1.1.113); Qu. (= cue) (1.2.83): *MA* 2.1.305; *H5* (F) 3.6.123; *R3* (F) 3.4.26 (Qu., Q. and Q); rellish (2.1.165); roule (= roll) (5.2.38); rore (5.2.196); sayd (4.1.29): *Ham* 1.3.85, 2.2.188, 313; *TC* (Q) 3.3.260; *VA* 333 (not very common in Shakespeare); sed (= said) (2.1.167): *AW* 1.3.140, 4.3.148; *AC* 4.4.28 (rare in Shakespeare); sence (= sense) (2.1.71); shew(es)* (2.3.292); sillable (4.2.5); Souldier* (2.1.36); stroake (1.3.158); subborn'd (3.4.154): *Son* 125.13 (subbornd); *CE* 4.4.82 (subborn'd); *Mac* 2.4.24; (subborned) (14 recorded); suddain (2.1.270); Sybell (= sibyl) (3.4.72): *TS* 1.2.70 (Sibell); *TA* 4.1.105 (Sibels) (5 recorded); syen (= scion) (1.3.333): *H5* 3.5.7 (Syens); *WT* 4.4.93 (Sien) (3 recorded); tearme* (1.1.38); tirranous (3.3.452): [tirr-] *AW* 1.1.50; *KL* (F) 3.4.2; *Ham* 2.2.460 (tirranus); vertue* (1.3.290); Warriour (2.1.180); Wensday (3.3.61): *CE* 1.2.55; *Cor* 1.3.59; *MV* 2.5.26 (ashwensday).

This is not a complete list: it could easily be expanded. I have not included some groups of characteristic spellings, common in Q *Othello* and elsewhere, all the members of which need not be cited as individual words. (1) Shakespeare's very frequent substitution of *y* for modern *i* (in Q *Othello*: ayme, ayre, choyce, dye, flye, lye, etc.); (2) *-oo-* for *-o-* (approoue, boord, etc.); (3) the doubling of consonants (abhorre, parrallell, etc.); (4) *in-* for *en-* (inchanted, indure, infetter'd, inforce, ingender'd, etc.); (5) *-full* for *-ful* (faithfull, fearefull, lawfull, lustfull, pittifull, powerfull, etc.) The same characteristic spellings are found in the good quartos, and four of the five groups occur in Hand D of *Sir Thomas More*. The absence of group (4) from *More* (where, on the contrary, we find enstalls and entreate) serves as a reminder that Shakespeare's 'characteristic' spellings are not his invariable spellings.

Some of the characteristic spellings coexist in Q *Othello* with alternative spellings which, in most cases, are also used in other Shakespearian texts: e.g. *sayd* and *sed*, *battaile* and *Battell*. With this last pair we may compare *JC* 5.1.14–16, where *Battell* and *Battaile*, both 'Shakespearian' spellings, are just three lines apart. In *Sir Thomas More* Shakespeare wrote Countrie, Country and Countrey on two consecutive lines, and other variable spellings of the same words were also written close together (see p. 117).

Some infrequently used words, lacking a replica spelling in Shakespeare, may nevertheless count as 'Shakespearian' for special reasons. Thus *shund* (= shunned, 1.2.67) illustrates Shakespeare's *-nd* ending (instead of *-nned*), as in

Son 62.10 (tand = tanned), *MND* 3.2.142 (fand = fanned), *MV* 4.1.46 (baind = banned, i.e. poisoned), *Ham* 2.2.554 (wand = wanned).

Even though several of the 'Shakespearian' spellings listed above were not uncommon, the stock of spellings shared by Q *Othello* with other Shakespeare texts (notably with *Hamlet* Q2) cannot be ascribed to sheer coincidence. To put it another way: a decided preference for *shew* (instead of *show*), or for *vertue* (instead of *virtue*), or for *sence* (instead of *sense*), was not unusual, taking each word individually. But how many other writers shared Shakespeare's preference for *shew* and *vertue* and *sence* and all the other strong or occasional preferences listed above? The large number of 'Shakespearian' spellings in Q persuades me that, despite all that has been said in favour of a scribal transcript serving as Q copy (see p. 41), Q could have been printed from Shakespeare's foul papers.

Q's stage directions, Greg thought, 'might all have been written by the author'.[1] Some are unique in Shakespeare (*'he stifles her'*, 5.2.82; *'The Moore runnes at* Iago', 5.2.232).[2] Others echo or resemble unusual directions found elsewhere in the canon. *'Enter* Cassio, *driuing in* Roderigo' (2.3.140) anticipates *'Enter Ariell, driuing in Caliban'* in *The Tempest* (5.1.255), a play written and printed later, and echoes *'enter Ioane de Puzel, driuing Englishmen before her'* (*1H6* 1.5.0); 'driving in' in *The Tempest* is particularly interesting – since Q *Othello* seems not to have been a playhouse manuscript (see p. 37), Shakespeare himself, not a playhouse scribe, must have repeated this direction.[3] *'Brabantio at a window'* (1.1.80) may be compared with *'Enter the King, and Buts, at a Window aboue'* (*H8* 5.2.10); *'Enter* Barbantio [*sic*] *in his night gowne'* (1.1.157) with *'Enter the King in his night-gowne'* (*2H4* 3.1.0) and *'Enter Iulius Caesar in his Night-gowne'* (*JC* 2.2.0); *'Enter* Montanio, *Gouernor of* Cypres' (2.1.0) with *'Enter Leonato gouernour of Messina'* (*MA* 1.1.0); *'A bell rung'* (2.3.153) with *'A Bell rings'* (*Mac* 2.1.61); *'Emillia calls within'* (5.2.84) with *'One cals within* Iuliet' (*RJ* 1.5.143). The nameless *'One within'* (1.3.12) is characteristic of Shakespeare: compare *RJ*, above, and *'Enter one to Richard with meate'* (*R2* 5.5.94) and *'Enter one with letters'* (*1H4* 4.1.12).

These stage directions reinforce the impression given by Q's spellings and Q's misreading (see pp. 41–5): the copy for Q was either a transcript close to the foul papers or the foul papers themselves.[4]

APPENDIX D: FIRST FOLIO 'SWIB' FIGURES

Definition: 'Swib' forms (i.e. single words in brackets) are included in these lists if printed as one word, or as two words jointed by a hyphen or apostrophe. Thus 'methinks', 'me-thinks' and 'quoth'a' are included, 'me thinks' and 'quoth he' excluded.

Swib figures for the good quartos are listed on pp. 59, 61. For the possible significance of swib forms see pp. 59–76. In this appendix I omit swib vocatives, which are less revealing than other swib words, but include them in the total

count for each play. The Through Line Numbering of the *Norton Facsimile*
follows every swib word, and the compositor is then identified as A, B, etc., as
in Charlton Hinman's *Printing and Proof-Reading*; where Howard-Hill's compositor analysis differs, it follows Hinman's in square brackets.[1] I have ignored
later attempts (not always convincing) to reallocate some Folio pages to even
more compositors, being chiefly concerned to show that more than one compositor often set the same word as a swib – that is, to prove that compositor
preferences do not explain the phenomenon, though no doubt no two men
reproduced copy in exactly the same way. It should be remembered that,
according to Hinman's breakdown, compositor A set the equivalent of about
194 full Folio pages, B set 445, C set 120, D set $35\frac{1}{2}$ and E set $71\frac{1}{2}$:[2] hence the
fact that swib totals differ from man to man. Howard-Hill changed these
figures, but not dramatically: B still remains responsible for about half the
Folio. The plays are arranged, below, in the sequence of the First Folio.

The Tempest: *inuisible* 1535A (stage direction). Total, 14.

Two Gentlemen: hap'ly 15A, vnworthily 1098C, senceles 1213C (letter),
Spaniel-like 1636A. Total, 33.

Merry Wives: la 236A, I'faith 402A, indeed 537C, quoth'a 677C, be-like 1203C,
forsooth 1275B, alas 1442B, good-heart 1712B, forsooth 1747B, *Faire* 1844
[?F], *Lapis* 1849 [?F], singly 2359A. Total, 66.

Measure for Measure: Authority 211D [D + C], soe 214D [D + C], oh 1412D
[D + C], be-like 1980B. Total, 17.

Comedy of Errors: vnhappie 204 ?D [C + D]. Total, 1.

Much Ado: total, 2.

Love's Labour's Lost: company 1411C* [C]. Total, 2 (both in Q).

Midsummer Night's Dream: perforce 396B, perforce 958D, forsooth 1257D,
1327D (the last three in Q or Q2). Total, 4.

Merchant of Venice: total, 0.

As You Like It: forsooth 1548B, *videlicet* 2008C. Total, 4.

Taming of the Shrew: Belike 408B, insooth 831B. Total, 2.

All's Well: *then* 1462B (letter). Total, 3.

Twelfth Night: perchance 576B, mistaken 691B, sau'd 1729B, henceforth
2331B. Total, 11.

Winter's Tale: indeed 40A, good-deed 99A, Priest-like 326A, Counsaile 543A,
alas 931B, missingly 1644B, frighted 1931B. Total, 76.

King John: ah 1353C, thus 1918B.[3] Total, 12.

Richard II: total, 18 (some from Qq).

1 Henry IV: neglectingly 374B, forsooth 462B, quoth-a 675B, byrlady 1382C,
forsooth 2547C, willingly 2951B. Total, 8.

2 Henry IV: haply 86B, Rebellion 253B, 258B, winking 534B, almost 550B,
indeed 979B, indeede 1971A, mis-order'd 2134C, certaine 2517C, alacke
2770B, vainly 2782B, quoth-a 3048B, lately 3176B, hence 3264B. (Epilogue:
indeed 3329, 3333, 3350.) Total, 60.

Henry V: England 315A, Scot 316A, almost 374A, 727B, indeed 858A, pera-
duenture 2009A, wretches 2333A, English 2998A. Total, 11.

1 Henry VI: perhaps 1480A, vnworthily 1762B, forsooth 1908B. Total, 5.

2 Henry VI: forsooth 1887B, indeede 2678B. Total, 5.

3 Henry VI: haply 1195B, vnwares 1199B, perhaps 1347B, Loue 3157B (in
square brackets). Total, 10.

Richard III: forsooth 510B, belike 531B, trembling 897B, almost 1243B, vngra-
cious 1255B, almost 1476B. Total, 11 (some in Q3 or Q6, most new in F).

Henry VIII: too 1236C, Shall 1449B. Total, 6.

Troilus and Cressida: indeed 474B, me 630B, forsooth 632B, ful 861B, alas
1124B. Total, 9 (3 as in Q).

Coriolanus: almost 340B, forsooth 2186A/B, sometime 2461B, almost 3260B.
Total, 7.

Titus Andronicus: worthily 48B, vnaduised 593E. Total, 3 (2 as in Q).

Romeo and Juliet: exquisit 237E (so Q2). Total, 1.

Timon of Athens: alas 2166B. Total, 2.

Julius Caesar: perhaps 134B, almost 351B, perhaps 553A, alas 803B, almost
1187E. Total, 8.

Macbeth: alas 1798B. Total, 3.

Hamlet: sometimes 1248B, perhaps 3018E. Total, 3.

King Lear: perchance 1638B. Total, 4.

Othello: hoa 199E, vnbonnetted 227E, hoa 792B, doubtlesse 1873B, indeed
2188B, pish 2418B[E], indeed 3490B, belike 3624B. Total, 34 (see also
p. 61).

Antony and Cleopatra: prythee 2820B. Total, 6.

Cymbeline: perchance 535B, happily 2237B, Greefe 2322B, wretch 2868B, alas
3166B. Total, 32.

Before one attempts to interpret these lists, some knowledge of the habits of
other writers will be useful. I have looked at several, and think that Middleton's are interesting. Some of Middleton's plays contain no swib words at all –
Michaelmas Term (1607), *The Phoenix* (1607), *A Chaste Maid in Cheapside* (1630).
Some have a few, roughly the same number as we find in most of Shakespeare's
texts: *Blurt Master Constable* (1602) has dismounted A3b, Melancholie D1b,
reading E2a, Ganimed G4b, Both H2b; *A Mad World My Masters* (1608) has
yfaith G4a; *The Roaring Girl* (1611) besides A4a, Sebastian, gentlemen B3b,
Dapper K2a. For our purposes *The Family of Love* (1608) is the most important:
the swib words here are indeed B4a, perhaps E1b, forsooth G3a, three of the
commonest swibs in Shakespeare.

The question now arises whether swibs were in such general use that they
have no evidential value whatever. This may be true of some but not, I think,
of all. An uncommon word like 'unworthily', which occurs just twice in the
whole of Shakespeare, in two plays probably written close together (*Two
Gentlemen* TLN 1098C, *1 Henry VI* 1762B), looks like an authorial swib in

origin; or, near the other end of his career, compare 'Very wisely (Puppies.)' and 'As many Inches, as you haue Oceans (Puppies.)' (*Winter's Tale* 2589A, *Cymbeline* 242B⁴) (vocatives, therefore not entered in my lists). The fact that different compositors set the same word as a swib in the same text almost certainly means that this was the copy spelling – as in *Julius Caesar* (perhaps, A and B; almost, B and E), or in *1 Henry IV* (forsooth, B and C). And the fact that the commoner swibs in Shakespeare were set in a number of texts by a number of compositors points the same way: 'indeed' by A (*Winter's Tale*), B (*2 Henry VI*), C (*Merry Wives*); 'perhaps' by A (*1 Henry VI*), B (*3 Henry VI*), E (*Hamlet*), and in the *Sonnets* (see p. 61). Even when one Folio compositor alone set a common swib, confirmation comes from non-Folio texts that this swib may nevertheless derive from Shakespeare: 'alas' was set by B in *Merry Wives, Winter's Tale, Timon, Julius Caesar, Macbeth* and *Cymbeline*, so one wonders whether this swib originated with B rather than in his copy. But swib 'alas' also occurs in *Lucrece* and in Q *Troilus and Cressida* (see p. 61): its non-appearance in Folio pages set by A, C, D, etc., may simply be due to B's much larger share in the Folio, or his greater propensity to reproduce swib spellings.

Compositors and scribes might react to swibs as to unusual spelling or punctuation, suppressing or introducing them as they saw fit. Taking this into account, and also the occurrence of some of Shakespeare's repeated swibs in non-Shakespearian texts, are we justified in ascribing most of the swibs in Shakespearian texts to the author? I think that we are, except when the statistical needle registers a startling aberration (as in the case of the Crane transcripts), the Shakespearian swibs being so widely dispersed in Quarto and Folio texts and, for the most part, so evenly, considering the total number of words per play. To look at the question another way, we are not entitled to assume that swibs found in other authors (e.g. indeed, perhaps) were *not* written by Shakespeare, for why should he be precluded from writing and spelling as others did? We know from the Pavier quartos that Jaggard's compositors 'did not have a habit of wantonly multiplying single words in brackets' (see p. 60); B set about half of the Folio pages, presumably *he* found the swibs he set in his copy. The swib figures for the other Folio compositors are sufficiently like B's to justify the inference that they, too, followed copy when they placed single words in brackets.

Assuming, then, that swib words in plays that contain up to a dozen or so are mostly Shakespeare's, and that Crane texts will tend to contain more, what are we to make of texts that fall between these extremes? I suspect that special factors will be involved, as in F *Richard II*, where the 18 swibs include several from earlier quartos. In *Cymbeline* (32 swibs) the special factor could be Crane. This Folio text, set entirely by compositor B (according to Hinman; Howard-Hill reassigned five pages to E), divides into two unequal halves, as I pointed out in 1967: to the end of 2.4 it prints *O* consistently as *O* (17 times); from 2.5 it prefers *Oh* (56) as against *O* (6).⁵ Accepting this division, the

Oxford editors thought 'that the Folio copy was a Crane transcript of another manuscript of mixed provenance'.[6]

Editors used to classify the manuscripts from which Folio texts were printed as foul papers, prompt-books, fair copies, private transcripts – as if they were texts very like the dramatic manuscripts that happen to survive. If, however, they were prepared specifically as copy for the Folio they would differ from most of the dramatic manuscripts known to us in their intended function and, in some cases, in their physical appearance. Act and scene numbering would be marked for the benefit of Folio readers, for a start; if in fact they served as printer's copy, compositors' smudges would be unavoidable and consequently these manuscripts would not appeal to the usual collectors, and would more easily perish. Again, if the printer was in a hurry, the actual writing of the manuscripts might have to be speeded up, and this could be done by dividing the work down the middle, between two men.

The Oxford editors said of *Cymbeline* that 'it is, as yet, impossible to be sure whether the change of hands occurred in the Folio copy itself, or in the manuscript from which the Folio copy derived'.[7] Other Folio texts divide, like *Cymbeline*, more or less down the middle, if their swib count can be taken as indicative. *King John* has 12 swibs, beginning in Act 3 (1033C); *1 Henry 6* has 5, beginning in Act 3 scene 2 (1480A); *2 Henry VI* has 5, beginning in Act 3 (1588A); *Macbeth* has 3, beginning in Act 3 scene 4 (1308A/B); *Julius Caesar* has 8, the last in Act 3 scene 2 (1753B). On their own these figures prove nothing; taken together they indicate possibilities that still need to be explored, and reveal Crane's challenge and elusiveness for editors of the future.[8]

APPENDIX E: THE FOLIO TEXT OF *2 HENRY IV* AND RALPH CRANE

(Folio line-references are to the Through Line Numbering or TLN in the *Norton Facsimile*, edited by Charlton Hinman (1968). Where necessary, the TLN is followed by a letter A, B, etc., indicating the compositor who set the page, according to the compositor analysis in Hinman's *Printing of the First Folio*.)

The text of F *2 Henry IV* in some ways resembles the text of F *Othello*, and has been ascribed to Ralph Crane. The ascription, first made by J. Q. Adams and cautiously endorsed by M. A. Shaaber, was 'doubted by careful observers', said W.W. Greg.[1] Howard-Hill, while staking no claims for this text, warned in 1972 that we must not lose sight of it: '*2 Henry IV* is a text which demands closer examination for possible Crane influence'.[2] I agree with Howard-Hill, the more so since F *2 Henry IV* has several links with Crane texts and with F *Othello* not noted by previous commentators.

(1) M.A. Shaaber. 'I think it quite likely that the MS. used by the F printers was a transcript of the play made by Crane or by some other professional scribe of similar working habits.' 'A scribe with some experience in handling playhouse MSS., a man like Ralph Crane, possibly Crane himself, was

engaged to prepare the new draft of the play. For this purpose, he was provided with the official prompt-book of the play.'[3]

(2) A.R. Humphreys[4] was struck by 'a strong penchant for unexpected hyphens' in F *2 Henry IV*. 'With *Othello*, the *Henry IVs* are the most heavily expurgated of F's plays . . . . Dr Alice Walker argues that expurgation was editorial in origin, rather than a prompt-book matter.' Humphreys added that 'a great number of Q's colloquialisms, archaisms, rusticisms, and apparent solecisms are turned into "proper" forms. This is one of F's most remarkable features [in *2 Henry IV*].' The features that distinguish F from Q, we can now see, support the case for Crane as scribe of the F manuscript. For Crane's penchant for hyphens and resistance to colloquialisms, etc., see pp. 63, 69.

(3) Swib count. There are 57 swibs in F *2 Henry IV* (or 60 if we include the epilogue), the third-highest figure in the Folio after *The Winter's Tale* (76) and *Merry Wives* (66), two 'Crane' texts. Some of the 57 occur again in Shakespeare (see p. 162) and/or in Crane, and one deserves a special mention: certaine (*2 Henry IV* 2517C). Not printed as a swib elsewhere in Shakespeare, but also found as one in Crane's *Demetrius* 2971.

(4) Verb and pronoun hyphened: figge-me (3143B). Not hyphened in Q. A common hyphen in Crane's work (see p. 64).

(5) *'Saue* [with apostrophe]: 1137C, 3106B, 3253B. Q has 'God saue' in all three cases. This spelling occurs only in Folio 'Crane' texts (not in other F texts), in the work of several compositors; it also occurs in F *Othello* (see p. 66). Taylor writes that 'in Crane plays "God save" never appears; the apostrophied alternative occurs seven times, twice unmetrically'.[5] In *2 Henry IV*, Q's 'God saue' becomes either ''Saue' or 'Saue' seven times (i.e. 'God' disappears) – another link with Crane.

(6) *By this hand*: a mild oath, left unexpurgated in many other texts, but omitted from F *Othello* 2521B and from F *2 Henry IV* 829B, 1180C, and omitted twice from Crane's transcript of *A Game at Chess* (L), 333, 706.

(7) *good-sooth* (1064C): related, I have suggested (p. 66), to hyphened 'Good-faith' in F *Othello*. Q prints 'good faith'. Crane, it may be noted, hyphened 'good' and the following word elsewhere (an occasional practice), as in *Game* (L) 554 Good-men (Middleton's holograph, T, reads 'Goodmen'); good-speed (*Witch* 667); good-heart (*Merry Wives* 1712B); good-deed (*Winter's Tale* 99A).

(8) Verb and adverb hyphened: rode-on 115B, Leane-on, giue-o're 223B, fub'd-off 645B, hooke-on, hooke-on 755–6B, Come-on 1534C (3 times), Go-too 1762–1828C (5 times), sway-on 1890A. Q omits all these hyphens. This characteristic 'Crane' hyphen (there are more than three dozen instances in *The Witch*) also occurs in *Two Gentlemen*, *Merry Wives*, *Measure for Measure*, *Winter's Tale* (all 'Crane' texts) and in F *Othello*. Elsewhere in the Folio it is rare, and seems to be used only when the verb and adverb function together as a noun or adjective: that young start-vp (*Much Ado* 404A: so Q); blush-in cheekes by faults are bred (*Love's Labour's Lost* 405C: so Q); a more comming-

on disposition (*As You like It* 2023C); my weau'd-vp follyes (*Richard II* 2151A); they wisht-for come, your vnthought-of Harry (*1 Henry IV* 307 ?B, 1961C); the vnlook'd-for Issue, our hop'd-for Hay, no hop'd-for Mercy (*3 Henry VI* 1655A, 2667A, 2918A); your su'd-for Tongues (*Coriolanus* 1611A); a made-vp-Villaine (*Timon* 2320B); That euer I should call thee Cast-away (*Antony and Cleopatra* 1794B); The falne-off Britaines (*Cymbeline* 2203B). Even if I have missed one or two instances in re-reading the Folio, which is not impossible, the profusion of instances in *2 Henry IV*, comparatively speaking, is as significant as their grammatical function, which differs in the non-Crane texts. On the other hand, some of the very same hyphened words appear in *2 Henry IV* and in Folio 'Crane' texts: for example, 'come-on' and 'go-too' (three and five times in *2 Henry IV*) are both found in F *Merry Wives*, a text that includes Go-too 1384B, Come-on 1438?, peere-out 1921B, drawes-on 2470B and 2483B. Compare also come-on in *Two Gentlemen* 879C, *Winter's Tale* 621A and 2220B, and go-too in Crane's *Demetrius* 2497 and *Witch* 1799. The involvement of compositors A, B and C in the Folio's 'come-ons' and 'go-toos' supports the view that the hyphens here are scribal.

(9) '*Dramatis personae*' list. The list that follows *2 Henry IV* differs from those that follow other 'Crane' texts in the Folio (see p. 71), perhaps because it had to fill a blank page. Nevertheless, the existence of such a list again suggests the pos-sibility of Crane's presence in F *2 Henry IV*. Of the seven lists in the Folio, four are in acknowledged 'Crane' texts, two are in *Othello* and *2 Henry IV*, and the seventh comes at the end of *Timon* (needed to fill the recto of an otherwise blank leaf).

(10) *has-hath* changes. Q 'has' becomes 'hath' in F six times: 867B, 892B, 1263C, 1275C, 1764C, 1853C. For similar changes in F *Othello* see p. 68. There are no such Q–F variants in *1 Henry IV*.

(11) Despite the similarities of the F texts of *2 Henry IV* and *Othello*, we must also take account of significant differences.

> It would be convenient to attribute the expurgation of profanity and collo-quialism in *2 Henry IV*, *Hamlet*, and *Othello* to a single interfering scribe . . . . But any such hypothesis runs into formidable difficulties. *Othello* strongly prefers 'Oh'; *2 Henry IV* as strongly prefers 'O'; *Hamlet* prefers 'Oh', but much less consistently than *Othello*. *2 Henry IV* changes 'and' to 'if' more than two dozen times; *Hamlet* and *Othello* make the same change only six times between them. *Othello* has 31 exclamation marks, *Hamlet* only 17, and *2 Henry IV* only 8; *Hamlet* 44 round brackets, *Othello* 137, *2 Henry IV* 272.[6]

For these and other reasons, and because we know enough about the composi-tors responsible for F *2 Henry IV* and F *Othello* to be able to say that these textual differences pre-dated the printing of the plays, it may be thought that the same scribe, Ralph Crane, could not have produced texts as unlike each other as F *2 Henry IV* and *Othello*. To which I reply: yes – and no. We would not anticipate such discrepancies if the texts from which Crane copied were both in the same hand – but were they?

As I have suggested,[7] following Fredson Bowers, 'the printing of a text may be taken as the destruction of that text'. Therefore, if we accept the consensus that F *2 Henry IV* derived, somehow or another, from Q and an authoritative manuscript, we have to reckon with two manuscripts: one supplied for and destroyed by the F printer, and one that transmitted authoritative readings not found in Q (eight longer passages and, in the words of A.R. Humphreys, 'many apparently authentic words and short phrases which the Folio contains and the Quarto does not'[8]). The owners of a manuscript containing so much unpublished material would have been short-sighted had they allowed the printer to lay his inky hands on it, and in effect to destroy it; the hypothesis that F *Hamlet* and F *Othello* were printed from a copy of Q (corrected with the help of a manuscript) has now lapsed,[9] and it is equally improbable applied to *2 Henry IV* – consequently I conclude that F *2 Henry IV* was set up from a manuscript, one that conflated Q and the 'authoritative manuscript'.

The puzzling fact that F *Othello* and F *2 Henry IV* share a number of special 'Crane' spellings and yet differ in other textual characteristics can now be explained. In each case a Crane manuscript served as printer's copy, but the Crane manuscript of *2 Henry IV* was itself copied from another scribal manuscript, one with many distinctive features not usually found in texts close to Shakespeare's papers, such as the other good quartos. The earlier manuscript of *2 Henry IV* was not, after all, 'authoritative', except in preserving passages and variants that would have perished without it. Crane, as was his custom, retained some of the scribal oddities of his predecessor and introduced some of his own, outlined in this appendix. Hence the striking differences with *O* and *Oh* spellings: *O*, 44; *Oh*, 1 (F *2 Henry IV*); *O*, 52; *Oh*, 117 (F *Othello*). Taylor, apparently unaware that F *2 Henry IV* and F *Othello* might be 'Crane' texts, has shown[10] that 'Crane reproduced whichever spelling [either *Oh* or *O*] he found in his copy'.

APPENDIX F: THE EDITING OF Q2 *OTHELLO*

The second Quarto of *Othello* (Q2: 1630) deserves more attention than it usually receives from editors. It reprints the first Quarto (Q) but frequently prefers F, or compromises between Q and F, taking something from each; and sometimes it differs from both Q and F. An edited text, it was diligently prepared by a person who probably relied on his intelligence to resolve difficulties. The older view, that he may have had access to a lost manuscript, was shown to be unlikely by Charlton Hinman:[1] yet the Q2 editor could have changed Q readings because he knew the play well as it was performed in the theatre. Each of these possibilities would give a different kind of authority to Q2 readings. In the absence of certainty my guess is that the Q2 editor drew on his native wit, and perhaps on his recollection of the play as acted, not on a manuscript. As an informed and interested near-contemporary he has some 'authority', perhaps more than any later editor, yet Q2 must be treated with caution.

Although we may be uneasy about accepting Q2 as an independent authority, clearly derivative as it is from both Q and F, the procedures of the Q2 editor can help us in other ways. For his editorial situation almost repeated that of the editor of the F text, and we may understand some of the F editor's puzzling choices by observing the Q2 editor at work. It appears that in both cases the editor used two texts to prepare his own: the F editor used Q and a manuscript, the Q2 editor used Q and F. How can we explain the fact that each editor, with two texts in front of him, sometimes preferred an inferior reading (inferior, that is, in the judgement of later editors), when an acceptable and better reading also lay at hand?

(1) Q2 adopts nonsensical Q readings: Vpon this *heate* I spake (1.3.167; *heate* Q; *hint* F); *rist* your three fingers (2.1.173; *rist* Q; *kiss'd* F); He shall in *strangest*, stand no farther off (3.3.12; *strangest* Q; *strangenesse* F); Patience *thy* young and rose-lip'd Cherubim (4.2.64; *thy* Q; *thou* F).

(2) Q2 interpolates inferior F readings: Officers of *might* (1.1.180; *night* Q; *might* F); knowes all *quantities*, with a learned spirit (3.3.263; *qualities* Q; *Quantities* F); From any *other* foule vnlawfull touch (4.2.86; *hated* Q; *other* F).

(3) Q2 interpolates nonsensical F readings: Would you, the *superuision* grossely gape on (3.3.398; *superuisor* Q; *super-vision* F); All's one, good *father*; how foolish are our minds (4.3.21; *faith* Q; *Father* F).

We can account for (1) as lapses of attention, and for (2) as errors of judgement on the part of the Q2 editor. He perhaps anticipated later editors in thinking F a better text than Q, hence in some cases of doubt (e.g. [2]) might prefer F. (The fact that Q2 reprinted from corrected Q, not from corrected F, does not mean that the Q2 editor thought Q the better text: the Q2 publisher had acquired his 'copy' of *Othello* from Walkley, hence used Walkley's Q as the basis of Q2.) But why should the Q2 editor delete good Q readings (as in [3]) and substitute nonsense? Whether F's *good Father* was this text's clumsy alternative for profanity or a misreading (as it was in Q2 *Romeo and Juliet* 4.4.21), F's *good Father* and *super-vision* are plainly wrong. If Q2 was printed from a hand-corrected version of Q, as is generally supposed, this seems to imply that the Q2 editor crossed out words that made sense and inserted instead words that did not make sense. Why would an apparently intelligent editor act so strangely?

Before we try to answer this question, let us be clear about his editorial policy. He took a great deal of trouble: most visibly in restoring from F passages omitted from Q, some of them lengthy (these will have been written on separate sheets of paper and possibly pasted into Q). He deleted Q's profanity, usually substituting F's diluted alternative, though not always satisfied with F. Compare 1.1.32:

And I, God blesse the marke, his Worships Ancient.

Q

And I (blesse the marke) his Mooreships Auntient.

F

And I Sir (blesse the marke) his Mooreships Ancient.

Q2

Q2 often interpolated brackets from F but, interestingly, omitted almost all the F swibs (single words in brackets); it repunctuated, relined the verse, and even changed some Q passages in roman to F's italics (pp. 24, 25). Nothing was too small to catch the Q2 editor's attention: Q *spoke* (2.1.74) becomes FQ2 *spake*, Q *What, now?* (5.2.106) becomes FQ2 *What? now?* And, always alert, the Q2 editor sometimes rejected both Q and F.

1.3.38 resterine Q; re-stem F; resterne Q2; 2.2.6 minde Q; addition F; addiction Q2; 3.3.109 By heaven he ecchoes me Q; Alas, thou ecchos't me F; why dost thou ecchoe me Q2; 3.3.389 (Q omits); My name F; her name Q2; 3.3.458 (Q omits); Neu'r keepes retyring ebbe, but keepes due on F; Ne'r feels . . . Q2; 4.2.157 (Q omits); Delighted them: or any other Forme F; Delighted them in . . . Q2; 4.3.39 (Q omits); The poore Soule sat sining (corrected to 'singing'), by a Sicamour tree F; . . . sate sighing . . . Q2; 5.2.13 That can thy light returne Q; . . . Light re-Lume F; . . . light relumine Q2.

Several of these Q2 emendations have passed into the *textus receptus*. Whatever we may think of them individually, they reveal a careful mind at work, as do other striking changes in this text.

So we have an editor with 'an active, alert editorial intelligence', as Thomas L. Berger aptly described him,[2] one who sifted and corrected the text with diligence and yet, now and then, proceeded with extraordinary carelessness, notably when he substituted F's nonsense at points where his copy-text, Q, seems acceptable. Now we should not expect an editor in the year 1630 to be equally careful on every page of his text (this is too much to ask for even three-and-a-half centuries later), yet the more painstaking he proves in general the more surprising and out-of-character his individual lapses.

The Q2 editor, however, was not alone in his lapses. Some of the very readings that I have called inferior or nonsensical were chosen not only by Q2 but also by F, and in each instance in preference to Q's 'better' readings. Had only one man, either Crane or the Q2 editor, chosen so strangely we might have dismissed his decisions as careless or quixotic. When two men independently select the same inferior or nonsensical reading, and the Q2 editor actually crosses out a better reading, as he must have done, and writes in one that we think self-evidently inferior, such an explanation will no longer serve. As I have suggested (p. 100), the independent testimony of F and Q2 must mean that by the 1620s Shakespeare's language was felt to be puzzling – sometimes 'obscure', sometimes 'not to be understood'. But he had acquired the status of a classic; the First Folio had firmly established his reputation and admirers were already making pilgrimages to Stratford.[3] In 1633 Prynne thought it deplorable that 'Shackspeers Plaies are printed in the best Crowne paper, far better than most Bibles.' Bardolatry had started: in these circumstances it is not surprising that Shakespeare's language, even if sometimes baffling, was revered as 'Delphick lines' (the words of Milton in 1630). Crane's choice of inferior readings can be blamed on Shakespeare's manuscript, which was often illegible and underpunctuated, forcing him to resort to guessing, and it can be blamed on his respect for Delphic Shakespeare. The Q2 editor, on the other hand, had no difficulty in reading his two texts, both of which were printed, and presumably switched to F's inferior readings out of respect for Shakespeare and for that 'live-long monument', the Folio. Modern editors are in no position to criticise the first two editors of *Othello*, for have they not all chosen to print inferior variants now and then, out of misplaced respect for 'the better text'?

Notes

If a book cited in the notes was published or co-published in London, no place of publication is indicated.

1 INTRODUCTION

1 Paul Werstine recently questioned the views of W. W. Greg and the 'New Bibliography' concerning foul papers: see Appendix A.
2 Arber, *Transcript*, IV, 59. I have changed some of Arber's capitals and bold type to roman.
3 See Hinman's *Norton Facsimile*, p. xxiv.
4 Greg, *First Folio*, p. 358, n. 7.
5 Chambers, *William Shakespeare*, I, 459.
6 For Q's press variants see Hinman, *Othello 1622*; for F's, Hinman, *Printing and Proof-Reading*.
7 Greg, *First Folio*, p. 359.
8 For a comparison of the stage directions in Q *Othello* with Shakespeare's other texts see Appendix C, p. 161.
9 Wells and Taylor, *Textual Companion*, p. 477.
10 See, for example, Robert K. Turner, *MP* (1973–4), 71, pp. 191–6; Richard Proudfoot, *SS* (1972), 25, pp. 194 ff.
11 See Proudfoot, loc. cit.
12 Taylor's argument is summarised in more detail on p. 93.

2 REVISION?

1 Nevill Coghill, *Shakespeare's Professional Skills* (1964), p. 167.
2 *Ibid.*, p. 179.
3 *Ibid.*, p. 189.
4 *Ibid.*, p. 180.
5 *Ibid.*, p. 198.
6 'Shakespeare's Revised Plays: *King Lear* and *Othello*', *The Library*, 6th Series (1982), IV, pp. 142–73, p. 162.
7 *The Division of the Kingdoms: Shakespeare's Two Versions of 'King Lear'*, ed. Gary Taylor and Michael Warren (1983).
8 Honigmann (as in n. 6), p. 169.
9 *Macbeth*, 4.1.39.
10 Taylor (as in n. 7), pp. 89, 93. Compare Warren, *ibid.*, p. 49.
11 4.3.29–52, 54–6, 59–62 and 5.2.244–6.

12 Cf. Arden 3 *Othello*, Appendix 1 ('Date')

13 See pp. 39–40.

14 Richard Proudfoot comments (privately) that the F lines omitted by Q (4.3.85–102), being in verse, make Desdemona's final couplet less suddenly sententious than Q.

15 Richard Proudfoot observes (privately) that a song would take more time than a speech: the Q 'cuts' would save a little more time than 8 minutes.

16 See Greg, *First Folio*, pp. 110–11, 233.

17 See pp. 39–40.

18 Greg, *First Folio*, p. 368.

19 I am thinking of passages such as the following: (a) 'I humbly beseech you proceed to th'Affaires of State' (1.3.221; 'Beseech you now, to the affaires of the state', Q); (b) 'And let me finde a Charter in your voice / T'assist my simplenesse. / Duke. What would you Desdemona?' (1.3.247–8; '*And if my simplenesse. – / Du. What would you – speake.*' Q). It will be noticed that in each case F's revision, if revision it is, upsets the metre, whereas Q, which is usually so indifferent to metrical considerations, scans correctly; also, that both (a) and (b) come from the very scene in which we have observed (pp. 16–17) other instances of revision leading to metrical irregularity.

I do not suggest that these two passages, or the five cited on pp. 16–17, were printed exactly as Shakespeare wrote them. Minor corruptions could have survived in both Q and F versions, as so often elsewhere. For instance, I assume that in (1) on p. 17 the (unpunctuated) manuscript read 'Why at her fathers', and that the F scribe or compositor, thinking this was a question, added the question mark.

20 Greg, *First Folio*, p. 367.

21 Honigmann, *Stability*, p. 110.

22 *Ibid.*, pp. 14–21, 27–33.

23 Greg in *SQ* (1956), VII, p. 103.

24 Honigmann, *Stability*, p. 25.

25 *Ibid.*, p. 15, n. 5.

26 Bowers, 'Authority, Copy', p. 21. See also p. 25: 'It is especially unfortunate that some critics are still under the influence of Greg's rigid dichotomy that if the copy were not foul papers it had to be the prompt-book.'

3 THE QUARTO PUBLISHER AND PRINTER

1 *The Library* (1925), VI, pp. 271–7.

2 L. Kirschbaum, 'Walkley's Supposed Piracy of Wither's *Workes* in 1620', *The Library* (1938–9), XIX, 339–46.

3 See Appendix B.

4 Hinman, *Othello 1622*, p. xv. It is worth noting that the printing of *The Maid's Tragedy* of 1619 was also interrupted. Greg observed that the text 'was printed in two sections, B–G and H–L, in slightly different types . . . . This might suggest that the copy was divided between two compositors . . . . It is, however, more likely that composition was interrupted . . . or possibly that the work was completed at another press' (*Bibliography*, vol. 2: *The Maid's Tragedy*, 1619). Although *The Maid's Tragedy* was printed by N. Okes for F. Constable, i.e. Walkley was not directly involved, the close association of Okes and Walkley in the issuing of so many plays belonging to the King's Men suggests that the fate of *The Maid's Tragedy* is part of our story. See also *The Dramatic Works in the Beaumont and Fletcher Canon* (general editor, Fredson Bowers), 1966–, II, 6, n. 3. It should be added, however, that 'shared printing', which was not very unusual, need not have involved lengthy interruptions or suspicious circumstances (see Blayney, as in n. 20, General Index, 'shared printing'). In the case of Thomas Walkley the suspicious circumstances emerge from his lawsuits.

5 See Appendix B, p. 154.

6 PRO, Prob 11/147 (109 Clarke), will of Thomas Snodham; Prob 11/148 (24 Hele), will of Elizabeth Snodham.

7 Quoted by Henry R. Plomer, *A Dictionary of the Printers and Booksellers . . . from 1641 to 1667* (printed for the Bibliographical Society, 1907): 'John Beale'.

8 K.W. Cameron, '*Othello*, Quarto 1, Reconsidered', *PMLA* (1932), XLVII, pp. 671–83.

9 I take it that 'recovered' means acquired (or repossessed?).

10 Greg, *First Folio*, p. 357.

11 *Ibid.*, pp. 15–16.

12 *Ibid.*, p. 24.

13 Chambers, *William Shakespeare*, I, 136.

14 See p. 25.

15 See Greg, *First Folio*, p. 36, n. 3, and Sidney Thomas in *SQ* (1976), XXVII, p. 186 ff.

16 *Thierry and Theodoret* (1621) was not replaced by an improved text.

17 For Burbage's will see *Playhouse Wills 1558–1642*, ed. E. Honigmann and Susan Brock (Manchester, 1993), pp. 113–14. This was a nuncupative will, declared by the testator before witnesses but not written or signed by him. Had Burbage's death been expected he would not have put off the making of his will till the day before his death.

18 For Jaggard's will see *ibid.*, pp. 122–3.

19 See Gerald D. Johnson, 'Thomas Pavier, Publisher, 1600–25', *The Library*, 6th Series (1992), XIV, pp. 12–50. Apart from the quartos of 1619, Pavier only entered or published plays from 1600 to 1611, specialising from then on in devotional works. On 14 June 1619 Pavier was elected one of the three new assistants 'and thereafter he regularly sat on the governing board of the Company'; in 1622 he was elected Under Warden. It is hard to believe that he knowingly participated in the faking of the dates of the 1619 'Pavier' quartos just before or just after June 1619, a critical month in his career as a stationer. Johnson notes that Greg, who originally saw Pavier as the instigator of the quartos, later wrote more cautiously 'Who was the responsible person behind the venture is not on the face of it very clear' (*First Folio*, pp. 13, 15). And Johnson sums up that, 'seen in the context of Pavier's other publications in the last decade of his career, his involvement in the publication of the plays known as the Pavier quartos appears incongruous' (p. 35).

20 See Peter W.M. Blayney, *The Texts of 'King Lear' and their Origins*, vol. 1 (New Cambridge Shakespeare Studies and Supplementary Texts Series, Cambridge, 1982), pp. 298–9.

21 *Ibid.*, p. 28.

22 *Beaumont and Fletcher* (ed. Bowers) (as in n. 4), I, p. 396.

23 Robert K. Turner, *ibid.*, II, p. 16.

24 Turner, *ibid.*, I, p. 396.

25 For the documents summarised in this chapter, and for Walkley's epistle to the reader printed in Q *Othello*, see Appendix B.

4 THE QUARTO TEXT

1 Greg, *First Folio*, p. 357.

2 Hinman, *Printing and Proof-Reading*, I, 28–9.

3 Hinman, *Othello 1622*, Introduction, p. v.

4 '*The Spanish Tragedy* – a Leading Case?', *The Library* (1925), VI, pp. 47–56.

5 The first Quarto of *A Midsummer Night's Dream* (1600) has an unusual partiality for colons: I assume that they are post-Shakespearian.

6 See p. 40.

7 E.g. 2.1.175 an–and; 2.3.274 light–slight; 2.3.338 wer't to–were to; 2.3.369 Do'st–Dos't; 3.4.176 No–Oh; 5.2.162 O–hoa.

8 Cf. *Hamlet*, ed. Philip Edwards (The New Cambridge Shakespeare, 1985), p. 145; ed. G.R. Hibbard (The Oxford Shakespeare, 1987), p. 238.

9 Alice Walker believed, more damagingly, that Q contains 'a solid core of variant readings only explicable as memorial perversions' (*Textual Problems*, p. 138). Many of these 'perversions' were defended by M.R. Ridley in Arden 2 *Othello* (pp. 217–22) and in my *Stability*, p. 102 ff.

10 Honigmann, 'Re-Enter the Stage Direction', p. 123.

11 Greg, *First Folio*, p. 110.

12 *Ibid.*, pp. 368, 369.

13 *Ibid.*, pp. 360, 357.

14 See Appendix C, p. 161.

15 Greg, *First Folio*, p. 361.

16 *Ibid.*, p. 297.

17 Honigmann, 'The First Quarto of *Hamlet* and the Date of *Othello*', *RES* (1993), XLIV, pp. 211–19.

18 See Chambers, *William Shakespeare*, II, 327–8. I have partly modernised the spelling.

19 *Twelfth Night* may, however, date from c. 1599: see my *Shakespeare's Impact on his Contemporaries* (1982), pp. 100–3. If so, the same boy actor could still have been the first performer of Viola and Desdemona, though not at the same time. For the 'casting' requirements of *Twelfth Night* and *Othello*, which are exceptionally alike, see Arden 3 *Othello*, Appendix 1 ('Date').

20 Greg, *First Folio*, p. 357, n. 6.

21 Cf. Hand D in *Sir Thomas More*, l. 175, 'stilnes'; '-*nes*' (for '-*ness*') was Shakespeare's preferred spelling, but Q *Othello* has fairenesse, blacknesse, worthinesse, tendernesse, madnesse, etc. (2.1.129, 133, 209, 230, 309).

22 Hinman, *Othello 1622*, pp. xiv–xv.

23 *Ibid.*, p. vi.

24 The suggestion that the Quarto manuscript (which I have called Aa) was copied from Shakespeare's foul papers by two scribes (*Stability*, pp. 112–13) is independent of the compositor analysis that follows; if Walkley commissioned Aa as printer's copy it would have speeded up the whole operation to employ two scribes. I should add that other play-texts were perhaps sometimes written by two scribes, though more often than not they divided their stints more or less down the middle, i.e. each scribe copied one to two thousand consecutive lines. See p. 165.

25 See the articles on these plays in *SB* 1956, VIII (J. R. Brown on *Malfi*); 1961, XIV (R.K. Turner on *Thierry*).

26 See Nigel Bawcutt on Crane's probable role in the abridgement of the Malone manuscript of *A Game at Chess* (MSR *Collections*, vol. XV, 1993, p. 15), and T. Howard-Hill in *SS* (1992), 44, pp. 113–29.

5 THE PRINTER OF THE FOLIO TEXT

1 E.E. Willoughby, *A Printer of Shakespeare: The Books and Times of William Jaggard* (1934), p. 149.

2 Quoted by Willoughby.

3 For the 'Pavier' quartos cf. Greg, *First Folio*, pp. 9–16.

4 W.S. Kable thought that all the 'Pavier' quartos were set by compositor B (*The Pavier Quartos and the First Folio of Shakespeare*, Shakespeare Studies Monograph Series, 1970, p. 13). In 1971 and 1972 John F. Andrews and Peter Blayney independently disagreed with Kable, and in 1982 Richard Knowles claimed that three

compositors set Q2 *King Lear* (Knowles, 'The Printing of the Second Quarto (1619) of *King Lear*', *SB* [1982], 35, pp. 191–206).

5 D. F. McKenzie, 'Compositor B's Role in *The Merchant of Venice* Q2 (1619)', *SB* (1959), 12, pp. 75–90.

6 I return to the Pavier quartos on p. 138.

7 An intermediate quarto of *Henry V* (Q2: 1602) agrees with Q 1600 in these readings: i.e. the transpositions originated in Q3.

8 Line references are to Cambridge 1 (ed. 1893), vol. 9. The fallacies inherent in the policy of following 'the better text' are discussed in more detail in chapter 12 (p. 142).

9 Honigmann, 'Indifferent Variants', pp. 191–4. Compare Taylor and Jowett, *Shakespeare Reshaped*, pp. 101–2: *Yes* and *I* were substituted for profanity. This confirms my guess that *yea* was changed to *yes* and *I* for the same reason.

10 Line references are to Spevack's *Concordance*.

11 See Topsell's *The Historie of Serpents* (1608), 'To the Reader'.

12 See Chambers, *William Shakespeare*, II, 218.

13 Walker, *Textual Problems*, pp. 93, 35.

6 THE FOLIO SCRIBE AND TEXT

1 See p. 5.

2 Some words could be printed as one or two (methinks or me thinks): for an explanation of the procedures adopted see p. 161.

3 Howard-Hill, 'New Light on Compositor E of the Shakespeare First Folio', *The Library*, 6th Series (1980), VI, pp. 156–78.

4 For compositor B see chapter 5, n. 4.

5 Howard-Hill, *Ralph Crane*, pp. 36, 131.

6 *Ibid.*, p. 71.

7 The Malone manuscript (M) has now been published, after the completion of this chapter: see the Malone Society's *Collections*, vol. XV, 1993. The editor, Nigel Bawcutt, cites the Trinity manuscript's Through Line Numbering, as I do, as well as an independent line numbering for M. Since M omits roughly one-third of the full text of *Game* and is untypical (though most interesting) in its splicing of lines and fudging of omissions, I use the Lansdowne manuscript (L) more than M to illustrate Crane's scribal habits.

8 Howard-Hill, *Ralph Crane*, pp. 39–42.

9 It is a curious fact that the only two non-vocative swibs in *King John*, (ah) and (thus), both unusual, are also found in Crane's MS. Rawl. poet. 61 (ff. 44b, 66a, 96a), and in his Rawl. MS. D 301 (ff. 6b, 7a) (both in the Bodleian Library).

10 *Demetrius* (MSR), p. ix.

11 Hinman, *Printing and Proof-Reading*, I, 210.

12 The references are to Dover Wilson's *The Manuscript of 'Hamlet'*, II, p. 370 ff.

13 The references are to Cambridge 1. It should be noted that 'has' becomes 'hath' in some of the 'Pavier' quartos (e.g. *Pericles*), but never more than two or three times, as again in F *King Lear*. The twenty-two variants in *Othello* are in a different order of magnitude.

14 I count 'ha's' and 'h'as' as 'has' spellings.

15 The references are to Dover Wilson (as in n. 12).

16 See p. 37; *Stability*, pp. 37–9; Arden 3 *Othello*, 1.3.17n. For *Dramatis personae* lists in the Folio see also Barbara A. Mowat, 'Nicholas Rowe and the Twentieth-Century Shakespeare Text', in *Shakespeare and Cultural Traditions*, ed. Tetsuo Kishi *et al.* (Newark, Delaware, 1994), pp. 314–22.

17 Gary Taylor in Taylor and Jowett, *Shakespeare Reshaped*, p. 72.

18 Wells and Taylor, *Textual Companion*, p. 604; see p. 164, above.
19 Howard-Hill, *Ralph Crane*, pp. 71, 62.
20 Howard-Hill, 'Shakespeare's Earliest Editor', p. 114.
21 Cf. Paul Werstine, 'Narratives about Printed Shakespeare Texts . . .', *SQ*, (1990), XLI, pp. 65–86, and my comments in Appendix A.
22 *King Lear*, TLN 1147–8.
23 For holly (= holy) see *Barnavelt* 2404, 2881; *The Witch* 2104; *Game* (L) 357, where Middleton (T) wrote 'holie'.
24 Curiously, F *Richard II* (but not Q) spells 'holliday' at 3.1.44: compare the Crane texts of *Tempest* 4.1.136 ('holly day') and *Merry Wives* 3.2.68 ('holliday').
25 Two other signs of patching may be mentioned. In F *Hamlet* the first column of the second page includes nine pairs of brackets. Neither the first page nor the second column of page 2 has any brackets: it looks as if the copy for the first column of page 2 was defective and someone addicted to brackets (Crane?) supplied a clean text. The first page of F *Much Ado* prints two swib vocatives, the only two swibs in this text (they are not found in Q). Since the first leaves of a manuscript or printed book are more vulnerable than the rest, a written replacement may have been inserted.
26 See Greg, *First Folio*, p. 439, n. 1.
27 Wells and Taylor, *Textual Companion*, pp. 468, 501.

7 MANUSCRIPT B

1 See Taylor and Jowett, *Shakespeare Reshaped*, p. 109.
2 Wells and Taylor, *Textual Companion*, pp. 476–8.
3 See *Shakespeare Reshaped*, pp. 76, 79, and also 83–5, 116 and *passim*.
4 *Ibid.*, p. 85.
5 Greg, *First Folio*, p. 152. For Crane's expurgation of profanity see also Howard-Hill, *Ralph Crane*, p. 133, and 'Shakespeare's Earliest Editor', pp. 122–3.
6 Honigmann, 'Indifferent Variants', pp. 191–4. Cf. p. 56, above.
7 *Shakespeare Reshaped*, pp. 83, 119.
8 Bowers, 'Authority, Copy', p. 15.
9 *Ibid.*, pp. 15–16.

8 MISREADING

1 For different views of the date of Shakespeare's addition ('Hand D') in *Sir Thomas More* see Scott McMillin and Gary Taylor in *Shakespeare and 'Sir Thomas More'*, ed. T.H. Howard-Hill (New Cambridge Shakespeare Studies and Supplementary Texts, 1989), pp. 71, 122; Alfred W. Pollard (ed.), *Shakespeare's Hand in 'The Play of Sir Thomas More'* (Cambridge, 1923), pp. 23, 31; *Sir Thomas More*, ed. V. Gabrieli and G. Melchiori (The Revels Plays, 1990), pp. 26–7; E.A.J. Honigmann, 'The Play of *Sir Thomas More* and Some Contemporary Events', *SS* (1990), 42, pp. 77–84.
2 J. Dover Wilson, *The Manuscript of 'Hamlet'*, I, p. 106 ff.
3 *Ibid.*
4 Cf. *Hamlet* 3.1.98: lost (Q2), left (F).
5 Cf. *Hamlet* 3.1.154: mo (Q2), more (F).
6 Compare also 1.3.220: eare Q, *eares F (discussed on p. 91); 1.3.393 eare Q, eares F.
7 'Surprisingly, Shakespeare never uses "O heaven" in the unexpurgated text of any play written before the "Acte to restraine Abuses of Players"' (Taylor and Jowett, *Shakespeare Reshaped*, p. 91).
8 See n. 1, above.

9 Cf. Sir E. Maunde Thompson in *Shakespeare's Hand*, ed. Pollard (as in n. 1, above), pp. 63–7.
10 Another possibility that we should keep in mind: the three pages in Hand D could be a fair copy taken from an earlier draft, interrupted by short bursts of free composition as the process of copying prompted afterthoughts (Honigmann, *Stability*, p. 28). If the manuscript of *Othello* transcribed by the F scribe was in Shakespeare's hand, as I suggest (p. 86), this too would have been an authorial fair copy which contained afterthoughts, but it seems to have been far less easy to read than Hand D in *Sir Thomas More*.
11 Maunde Thompson (as in n. 9), pp. 70, 71.
12 See Honigmann, 'The First Quarto of *Hamlet* and the Date of *Othello*', *RES* (1993), XLIV, pp. 211–19.
13 See Honigmann, *Stability*, p. 153 ff.

9 THE RELATIONSHIP OF THE QUARTO AND FOLIO TEXTS

1 See Greg, *First Folio*, p. 363; Bowers, 1964, p. 171.
2 J. G. McManaway, *SS* (1953), 6, p. 166.
3 Harold Jenkins, 'The Relation between the Second Quarto and Folio Text of *Hamlet*', *SB* (1955), VII, pp. 69–83; compare also his edition of *Hamlet* (The Arden Shakespeare, 1982), p. 73.
4 Robert K. Turner, *MP* (1973–4), 71, pp. 191–6.
5 Taylor, 1983, p. 57.
6 *Ibid.*, pp. 45–6.
7 *Ibid.*, p. 59.
8 Walker, *Textual Problems*, pp. 157–8.
9 Walker, 1952, pp. 19–20.
10 *Ibid.*, p. 21.
11 Walton, *Quarto Copy*, pp. 183–94.
12 Bowers, 1964, p. 171.
13 Cf. Greg, *First Folio*, pp. 110, 220, 233; Honigmann, *Stability*, pp. 80, 84, 96 ff., 127–36.
14 Greg, *First Folio*, pp. 365, 367–8.
15 *Ibid.*, p. 369.
16 *Stability*, p. 2 and chapter 5.
17 I assume that the stop after 'appetite' was not Shakespeare's, that Crane copied it from Q and at the same time misread his manuscript's *againe* as *a game*.
18 For the quotations see my paper on 'Shakespeare's "Bombast"' in *Shakespeare's Styles: Essays in Honour of Kenneth Muir*, ed. Philip Edwards *et al.* (1980), pp. 151–62.
19 *Ibid.*, p. 155.
20 For the Q2 editor see also Appendix F.
21 Greg, *First Folio*, p. 370.
22 *Stability*, pp. 13–16.

10 LINEATION AND SCANSION

1 See Paul Bertram, *White Spaces in Shakespeare: The Development of the Modern Text* (Cleveland, Ohio, 1981), pp. ix, 28–9, 65.
2 *Ibid.*, p. 29.
3 Abbott, *A Shakespearian Grammar*. Many other books have appeared on Shakespeare's grammar and versification, but Abbott remains useful for reference and examples. For a later discussion see George T. Wright, *Shakespeare's Metrical Art* (1988).

4 Extra-metrical interjections and interruptions are printed in italics.
5 For example 1.1.93; 2.1.24, 102; 3.1.40; 3.3.40, 93, 95, etc.
6 For example 1.2.85; 1.3.43–4; 2.1.65, 193; 3.3.260–1, 433–4, etc.
7 Abbott, §453a.
8 See, for example, Stanley Wells's *Modernizing Shakespeare's Spelling* (Oxford Shakespeare Studies, 1979), pp. 18–27.
9 The line references are to the Through Line Numbering of Michael Warren's edition of *King Lear* (1619) in *The Complete King Lear 1608–1623* (1989).
10 Paul Werstine has shown how the First Folio compositors changed line division in different ways when they set verse from printed copy ('Line Division in Shakespeare's Dramatic Verse: An Editorial Problem', *AEB* [1984], VIII, pp. 73–125), and usefully reminds us that in *Demetrius and Enanthe* the Malone Society editors 'find [Ralph] Crane apparently relining the text ten times' (p. 77).
11 Plays first printed in the First Folio are cited from Hinman's *Norton Facsimile*, with the Norton Through Line Numbering.
12 Crane frequently changed Middleton's 'I'me' to 'I am' or 'I'am' in the Lansdowne MS. of *A Game at Chess* (lines 1119, 1214, 1264, 1412, etc.), and this suggests that Crane could be responsible for 'I am' spellings in F *Othello*.
13 Crane changed Middleton's 'I haue' to 'I'haue' in the Lansdowne MS. of *A Game at Chess* (lines 303, 314, 384 [twice], 388, etc.) and clearly 'heard' *I have* as *I've*.
14 See A.C. Partridge (as on p. 111), p. 15.
15 *A Game at Chess* by Thomas Middleton (1624), edited for the Malone Society by Trevor Howard-Hill (1990).
16 Chambers, *Elizabethan Stage*, II, p. 329.

11 PUNCTUATION

1 See p. 51.
2 See p. 93.
3 In the good quartos, of course, punctuation is not always equally light because different printers were involved: see p. 174 n. 5.
4 For Folio colons see also pp. 66–7.
5 For Folio question marks see also p. 53.
6 It will be clear that I disagree with Michael Warren's argument that 'future scholarly editions of Shakespeare must ... treat the original punctuation with far more respect' ('Repunctuation as Interpretation in Editions of Shakespeare', *English Literary Renaissance* [1977], 7, pp. 155–69). Warren defended the 'original punctuation' of three Folio texts (*The Tempest, Julius Caesar, Cymbeline*), apparently unaware that *The Tempest* had been identified as a 'Crane' text and inevitably unaware that *Cymbeline* might one day be claimed for Crane. Yet even if we disregard Crane's pervasive repunctuation of texts that he transcribed (see p. 128 above), the Folio compositors also changed the punctuation of their texts quite drastically. It is therefore misleading to describe the Folio's pointing as 'the original punctuation' (except in the sense that it is the earliest surviving punctuation, a very different matter) and, as I have argued, it deserves not 'far more respect' but, on the contrary, far less than generations of editors have given it. I agree with Warren, however, that modern punctuation, unless very lightly marked, will be 'potentially confining, neutralizing, or distorting.'

12 SOME CONCLUSIONS

1 A.E. Housman, *Selected Prose*, ed. John Carter (1961), p. 61, from the Preface to *Juvenal* (1905).

2 Greg, *Editorial Problem*, p. xxx.
3 See Fredson Bowers, 'Established Texts and Definitive Editions', *PQ* (1962), XLI, pp. 1–17: 'it is even possible that the most authoritative edition in respect to accidentals may not be the same as the most authoritative edition in respect to substantives' (p. 4). Compare also David Foxon, 'Greg's "Rationale" and the Editing of Pope', *The Library* (1978), 33, pp. 119–24.
4 Line references are to the following editions: *The Complete King Lear*, ed. Michael Warren (1989); the Revels editions of *Yorkshire Tragedy* and *Oldcastle*; the New Variorum edition of *Merchant of Venice* (ed. H.H. Furness, 1888, etc.: in this edition Q1 and Q2 are cited in the wrong order). All other 'Pavier' texts are cited from vol. 9 of Cambridge 1 (2nd edn, 1893), ed. William Aldis Wright.
5 See also p. 53.
6 'This early stage' has lasted for some time: cf. Honigmann, 'Indifferent Variants', *passim*.
7 See Honigmann, *Stability* (1965); Grace Ioppolo, *Revising Shakespeare* (1991); and reviews in *YES* (1993), 88, pp. 941–2, and *NYRB* (25 October 1990), XXXVII, pp. 58–60.
8 See Frank Kermode's 'Disintegration Once More', in the *Proceedings* of the British Academy (1994), 84, pp. 93–111.
9 Wells and Taylor, *Textual Companion*, p. 510.
10 Housman, (as in n. 1), p. 36, from the Preface to *Manilius* I (1903). I have changed Housman's 'MS.' to 'text'.
11 I avoid the word 'copy-text' because, as indicated in this chapter, I do not copy the chosen text (in the case of *Othello*, the Folio) wherever 'copy-text editors' have done so. For the gradual increase of scepticism concerning 'the rationale of copy-text', see W. Speed Hill in *Documentary Editing* (June 1994), 16, p. 32.
12 See Honigmann, 'Re-Enter the Stage Direction'.

APPENDIX A: SHAKESPEARE'S 'FOUL PAPERS'

1 'Narratives about Printed Shakespeare Texts: "Foul Papers" and "Bad" Quartos', *SQ* (1990), LXI, pp. 65–86; see also Werstine in *Renaissance Drama*, NS, XIX, 1988, pp. 149–73.
2 *The Complete Works of John Webster*, ed. F.L. Lucas (4 vols, 1927), II, pp. 286–8. Spelling modernised.
3 Quoted in Honigmann, *Stability*, p. 17.
4 See Greg, *First Folio*, p. 107. Spelling modernised.
5 *Stability*, pp. 17–18.
6 *Ibid.*, pp. 172–92.

APPENDIX B: THOMAS WALKLEY AND JOHN EVERARD (CONTINUED)

1 Public Record Office, C3 390/88.
2 PRO, C3 392/63.
3 See especially C33/145, ff. 1213, 1262, 1288, 1298; C33/146, ff. 1403, 1444 (PRO).
4 C33/145, f. 1298b.
5 PRO, Prob 11/140 (82 Savile).
6 Prob 11/141, f. 129a.
7 This is from the original will, Prob 10/397.
8 John Everard, *The Gospel-Treasury Opened* (2nd edn, 1659): from the epistle by R. Harford.
9 I have not seen a manuscript by Everard translated from German 1628–36, in the Folger Shakespeare Library (V.a.222).

APPENDIX C: 'SHAKESPEARIAN' SPELLINGS IN Q 'OTHELLO'

1 Greg, *First Folio*, p. 360.
2 But compare 'Glosters men rush at the Tower Gates' (*1H6* 1.3.14), 'The murderers rush in' (*R2* 5.5.104).
3 In Q *Othello* and F *Tempest* 'driving in' seems to mean 'driving on-stage' whereas 'in' in stage directions more commonly means 'off-stage'. Compare *within* (*Oth* 1.3.12, 5.2.84), and *Cor* 1.8.13, '*Martius fights til they be driuen in breathles*'; *Lust's Dominion*, '*The rest ioine and drive in the Moors*' (Dekker, IV, 185).
4 For 'Shakespearian' spellings in Q see also Honigmann, *Stability*, p. 118.

APPENDIX D: FIRST FOLIO 'SWIB' FIGURES

1 Hinman, *Printing and Proof-Reading*, II, p. 518. Hinman's compositor assignments have to be modified in the light of later findings by T.H. Howard-Hill: 'The Compositors of Shakespeare's Folio Comedies', *SB* (1973), XXVI, pp. 61–106, and 'New Light on Compositor E of the Shakespeare First Folio', *The Library*, 6th Series (1980), II, pp. 156–78.
2 Hinman, *Printing and Proof-Reading* II, p. 518.
3 See chapter 6, n. 9.
4 See also p. 72: *Cymbeline*, like *The Winter's Tale*, may be printed from a Crane transcript, in which case Crane might be responsible for these swibs.
5 Honigmann, 'Indifferent Variants', p. 200, n. 3; Wells and Taylor, *Textual Companion*, p. 604.
6 Wells and Taylor, *Textual Companion*, p. 604.
7 *Ibid.*
8 See p. 73 (Crane might have inserted pages in manuscripts written by others, or might have corrected such manuscripts) and chapter 6, n. 9 for *King John*.

APPENDIX E: THE FOLIO TEXT OF 2 *HENRY IV* AND RALPH CRANE

1 Greg, *First Folio*, pp. 269–72.
2 Howard-Hill, *Ralph Crane*, p. xi.
3 *The Second Part of Henry the Fourth* (A New Variorum Edition, ed. Matthias A. Shaaber, 1940), pp. 513–15.
4 *The Second Part of King Henry IV* (The Arden Shakespeare, ed. A.R. Humphreys, 1966), p. lxxiii ff.
5 Taylor and Jowett, *Shakespeare Reshaped*, p. 97.
6 *Ibid.*, p. 78.
7 See p. 80.
8 Humphreys (as in n.4), p. lxx.
9 See pp. 93–8.
10 Taylor and Jowett, *Shakespeare Reshaped*, p. 248.

APPENDIX F: THE EDITING OF Q2 *OTHELLO*

1 Charlotte Hinman, 'The "Copy" for the Second Quarto of *Othello*', in *Joseph Quincy Adams Memorial Studies*, ed. J.G. McManaway (1948), pp. 373–89.
2 Thomas L. Berger, 'The Second Quarto of *Othello* and the Question of Textual "Authority"', in '*Othello*' *New Perspectives*, ed. Virginia M. Vaughan and Kent Cartwright (1991), pp. 26–47.
3 Chambers, *William Shakespeare*, II, p. 239; see also E.A.J. Honigmann, *Shakespeare's Impact on his Contemporaries* (1982), pp. 36–7, on the impact of the First Folio, and *John Weever* (1987), pp. 68–71.

Index